NEGATIVE MEDIA

• • • **Sensing Media**
Aesthetics, Philosophy, and Cultures of Media
EDITED BY WENDY HUI KYONG CHUN AND SHANE DENSON

NEGATIVE MEDIA

Erasure and the Limits of Retention

ELLA KLIK

STANFORD UNIVERSITY PRESS
Stanford, California

Stanford University Press
Stanford, California

An earlier version of chapter 3, "Randomizing Particles into Televisual Oblivion," was originally published in *Television and New Media*: Ella Klik, "'We Should Have Had a Historian': Live Television and the Accident of the Moon Landing Tapes," *Television & New Media* 22, no. 7 (2021): 799–814; https://doi.org/10.1177/1527476420934764. Reprinted with permission.

Library of Congress Cataloging-in-Publication Data
Names: Klik, Ella, author.
Title: Negative media : erasure and the limits of retention / Ella Klik.
Other titles: Sensing media (Series)
Description: Stanford, California : Stanford University Press, 2026. | Series: Sensing media : aesthetics, philosophy, and cultures of media | Includes bibliographical references and index.
Identifiers: LCCN 2025024062 (print) | LCCN 2025024063 (ebook) | ISBN 9781503639768 (cloth) | ISBN 9781503645264 (paperback) | ISBN 9781503645271 (ebook)
Subjects: LCSH: Information storage and retrieval systems—Philosophy. | Communication and technology—Philosophy. | Communication and technology.
Classification: LCC P91 (print) | LCC P91 (ebook)
LC record available at https://lccn.loc.gov/2025024062
LC ebook record available at https://lccn.loc.gov/2025024063

Cover design: Bob Aufuldish, Aufuldish & Warinner

The authorized representative in the EU for product safety and compliance is:
Mare Nostrum Group B.V. | Mauritskade 21D | 1091 GC Amsterdam | The Netherlands | Email address: gpsr@mare-nostrum.co.uk | KVK chamber of commerce number: 96249943

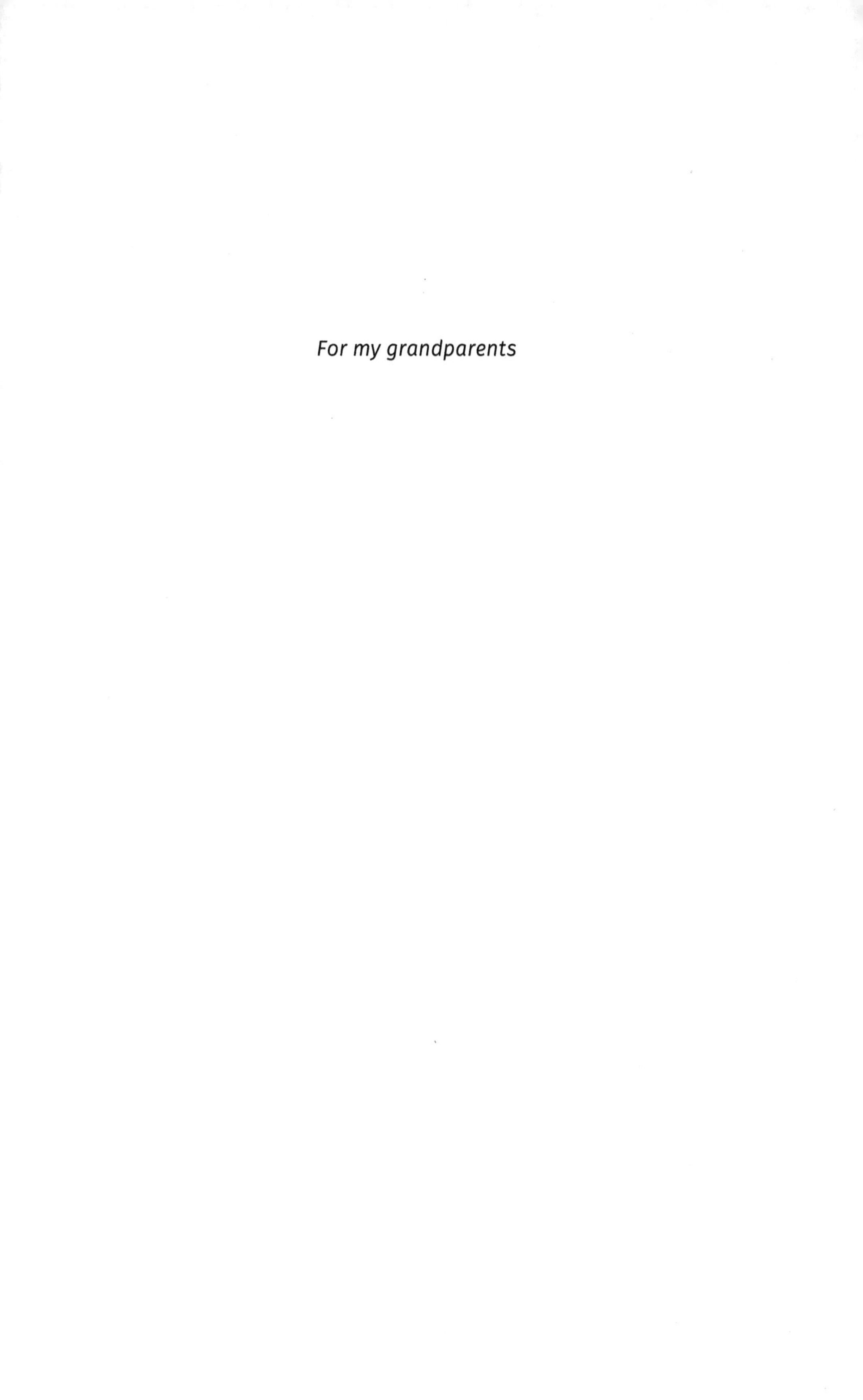

For my grandparents

CONTENTS

ACKNOWLEDGMENTS

Books, like all media objects, are products of entire networks—professional, institutional, technical, and social. They are assembled over time and bear the imprints of many encounters, unforeseen detours, hesitant erasures, and those serendipitous missteps that so often yield the most compelling realizations.

This work originated in a question that first emerged at New York University. It has since been rewritten more times than I care to admit and for far too many years. I owe an intellectual debt to Allen Feldman, who sought to provoke and encourage thought that resists simplification. I extend my deepest gratitude to Alexander Galloway, Jonathan Sterne, and Marita Sturken for their incisive critiques and generous engagement with this project from its earliest, most unruly stages. Jonathan, with his characteristic brilliance, once commented in passing that absence is often harder to grasp and explicate than presence. That simple but profound comment led me to reevaluate how I approached the matter of negativity in the context of media early on. Much of my interest in media history was also kindled by the work of Susan Murray, Mara Mills, and Lisa Gitelman.

Though the kind of writing we do may seem to require little more than the most basic conditions (a room, a desk, a laptop with internet access), it remains inescapably bound to material realities and labor structures. I have been extraordinarily lucky to receive institutional and financial backing at key moments in this project's development. This privilege feels increasingly rare in the face of academia's growing precarity. My time at the University of Southern California's Society of Fellows in the Humanities and the Cinema and Media Studies Department was one such opportunity, and I appreciate Tara McPherson's welcome into that intellectual community. Henry Jenkins's generosity of thought and kind advice taught me much about mentorship. Equally invaluable was my stay at New York University Shanghai, with particular thanks to Anna Greenspan, who fostered engaging conversations in an open and collaborative environment, a spirit I hope to extend one day to others. I also received additional support from the Polonsky Fellowship at the Van Leer Institute and the Institute for Human Sciences (IWM). Together, these opportunities, spanning institutions across the globe, afforded me the rare gift of time spent in the company of outstanding scholars. More recently, the Azrieli Faculty Fellowship provided essential resources at a moment when my efforts might have stalled under the weight of academic obligations and responsibilities.

Few single-authored monographs, strictly speaking, are written in isolation, though the act of completing one has long been imagined as such. So much of scholarship, after all, takes place through dialogue with others. One of the real pleasures of composing this book has been the chance to think alongside brilliant minds, some of whom I count as dear friends: Neta Alexander, Isaac Blacksin, Patricia Ciccone, Ruth Ezra, Christian Flow, Slava Greenberg, Meredith Hall, Yoav Halperin, Roni Hirsch, Matthew Hockenberry, Tamar Hoffman, Diana Kamin, Paula Kiel, Ben Mendelsohn, Diane Oliva, Ray Schrire, Nofar Sheffi, Nimrah Syed, Liran Razinsky, Daniel Wiley, and Hannah Zeavin. Their encouragement, recommendations, and occasional philosophical differences over coffee, Zoom, or drinks have made the process far more creative and, at times, far more bearable.

The irony is not lost on me that a book about reusing records could not have been completed without access to materials safeguarded by archives, collections, and museums. The Lemelson Center for the Study of Invention and Innovation, the Hagley Museum and Library, the Baker Library at Harvard Business School, Stanford's Special Collections, IBM Corporate Archives, the Thomas A. Edison Papers collection at Rutgers University, Whitney Museum of American Art, and the Internet Archive were integral (virtual and physical) sites for rummaging through well-known and overlooked historical sources. The librarians, archivists, and staff who facilitated this research have my enduring appreciation.

I would also like to recognize Sarah O'Brien, the series editors Shane Denson and Wendy Chun, and the reviewers, who read this work with care. Shannon Mattern's, David Parisi's, and Benjamin Peters's thoughtful and, at once, humbling feedback has helped refine and clarify the arguments laid out in the following pages. The patience of my editor, Erica Wetter, has been unwavering, and for that, I am truly grateful. Errors and omissions, as ever, remain entirely my own, and so too does the possibility that I have overlooked anyone whose input was no less essential.

An earlier version of chapter 3 was first published in 2021 in *Television and New Media*, which has kindly granted permission for its inclusion in this book.

Finally, to my family, Basia, Lilya, Alexander, Ron, Maria, and to my friends, who all have endured my long writing bouts and writer's blocks, stood by me through moments of uncertainty, and remained steadfast even when my work was an enigma (including to myself): your presence has mattered most.

Introduction

ERASURE: EVERYWHERE, NOWHERE, RIGHT HERE

••• On May 16, 2023, a blog post from Google (now a subsidiary of Alphabet), "Updating Our Inactive Account Policies," announced a seemingly innocuous Gmail policy change that stirred widespread criticism. Proclaiming its dedication to maintaining the safety and security of its user base, the company said it would begin deleting accounts that had been inactive for at least two years.[1] Despite the post's subdued tone, the news spread fast. In a matter of days, major news outlets reported on the statement, prompting users on social media platforms to protest on the grounds of continuity.[2] What would happen to the material that these account users had uploaded—say, to the video-hosting platform YouTube—that could not be found elsewhere? Would accounts and content created by deceased users be removed? At their root, these questions addressed the company's perceived disruption of users' expectations of data permanence. If the internet is indeed defined by a tension between endurance and ephemerality, then the company designed for the fleeting, while users placed their trust in lasting presence.[3] A few days after the announcement, Google edited its original post to claim it would only delete accounts not linked to YouTube videos. The public's growing ire regarding the shortened shelf life of their data only partly forced the company's hand. It finally purged the remaining inactive accounts as 2023 came to a close and has continued to delete abandoned accounts since.

Such instances of wholesale elimination appear, paradoxically, at a moment of widespread conviction that the internet no longer forgets—meaning, according to some popular claims, that erasure is neither necessary nor possible.[4] But this story reveals a more complicated relationship between abundant digital storage, commercial interests, and internet users. As rates for commercial cloud storage steadily decrease, the amount of stored data only grows, which means that data-hosting costs are nevertheless rising, at least for now.[5] What was ostensibly part of Alphabet's extensive bid to cut storage expenses across its various platforms and products, from Gmail to Google Photos and YouTube, became a battleground for a collectively produced cultural sphere. Incidents like this stress that undoing is no less technical and economic than it is social.

Like many other recent tugs of war between Silicon Valley corporations and their consumers, this episode should remind us that the pull of idealizing vast and eternally accessible digital archives akin to Jorge Luis Borges's "Library of Babel" is a problematic inheritance of imagined media pasts and unfulfilled utopian dreams. To truly grasp the power dynamics shaping contemporary media, it is essential to explore how and why this intricate mesh of private companies came to be perceived as a boundless and intangible cloud, overshadowing the material—and decidedly finite—repositories they rely upon. *Negative Media* delves into the historical and theoretical underpinnings of the prevailing belief that capturing something on various substrates, from paper to hard drives, necessarily leads to long-term retention and preservation. It investigates the circumstances under which the design and use of various technologies respond to the finiteness of storage space against promises of total recall. Throughout, deletion will be shown to resolve the topological and material challenges arising not only from scarcity but also, unexpectedly, from abundance. Although erasure is a process often mistakenly represented as working solely at the level of content, from a bird's-eye view, it has much to do with producing, abating commodity prices, and managing storage costs.

EVERYTHING IS FINITE AND NOTHING IS INFINITE

Embracing what might sound like a paradox—generative discard—this book is dedicated to things undone: wiped magnetic tapes, excised film reels, crossed-out letters, recycled phonograph records, and scrubbed digital files. Even in absentia, such matters deserve our attention and consideration. As objects entangled in complex social and physical relations, media are inevitably caught in an economy of sourcing, manufacturing, and consumption. Erasure is born out of this reality in that the process somewhat alleviates the physical confines of matter. Materiality, when taken as a way of thinking and orienting, offers an indispensable path into the complexities of modern technologies.[6] A particularly revealing vein of media scholarship attends to the tech industry's parasitic coexistence with nature, including its reliance on extracting once-abundant natural resources, mining rare substances, and voraciously consuming energy and water in the name of sustaining hyperproduction, which is now at the core of data capitalism.[7] In order to understand media commodities as material things, researchers turned to charting colonial histories, exploring labor and mining issues, and looking into disposal procedures. Yoking together accumulation, excess, and planned (and unplanned) obsolescence, Jennifer Gabrys follows the life of technical objects in an ever-evolving trajectory from the factory to the landfill; Nicole Starosielski foregrounds the sprawling planetary-scale efforts of constructing and maintaining the internet's infrastructure; and Kate Crawford and Jussi Parikka push the boundaries of media studies to encompass the imprints of production that have been etched into the geological strata of Earth. Cumulatively, these accounts stress the imperative of following post-digitality's horizontal (spatial) and vertical (temporal) trajectories of expansion across this planet.

What does this have to do with announcements such as that sounded by Alphabet? Though tech companies may promise their consumers opulent, limitless worlds, their goods and products are contingent on exhausting matter. For Sean Cubitt, two realities govern the material life of media: its substance cannot be mined endlessly, and it degrades over time. He writes: "Media are finite, in the sense both that, as matter, they are inevitably tied to physics, especially the dimension of time; and that their constituent elements—matter and energy, information and entropy, time and space, but especially the first pair—are finite resources in the closed system of planet Earth. Because they are finite, media not only cannot persist forever; they cannot proliferate without bounds."[8]

Simply put, there are natural and unnatural limits to the manufacture of media technologies and their shelf life once assembled. The extensions of humanity, as Marshall McLuhan would have it, are themselves bound by finitude. Since nothing can be built to last forever—not even archival initiatives inspired by post-apocalyptic fiction—waste sites amass in towering heaps now visible from outer space. The deluge of decommissioned electronics largely results from concerted industry efforts to artificially accelerate the rate of their physical degradation and disposability, a fact obscured by promises of bigger, better, and more durable future technologies.[9]

All this invites reflection on the multivalent relation between matter and economy, whereby production is a process that constantly vacillates between (promised) abundance and (looming) scarcity. "Scarcity" is a term interwoven in major writings about the industrialized world, from Thomas Malthus's anxieties about potential depletion caused by unchecked population growth to Karl Marx's class-based reading of distributional inequity.[10] The finiteness of nature, Fredrik Jonsson and Carl Wennerlind maintain, is fundamental to various, and at times conflicting, modern theories of economy.[11] Unsurprisingly, some of these models predicted (and continue to predict) that scientific mastery over the natural world could rectify the predicament of material boundedness—technical solutionism to the rescue.

The deterministic relation between economics and technological change was inverted in the mid-twentieth century by communication scholars who contended that media instead affect economic structures.[12] These sorts of arguments begin by identifying the emergence of writing to aid in stockpiling and counting goods. Next, they describe how the spread of information through written texts and later printed materials germinated new social and monetary forms of organization. When the telegraph was popularized in the nineteenth century, James Carey proclaims, it radically standardized market prices by collapsing space with near-instantaneous transmission. Rather than chasing the chicken-or-the-egg problem (which comes first, the market or technology?), insights from these opposing approaches can be combined to reveal an open feedback loop in which form and information are redistributed based on available materials.

Negative Media intervenes precisely at this point. My goal is to comprehend how notions of scarcity and, later, presumed abundance translate into design. By reframing such resource constraints as also intrinsic to media, reusability emerges as a condition of possibility for creation. Media history abounds with objects that embody this principle: erasable wax tablets employed by students and bookkeepers in ancient Greece, papyrus sheets repurposed by layering images and texts upon the same surface, scraping tools wielded by medieval scribes on parchment and vellum, and batch-produced reusable writing notebooks in the Renaissance period.[13] In the late eighteenth century, the import of rubber to Europe brought about the mass production of erasers, which replaced stale bread as the primary abrasive agent for removing unwanted written traces.[14] To be sure, undoing is hardly a modern conceit. Writers, scribes, accountants, diarists, secretaries, and poets have been erasing for as long as they have been marking things up. What we are witnessing today is the production of cultural objects, knowledge, and data at a scale and velocity once unimaginable, even though debates over "information overload" have raged for centuries.[15] In view of the sheer proliferation of content and the expanding networks of retentional objects, erasure itself has, in turn, become an infrastructural function.

The task at hand is to uncover the ways in which material considerations have been and are hardwired into the architectures of storage from the late nineteenth century to the present. Although this is an admittedly extensive period by historical standards, this timeframe allows me to consider illustrative cases that cumulatively outline media economies in an epoch in which production has been accelerated on all possible fronts. My exploration of reusable technologies thus opens with a chapter on Thomas Edison's proto–Silicon Valley vision of innovation in sound recording and concludes with a chapter unpacking the contemporary legacies of cyberutopians who believed that the internet could be limitless. Much as the phonograph once promised a technology that transcends the finitude of the human body and keeps something of it forever, the early web's creators and theorists envisioned a future where digital data could also be severed from its tangled, physical roots—those cables, drives, and peripherals—believing that this disconnection would resolve the age-old dilemmas of scarcity and finiteness. Analog storage space was to give way to data abundance, they proclaimed. "It is now possible to replace all previous information storage forms with one meta-bottle: complex—*and highly liquid*—patterns of ones and zeros."[16] Such liquidity encapsulates modern ideas about preservation as the default state of things, cemented by the propagation of archives, collections, museums, and libraries.[17] But digital media do disappear, and much of the disappearance is *by design*.

Insofar as erasure is a process engineered to introduce ephemerality into various recording systems, it alleviates the physical conditions of finiteness by offering a method for reusing the same substrate again and again. Given its physical nature, this is not solely a temporal relation but also a spatial one. Two intertwined movements—compression, folding inward, and expansion, radiating outward—represent the different trajectories that aim to solve the problem of storage. As a child of the 1990s, I still remember the sense of awe I felt when a friend handed me a CD with tens(!) of pirated Pantera tracks, rendering my Walkman instantly outmoded and the stacks of double-sided cassette tapes in my bedroom obsolete overnight. The gift of an MP3 player smaller than the palm of my hand just a couple years later left me reeling at how quickly this new device could collapse a carefully curated collection of physical media into a single object. It was also yet another example of how tech companies market progress and distinguish their products from previous makes and models by offering more memory in ever smaller enclosures. Again, this is nothing new. Since the late nineteenth century, as one substrate was replaced with another, declarations about increased storage capacity have been championed in promotional materials. For instance, the Edison Company boasted the ability of wax cylinders to capture sounds, first for mere seconds and later for minutes. When the cassette tape was introduced in the early 1960s, it was celebrated for being physically smaller than the vinyl record and holding up to twice its capacity.

In the ongoing quest for enhanced retention, storage becomes ever more compact. Throughout the twentieth century, each successful act of miniaturization fed into the conviction that this trajectory could linearly extend, one leap after another. Yet even tech outlets of the optimist kind (*Wired*, among others) are now sounding the alarm that we are approaching the physical limits of downsizing electronic components.[18] Content, too, is subject to the demands of minimization. Data compression techniques are routinely devised and implemented within a digital economy that, for all its promises, remains bound by a shortage of available space and bandwidth. To make things lighter—that is, fit for finite media and strained channels—digital technologies had to unlearn the indiscriminate recording habits of their analog predecessors.[19] Following the principle of sufficiency (what is "good enough" for the eye or the ear) renders whole categories of data superfluous to the primary aim of record making, allowing "excess" to be preemptively discarded.[20] From the crackling dawn of analog recording to today's streams, usability has required some type of tradeoff between keeping and deleting. This is a relation I call "adaptive retention," a way of describing how devices, machines, and systems built to hold onto things end up internalizing impermanence as the means by which they manage to retain anything at all. This, precisely, is what escapes simplistic distinctions between artificial short-term and long-term memory.

Regrettably, while the size of digital devices is shrinking, their presence in the landscape is ever more palpable. This reality, one might argue, stems from the sheer sweep of accumulation. Even the tiniest units, given enough time and space, begin to pile up. Computer drives, stacked atop one another, now form the guts of data centers in ways reminiscent of earlier furniture designs crafted to organize an overabundance of texts and media, whether in homes, offices, or libraries.[21] Tight storage space thus mutates into a territorial problem. Storage studies, if such a framework were to develop, would engage with retention in its complicated nonuniformity: as technical things (materials, containers, and formats); as quantities (stand-alone devices and information in aggregate or in bulk); as processes (holding, maintaining, operating, malfunctioning); and as cultural commodities (objects, services, devices, content). Only then could undervalued processes like erasure be fully examined and the circumstances around episodes such as Alphabet's account purges fully appreciated.

SENSE MAKING AND UNMAKING: NEGATIVE MEDIA THEORY

Deleting, expunging, canceling, wiping, rubbing off, demagnetizing, cutting out, scrubbing, scratching, obliterating, effacing, covering up, excising: these are but a few of the many terms used to denote a seemingly simple function. Although the multiplicity of descriptors reflects how pervasive these acts are, scholarly attention to practices of undoing in media production is disproportionately limited relative to the wealth of literature on inscription, documentation, and storage.

Erasure is thus found not at the center but in the cracks and crevices of media history and theory. Friedrich Kittler famously announced that media studies cannot escape the sensible.[22] In his view, because media technologies actively rework our perception of the world and even our sense of self, it is impossible for the field to fully account for its subject matter without addressing this fundamental yet elusive role. It goes without saying that investigations of sensibility prioritize the readily perceivable or moments of becoming perceptible, paying attention to negation only on the off chance and as nothing more than a boundary-setting operation (what is and is not). Attempts to address negation within the realm of sense making unquestionably raise methodological, epistemological, and ontological challenges. What form might media analysis take when media may not only be what they appear? Can the conceptual triad of withdrawal, deferred presence, and self-cancellation be mobilized to engage that which resists apprehension?

Advancing the concept of "negative media theory," Dieter Mersch attends to a peculiar quality of such forms: they function best when their inner workings go unnoticed.[23] Lines of thought that fall, or might be seen to fall, under this umbrella can be said to draw on mid-twentieth-century philosophical reflections on technology. Jacques Derrida extensively theorized this medial relation between language, technē, and the world. His body of work—from negative theology, through différance, to pharmacological supplements and spectral returns—is, in all its breadth, an ode to indetermination. Visually, in *Of Grammatology*, he also attempts to find another means of signification for the commonly ignored, or erased, as he puts it, artifice at the heart of philosophy. He settles on a strategy of crossing out key terms so as to bring to the forefront the impossibility of pure, unaided presence (~~a negation for the sake of visibility~~).[24] Himself no stranger to graphic experimentation of this kind, Martin Heidegger's work and his concept of the present-at-hand informs many contemporary theories of technological failure.[25] Thinking through simple household objects, Heidegger described the utilitarian relation between us and our tools, a relation that rests on indifference so long as the tools perform their expected tasks without interruption. Although Heidegger was critical of complex modern systems, his diagnosis of the inverse link between operability and (lack of) awareness is central to investigating media, even—or especially—of digital environments.[26] Finally, McLuhan marked a critical moment for the field more than half a century ago when he insisted that the meaning of a medium lies in its form and not just in the content that it brings forth. His now well-known dictum draws attention not only to what is apprehended but also to the materials and conditions that enable the reception of messages.[27]

One could argue that "negative media theory" is not a unified scholarly program but a current within contemporary thought. It is cumulative: a stray footnote, a piece followed by another piece, and then several monographs. Threaded together, these scattered fragments become provisional throughlines toward a reflection on the negative kernel at the core of mediality. To begin with, there is the question of how we orient ourselves toward the technical objects that cohabit with us in our everyday spaces and the uncertainty over whether an encounter is possible at all. Such thinking is fragmented and its echoes are many. Media's "tendency to erase themselves," so goes the argument, engenders a structure of relations where users suppress, or at the very least ignore, the technological aspects of production, transmission, and reception.[28] Sybille Krämer posits that users exist in an essentially negative relation that "enable something to emerge [. . .] while the 'deep structure' constitutes the non-visible medium."[29] The perceptible difference between what appears to the eye and the recessive technical grounds upon which capture of some sort takes place can be conceptualized, as Boris Groys suggests, as the front and the back of a painting.[30] The verso of the painting, or the inner mechanism of any other medium, is what he characterizes as a "submedial space" that is "structurally invisible."[31] Jay Bolter and Richard Grusin observe that such morphological matters are not unrelated to aspirations of abundance: "our culture wants to multiply its media and to erase all traces of mediation; ideally, it wants to erase its media in the very act of multiplying them."[32]

Is the reverse side ever registrable? Maybe, perhaps, not quite. Victor Stoichita cites an ancient tale of a woman tracing her lover's shadow image on a wall. From this moment of mimetic duplication, of presence entwined with absence, he claims that the origins of Western art emerge "in the negative.[33] Akira Lippit moves along a similar path in proposing "avisuality," where figures at the threshold of vision (internalities and externalities discernible only through cinema, X-rays, and the atomic bomb) become perceptible in shadow form.[34] This debate, in its strictest sense, however, is concerned with more than vision alone. The gaps, glitches, and breakdowns that seem to plague systems offer opportunities to think through the nature of mediation itself. By extension, we come to find, perhaps unsurprisingly, humanity and its limits, its relation to the Other and the otherness that it cannot directly comprehend, so we have learned from John Durham Peters, Amanda Lagerkvist, Amit Pinchevski, and Michel Serres.[35] This is all to say that the negative need not be regarded as unproductive. Even at the ends of communication, as Alexander Galloway, Eugene Thacker, and McKenzie Wark remind us, the theorist is never quite out of a job.[36] Admittedly, though, grappling with negative mediality is somewhat like walking a tightrope loosely tethered at both ends, always on the verge of snapping and leaving one suspended without ground.

Suppose we allow that constitutive aspects of the medium always recede from view (figuratively and literally). How can we study media in this obscurity as denying their own mediation? Both Mersch and Jens Schröter turn to modern art's propensity to reflexively represent its own production as a helpful point of departure. Robert Rauschenberg's notorious act of expunging a de Kooning drawing to produce the *Erased de Kooning Drawing* (1953), Mersch argues, shows the "facets and unknown dimensions [. . .] [of the] pictorial character of the picture."[37] This choice of example could not be more pertinent to this current discussion. Ironically, the iconic artwork was recently un-erased with the help of digital technology and made to reveal the traces of its original creator. Further, in 2007, artist Peter Baldes released *Erased de Kooning* in homage to Rauschenberg: one video features a screencast in which a file named "de Kooning" is marked for deletion and another in which Rauschenberg is erased from a photo of himself before the painting, by means of Photoshop. In *Deleted Rauschenberg* (2011), Adam Cruces picks up this thread. A screenshot of the familiar prompt, "Are you sure you want to permanently delete the item in the Trash?" is captured at the exact moment the "empty trash" button is clicked. Reframed by decades of multilayered commentary, Rauschenberg's *Erased de Kooning Drawing* appears to stand less in the domain of aesthetics proper than in the sphere of material engagements with media substrates and interfaces.

There's something instructive in just how banal these Rauschenbergs have become. The labor of deletion is executed by a machine in a manner entirely dissimilar to the taxing nature of the original act of image making through removal. Erasure is constantly performed as part of our daily engagement with digital media. It is not an anomaly. It is routine. The signs are everywhere, in the instruction manuals, in the gestures of everyday use, and in artworks. The issue is whether one ever pauses long enough to notice. Mundanity may be the key to erasure's underexplored status. Long before Bruno Latour posed his question about the scholarly neglect of technical objects, Gilbert Simondon had already diagnosed that "habitual repetition erases the awareness of structures and operations with the stereotypy of adapted gestures."[38]

This study is concerned with a specific subset of everything we may mean by erasure. Specifically, it traces *a spatiotemporal process where content*—whether texts, images, sounds, or data—*is cleared to allow its substrate to be reused.* With this general positioning in mind, unmaking, which enables content to be created, excluded, and then re-created within the same objects, becomes crucial to the discussion of how material limits are reconfigured within our systems, whether we are able or even care to notice.

TECHNOLOGIES TO ERASE WITH

In the spirit of negativity, I should first contend with what *erasure* does and does not mean, at least within the pages of this book. Certainly, the word itself means many things to many different writers and speakers all at once. It is regularly mobilized in political discourse, professional debates, and artistic contexts, to mention only a few arenas. The growing scholarly attention to everything negative covers such wide-ranging phenomena as failure, ruination, and noise.[39] Given its ambiguous nature—equal parts destructive and productive, figurative and literal, intentional and accidental, visible and imperceptible—erasure is too often mistaken for such related concepts. Although studying this negation in concert with others could yield a holistic understanding of the "undesirables" of mediation, it also curbs the analytical distinctiveness of each such one. Erasure here is not decay, not an accident or a forgetting as such. It is something entirely else. And to face it, as it were, requires distinguishing it from other, kindred negations. No sustained inquiry has yet been undertaken into reusability as the hidden facet of media production, and this book offers a preliminary contribution toward such an investigation.

Erasure is not destruction. Destruction forecloses the surface itself, and it therefore remains beyond the purview of this discussion, which centers on forms of erasure that both clear and conserve the substrate's capacity for reuse. Destructive practices like book burning or hard drive shredding treat content and carrier as indistinguishable, eliminating both in a single gesture. Conversely, erasure as defined above discloses the internal cleavage between "recorder" and "recorded on/in/within" that makes the machine function as it does. In methodological terms, to address media by means of their negative qualities means to refocus the analysis away from content that disappears to how and why it does so. Any attempt to account for it can only proceed through what persists, a double bind, no doubt. Undoing circles inevitably back to the underlying puzzle of why we devise technologies that are built to both create and erase. For the sake of brevity, the answer is that we do so because we must.

Erasure is not totally accidental. As a mechanism made to sustain production, unintentional erasure paradoxically illuminates the system at the very moment it misfires. A few years back, a friend pointed me to a podcast, knowing I would be drawn to a story of a daughter's heartfelt mission to locate decades-old footage.[40] She was searching for an interview with her father speaking from his hospital bed during the Vietnam War, which she, as a teenager, had taped over. In overwriting the recording, she enacted a routine gesture with adolescent indifference. It was only with time that the gravity of wiping an inconspicuous tape settled in. Deletion was never the intention, of course. Yet, as with countless other accidental episodes, this one unfolded because the technology was engineered to impose order, regulate, and keep entropy at bay through adaptive retention. It happened, as so many things do, because the system allowed it to, as I discuss in chapter 3.

It is hardly coincidental that Norbert Wiener, a principal architect of midcentury aspirations to optimize and systematize operations in human and nonhuman domains, invokes the act of erasure in the early passages of *Cybernetics: Or Control and Communication in the Animal and the Machine*: "That the machine contains an apparatus for the storage of data which should record them quickly, hold them firmly until erasure, read them quickly, erase them quickly, and then be immediately available for the storage of new material."[41] Thus, above all else, *Negative Media* proposes that although erasure appears to be an obstructive or accidental act, process, and feature, it is a crucial aspect of producing media objects in most forms.

Erasure is not a "natural" process. The deliberate and systematic unmaking of records and traces operates on a different register from the slow degradation of matter over time. Consider, for instance, celluloid rot and the nitrate-induced combustion of old film reels as mirror images of analog film's end of life: one withers gradually and slowly, while the other is rapidly reduced to ashes. Such material unraveling, though inevitable, can be slowed under the aegis of institutions that manage light exposure, maintain stable temperatures, and monitor humidity levels. Certainly, battling degeneration poses a gamut of challenges of "doing more with less," not the least of which is labor and maintenance costs, as well as procuring sufficient storage space.[42] Responding to these financial demands, approaches such as "more data, less process" or "graceful degradation" champion minimal archival interventions to meet the unique dilemmas posed by born-digital objects that have more recently emerged.[43] But the process of erasure I am concerned with is inherently interventionist. It occurs in the interval before corrosion sets in, when the physical medium remains intact and usable. Perhaps the term "operative erasure," which I adopt from Johan Fredrikzon and Chris Haffenden, might serve to distinguish deliberate, executable deletions from the inevitable transience of all physical things, none of which can truly endure through time.[44] The onset of decay is a fact of any matter, while operative erasure belongs to only certain designs. Generative negation represents neither closure nor finality but a moment that "unnaturally" makes space for the new.

Erasure does not invariably map onto forgetting. Individual and collective memory is often articulated through its supposed inverse; much of memory studies and a great deal of humanistic inquiry has long followed this conceptual path.[45] Forgetting's frequent near-assimilation to erasure is an added complication in an already difficult discussion. I turn to a paradigmatic psychoanalytic text to exemplify the thorniness of the memory/storage and forgetting/erasing chiasmus.

"If I distrust my memory," begins that brief and frequently revisited passage, "I am able to supplement and guarantee its working by making a note in writing."[46] Viewed anew through Derrida's deconstructive prism, Sigmund Freud's compact essay "A Note upon 'the Mystic Writing-Pad'" acquired belated status as a touchstone in media theoretical debates. Freud offers an analogy anchored in a deceptively unassuming device, enlisted to probe the stratification of perceptual processes and psychic trace-formation. The Mystic Writing-Pad functions in a manner distinct from the sheet of paper, upon which a thought might be hastily inscribed (a medium that Freud identifies as permitting a "permanent memory-trace," though one constrained by its finite "receptive capacity"). Unlike paper, the blackboard functions recursively. Praised for its unlimited receptive surface, the blackboard cannot retain marks over time. It is this incapacity that renders it an inadequate model for memory. On to the next. At this impasse, Freud turns to the Mystic Writing-Pad, the *Wunderblock*, an apparatus composed of "a slab of dark brown resin or wax [. . .] over the slab is a thin transparent sheet," for a schematic that may elucidate the conundrum of the mind. On the top layer, the user records impressions until the surface can hold no more or its content is deemed irrelevant. A single operation suffices to clear any marks: "All that is necessary is to raise the double covering-sheet from the wax slab by a light pull."[47] The pad's layers peel apart, the surface lifts, and traces, once visible, disappear. Yet Freud insists that, to the trained eye of a scholar or psychoanalyst, the wax below discloses what remains, an accumulation of what once passed across its surface.

This remarkably detailed engagement with technical affordances and retentional thresholds is undertaken in service of a project distinct from the one pursued in this book, and thus Freud devotes few words to negation in its own right. One might first observe that his account treats erasure as an operation of such apparent effortlessness and simplicity that it sidesteps the need for any elaboration. A recurring motif throughout these pages suggests otherwise: viewed from a different perspective (as Freud does when attending to the barely perceptible traces left on wax), erasure is only easy insofar as it has been meticulously, even laboriously, programmed. It is a complex operation in and of itself, one whose intricacy is rendered unremarkable by its alignments with procedural repetition.

Second, taken seriously, the analogy suggests something rather provocative. Erasing becomes a mere surface-level effect that grazes but never penetrates the barrier. Undoing does not extend to the depth of the storage layer, nor does—or can—it disturb the substrate in which the trace continues to reside. If Thomas Elsaesser is right to cast Freud as a theorist of media before media theory existed, and despite any intention on Freud's part, then we are left with the striking absence of a vocabulary through which negation might be meaningfully addressed.[48] Traces are displaced and absorbed into the folds of the substrate, accumulating incrementally atop what came before. Elsewhere, Freud more explicitly posits that the mind abolishes nothing. The superficially absent is merely repressed. "It is rather the rule than the exception for the past to be preserved in mental life."[49] To the extent that this text—and others in Freud's oeuvre—articulates a philosophy in which forgetting is structurally impossible, erasure is stripped of any consequence. His focus, to be sure, falls primarily on the interaction with the durable remnants entrenched in economies, libidinal or otherwise. However, the material operation, as we shall see in the following chapters, is by no means external to storage. It is conditioned by the substrate, functioning within it as a process that penetrates, disfigures, effaces, or overwrites and, in so doing, manages and changes the limits of storage capacity itself.

Which leads, in turn, to the next point I wish to make. Freud's essay treats the imprinted substrate as an archival space where writing persists as indelible indentations in wax. The wax cylinder, taken up in chapter 1, is another instance of the substance's longstanding role as a container for data, a lineage Freud links to ancient technologies previously mentioned. As for the phonograph, its promise of successful reproduction of sounds hinges on the thorough removal of any preexisting grooves. Paraphrased, the sediments that psychoanalysis takes as its objects of study are, for engineers of analog recording apparatuses like Edison's machine, debris that must be removed wholly to ensure the fidelity of future recordings. Their concern is no longer with residual signs or the conditions of their return, but with one imperative alone: that they must not. Analog media, then, treated remnants as frustrations that were best handled through negation. Still, outside the well-trodden paths of theories of forgetting, few conceptual tools help us make sense of this recurring intervention.

Last, Freud's Mystic Writing-Pad is also a historical object that once widely circulated and, to a degree, still does. R. John Williams excavates a parallel history of this "contrivance" that complicates its framing as a child's plaything, as did Freud's reception. It also functioned as a lightweight tool for making notations at the tip of one's hand. Contrary to the frivolous, lighthearted impression typically ascribed to toys, "the main selling point of the pad was that navigators could work out their sums on the fly, and then erase as needed (refreshing the space for additional calculations and eliminating the need to destroy paper in case of an emergency landing)," Williams explained of its utilization by the German Air Force during World War II.[50] Endurance, then, is an accident of design. Whether for incendiary or benign purposes, the device's functionality hinges on the blackboard's "infinite capacity," favoring rapid inscription and erasure, and rejecting the remainder as a potential obstruction.

For Kittler, the drive to stave off forgetting is entangled in a paradox whereby archives "for new books, new knowledge, new programs [. . .] had to be made erasable."[51] Because they seem to defy time, recording technologies are often presumed to serve permanence itself. The historical trajectories of various media systems, some covered in this book, suggest otherwise. Longevity is not necessarily their default, nor is permanence their encoded aim, given that infinity is a structuring myth. A better understanding of the tools that shape thought, being, and the possibility of thinking about being—as Kittler and Derrida each explore through their respective engagements with technics—requires examining not only what these devices and machines are presumed to do, but what they enact in the plural and beyond abstraction. This calls for attunement to the connections between strata, processes, and networks, which so often buckle under the weight of concepts such as forgetting or recollection.

Erasure is not only representational. Whereas acts of removal cannot be reduced to one political program, they frequently serve as instruments of normalization, marginalization, and silencing. Negation takes on myriad forms, persisting just at the threshold of detectability as a latent dimension of social control. Erasure sanctions bodies that do and do not generate value, a point of departure for chapter 4. Representational absences, in fact, double exclusionary practices that demarcate cultural life and continue to reproduce biases, dispossession, and precarity.[52] Accordingly, scholars, practitioners, and communities have long worked to expose the logics of exclusion that shape dominant narratives, undertaking the amplification of suppressed voices and the retrieval of stories effaced from archives, popular media, and collective memory.

What the system attempts to cast outside as surplus or residue remains tethered to its internal mechanics, a point extensively developed by Michel Foucault, Jacques Rancière, Gayatri Spivak, and many others.[53] One incisive tactic for asserting control over the sensible goes with and against representation. It is in the thick of this operational obscurity, Allen Feldman theorizes, that political power "dismediates" violence—so it may persist and intensify, unchecked, detected and undetected, and no less effective for it.[54] It leaves a deliberate negative trace that registers the forcible withdrawal of someone or something. Across centuries and millennia, such elimination manifested in practices operating across a range of substrates: rubbing out names of excommunicated persons from scrolls and stone, and their likeness from painting and statues in ancient Rome (*damnatio memoriae*); defacing illuminated manuscripts that contained nudity during the Middle Ages; whitewashing graffiti to restrict public communication in early modern England; removing oppositional figures from official photographs in Soviet Russia; censoring the circulation of lyrics and images deemed harmful to children in twentieth-century popular culture; blacking out governmental documents released under the Freedom of Information Act—the list goes on and on.[55] Injunctions against knowledge transfer such as these, which Peter Galison calls "antiepistemology," can only fail to fully seal information off. The spectacle of invisibility is, therefore, inadvertently also an aperture or point of ingress (anti-antiepistemology, perhaps?).[56] Chapter 2 examines in detail such a dynamic, less a lapse than a regulatory technique of power.

A final "not," which is also a note on method and incompletion. It would be foolish to pretend that a work about strategies dealing with storage space is itself not bound by character, word, and page counts, so allow me to briefly reiterate. The cases gathered across various technologies, locations, and periods are meant to be representative of a broader pattern of undoings, not to offer a comprehensive list. This work thus joins other efforts, including Gina Giotta's account of practices of effacing the human body, to make sense of media's materiality and finiteness.[57] To be clear, this is but one beginning among many, I hope. By way of tracing phases of experimentation and versioning, and attending to prototypes and formats, technology comes into view as a working definition rather than as an ontologically stable object of inquiry.

Each analysis opens with an account of a prevailing theoretical discourse surrounding a medium whose reusable character has not yet been thoroughly addressed. From that point onward, each chapter pivots to a different body of materials, using product design and industry perspectives as entry points into storage—conceptualized as an axis around which a fledgling industry begins to cohere. I stay close to issues surrounding encoding, formatting, and substrate concerns that bring designers, engineers, and early users to the decision to embed a negative function into devices otherwise meant to capture and potentially preserve. With a focus on moments of transformation, frustration, and contestation, this media archaeological method historicizes adaptive retention and the shifting values attributed to undoing as a feature.[58] Aggregating the disparate voices of scholars and workers, critics and commentators, whose perspectives at times diverge, if not directly conflict, necessarily yields a polyphonic account between the practical and theoretical.

As a result, the chapters resist symmetry. Some confront ontological debates, others stay with the pragmatic, and yet others trace how the ideological is inscribed in everyday design. Although each is grounded in its own distinct discourse of erasure, the overall gist of these stories is that, for those who conceived of and produced media used to record for almost two centuries now, erasure is a necessary feature, not an incidental bug, within systems tasked with the generation of objects and their retention. Debates about manufacturing, fabrication, removal, and use must not be divorced from considerations of appearances and withdrawals, nor should theorists relegate the former to the domain of historians and communication scholars alone.

From Edison's workshop to Google's data centers, across the following pages, the reader will encounter a recurring preoccupation with affordability, efficiency, and profit. Such concerns bring to the surface a constant tension between the markets' ambitions and the material limits that quietly govern them. Chapter 1 considers negation in early sound recording by focusing on one of Thomas Edison's short-lived inventions, the reusable wax cylinder phonograph device (1887–1913). Although Edison speculated that this groundbreaking contraption would have a variety of possible applications, many accounts dwelled on his proposition that the device would conserve the voices of the soon-to-be-dead. The phonograph became a sonic mausoleum par excellence.[59] What would it mean to think less about ghosts and more about the finitude and finiteness of matter? In rhetoric that runs counter to this hauntology, the Edison Company's promotional materials often noted the device's economic aspects for recording sound at home and in the office. Some models came with a shaver or a knife to remove the top layer of the cylinder. Far from preserving last words for eternity, customers were urged to trim costs by shaving off the top layer and cutting new grooves before having to purchase a fresh roll. The shaver counters the condition of scarcity by making space for what is yet to be recorded. That Edison tied ephemerality to sonic capture remains a marginal concern in the theoretical treatments of this medium. Although some sounds of the late nineteenth century have successfully been preserved, including his own voice, other cylinders were used and reused, owing to this design, not despite it.

Chapter 2 turns to the business of cinema. Film scholar Jean-Louis Comolli contended that "a subterranean history, a negative history, needs to be written. A history of what was not possible and what was eliminated could reveal the real dimension of what did take place. Shadows are a part of the picture."[60] Taking up Comolli's provocation on elimination, the analysis keeps with the physical cutting of celluloid strips. The chapter considers the legacies of avant-garde cinema pioneers such as Esfir Shub and Dziga Vertov with an eye to the material process of reuse. These early practitioners chronicled the technical editing process as a part of a moment in the newly erected union that could not be described as anything but undergoing a dire film stock crisis. Cutting and recutting films transformed under these conditions into aesthetic and political strategies to maximize the number of films derived from limited raw materials. All of this notwithstanding, their own prevailing theories of editing (*montage*) emphasized the psychological effects produced by the juxtaposition of disparate frames. The Soviet filmmakers, for the most part, circumvented the meaning of the physical act of severing, privileging cognitive and aesthetic explanations of the cinematic instead. Despite this divergence between theory and praxis, the cutting room floor is fertile ground. In this space, undoing is not merely a hindrance but a constitutive component of cinematic production, reshaping the boundaries of the industry's possibilities at that point in time.

Chapter 3 focuses on the Apollo 11 moon landing broadcast and its eventual fate in recorded form. In 2009, on the fortieth anniversary of the event, NASA admitted that its search for the original tapes containing documentation of this momentous event had come up short: the tapes had likely been overwritten sometime in the 1980s. Although the moon landing is a noteworthy event for media history, the vanishing of its recording passed with little more than a murmur.[61] As Susan Murray has more generally observed, this tendency reflects "the reluctance of many contemporary television studies scholars to engage with questions of technology, vision, and its relation to aesthetics."[62] Building on the circumstances that precipitated the disappearance of a significant material trace of human history, this chapter turns to NASA's widespread deployment of demagnetization of magnetic records and archival protocols. The erasure, however unintended, followed an operative logic embedded in the apparatus itself. It happened due to a protocol for managing scarcity by weighing data capture with the limitations of physical space, which even resource-rich state agencies could not ignore. The eventual loss of the moonwalk tapes—a failure that is at once unspectacular and monumental in terms of its exposure of a system of relations based on reuse—shines a light on the clash between an internal economy reliant on undoing and the will to keep materials of great historical worth.

Around the same time the moon landing was recorded, typewriting—the subject of chapter 4—became a key force driving excessive textual production. As Craig Robertson meticulously details, the proliferation of documents across bureaus in the late nineteenth century spurred the creation of the iconic filing cabinet, a vertical system that, he argues, compressed information and restructured office labor and the laborers' roles.[63] I follow another path, one that leads through practices meant to cut down on drafts and paper waste before anything had to be stored or filed. The chapter uncovers four strategies conceived to bring order and uniformity to office work and, more particularly, to normalize the secretary's body, a response to the mounting deluge of documents. Between the 1920s and 1970s, a group of inventions that pledged to cleanse the page of error arrived in rapid succession, each advancing the ideal of the flawless record. Some, like the now-famous Liquid Paper and IBM's proto–word processing Correcting Selectric II typewriter, performed notably well on the market. Not all fared as well, such as the laser eraser, which never quite found its niche. These technologies are part of a whole lineage of corrections, comprising efforts to eliminate typographical errors that have long troubled writing, copying, printing, and typing. As data volume swelled, undoing was said to ease production by reducing the need for multiple drafts and do-overs. It could not, however, save anyone from the error that inevitably came next.

Chapter 5 steps into contemporary debates surrounding deletion in the digital era, or the presumed lack thereof, to unpack a popular discourse about internet memory and its infinite promise. What role does negation have in a lifeworld that has seemingly achieved total recall? A major one. If we are to believe the assurances of tech companies, storage concerns are relics of the past. The dream of infinite memory, an archive without end, has its antecedents in early debates about networks, where the digital was posited as disembodied and unmoored from material constraints. "There is no trash in cyberspace because there is nothing material to be disposed of, and indeed, because everything may be kept."[64] Such utopian aspirations and the delusion of an unlittered virtual plane raise the question of whether abundance could replace scarcity as the defining technical condition. Victor Mayer-Schönberger suggests as much in his famous assertion that "the internet never forgets."[65] In an ironic twist, scholarship critiquing the neoliberal practice of unreserved data capture has inadvertently provided the perfect slogan for tech companies' marketing strategies: "let our cloud protect your data." From a practical standpoint, the chapter argues that grappling with the materiality of the internet must begin by acknowledging a simple fact. There is too much data to keep, and the cost of data collection en masse is climbing fast. Despite appearances, the unforgetting internet owes its memory to profit. Commodified, "memory" is another line item on a budget.

One

SHAVING WAX CYLINDERS, LAYER AFTER LAYER, UNTIL THERE IS NONE

This machine arose from the depths of time against time.[1]

• • • Nothing lasts forever, not even our sun. But if no organic substance does, can something else—say, a box—preserve the echoes of a living body for perpetuity? This was a question asked before the turn of the twentieth century. In 1877, Thomas Alva Edison unveiled a device that transcribed sound waves onto a recording medium and replayed them instantaneously. With the first successful demonstration of his phonograph, time was suddenly arrested, even mummified, according to some critics and theorists. The historical importance of this technical artifact stems not only from its ability to capture—others preceded Edison in this regard—but also from the phonograph's future-oriented capability of allowing listeners a chance to revisit past moments and times through boxed (oftentimes also described as "bottled" or "canned") sound.[2]

In the wake of late nineteenth-century advances in sound recording and photographic technologies, it has become conventional to view these apparatuses, which capture fleeting visual and auditory impressions, as revealing an undeniable truth bound up with the passage of time, namely, mortality. They offer a means of rejecting this finality through the promise of eternal recurrence. Despite early praise from popular outlets like *Scientific American*, which celebrated the phonograph's ability for "indefinite repetition"—a sentiment still echoed in today's discussions of cloud technology—mechanical vessels like the phonograph are far from infinitely enduring, nor were they designed to be.[3] With this tension in mind, this chapter thinks more carefully about substrates, finiteness, and how these intersect with ideas about human finitude.

I consider the phonograph as one manifestation of the problem of limits as weighed against the urge to boundlessly extend our short-lived existence on this Earth via external storage devices. In addressing the phonograph and its scholarly resonances, I am concerned with how media theory places death (finitude) along and at odds with technical capture. This is all while bracketing material scarcity (finiteness) when debating the essence of the phonograph as derived from the capacity to arrest time (finality). Turning to theory, one finds the withering human body at the heart of the phonographic project; by reexamining a brief interval in the history of this device and industry, I recover the exhaustion and depletion of matter as an equally important prism of inquiry.

Jeffrey Sconce, Carolyn Marvin, John Durham Peters, and many others have already recognized how popular media discourses have assimilated and continue to echo, to a certain extent, lingering notions regarding analog recording that were born out of the Victorian era, most pertinently in its preoccupation with mortality.[4] Each marvelous invention, upon its arrival, was heralded as a potential redress for the most intractable of human limitations. One might read these reflections and aspirations projected onto the phonograph through Amanda Lagerkvist's lens of "existential media," which are also "transcendent media: media that promise to transcend the ultimate boundaries, by allowing for relating across the threshold."[5] And the dead did speak. Edison, drawn to the idea that technology might somehow interrupt the finality of death, proclaimed that "speech has become, as it were, immortal."[6] In Edison's formulation, immortality is achieved when time (thus death) is filtered through an iterative machine—an annihilation of annihilation of sorts. Reading such an avowal out of context, however, obscures the fact that even this visionary businessman was quite unsure about the technology's particular nature or purpose as he announced its existence to the world.

In an article published in 1878, Edison famously detailed ten possible modes for sound recording to be employed and, no less crucially, commercialized in a variety of settings and for an array of clienteles. In this tentative introduction to the phonograph, Edison prophetically predicted, as Roland Gelatt suggests, many, if not most, contemporary uses of sound recording.[7]

1. Letter writing and all kinds of dictation without the aid of a stenographer.
2. Phonographic books, which will speak to blind people without effort on their part.
3. The teaching of elocution.
4. Reproduction of music.
5. The "Family Record"—a registry of sayings, reminiscences, etc., by members of a family in their own voices, and of the last words of dying persons.
6. Music-boxes and toys.
7. Clocks that should announce in articulate speech the time for going home, going to meals, etc.
8. The preservation of languages by exact reproduction of the manner of pronouncing.
9. Educational purposes; such as preserving the explanations made by a teacher, so that the pupil can refer to them at any moment, and spelling or other lessons placed upon the phonograph for convenience in committing to memory.
10. Connection with the telephone, so as to make that instrument an auxiliary in the transmission of permanent and invaluable records, instead of being the recipient of momentary and fleeting communication.[8]

As extensive as it is scattered, this often cited list spawned diverse scholarship grappling with the cultural, musicological, epistemological, and ontological meanings of the phonograph device, the phonogram record, and phonographic logic. For linguists and ethnographers, item 8 on the list marked the beginning of developing methodologies for studying spoken language and conserving vanishing ones, though not without introducing Western biases and the exploitation of the (recorded) Other; for disability scholars, the phonographic book of item 2 represents the ways in which physical challenges may not only be alleviated by scientific and technical developments but become their driving motor (perhaps even for Edison himself, who was already hard of hearing). For those interested in gadgetry, items 4, 6, and 7 (music boxes, toys, and clocks) seamlessly blend into a long technical lineage from ancient mechanical automata to virtual assistants. For musicologists, the list rightfully symbolizes the budding stages of a new musical mass market when aesthetic standards of quality had yet to be formed. In Emily Thompson's words, sound reproduction was achieved "before a need for its function had been identified."[9]

Despite the counsel of his colleagues, it took Edison nearly two decades to concede that consumer preference for prerecorded, nonerasable, non-reusable records had overtaken the primary use case he had envisioned, that of dictation. This, of course, was the function he had so fervently promoted in his marketing of the phonograph to bureaucrats and business professionals. That choice targeted a sphere of economic life where the ephemerality of captured ideas and dictated letters was considered not detrimental but utilitarian. With the phonograph placed in the interiors of the office, the transiency of its auditory recordings became part of the operational humdrum.

Surely, this type of operational and dynamic use is conceptually at odds with the durational aims of items 5, 8, and 10 (preserving family memories and languages, and producing recorded educational materials), through which Edison extols the potential for the "permanent and invaluable" over "momentary and fleeting communication." This line of thought has had a lasting influence on media theory's ongoing fascination with the ghostly, deathly, and eternally resonant. Such legacy is also related to Edison's own keen interest in solving the mysteries of the afterlife, a pursuit that was to culminate in the "spirit phone" (the fabrication of which he, perhaps regrettably, failed to complete).

As outlined in the introduction, my primary interest revolves not around the content produced by the phonograph—or that of any other technology invoked in this book—but rather around the designs and the means by which production is made possible in the first place. To echo Wolfgang Ernst: "The phonograph as a media artifact not only carries cultural meanings like words and music but is at the same time an archive of cultural engineering by its very material fabrication—a kind of frozen media knowledge that—in a media archaeological sense—is waiting to be unfrozen, liquefied."[10] The conundrum, then, is how to move beyond this chaotic Ur moment, captured in a list that championed competing and often contradictory imaginaries. From the phonograph's initial form to its solidification as a device that "had to become an archival medium" in the second decade of the twentieth century, the value of long-term durability has undeniably persisted while the allure of ephemerality has steadily waned.[11]

Nevertheless, this chapter dwells on the reusable cylinder's historically short stint before the phonograph ultimately evolved into a stable and nonreusable storage medium. This discussion aims to dislodge the phonograph from its exclusive association with the *archival* (whether preserving music or traces, near-extinct dialects, or human lives) and instead reposition it within a genealogy of erasable media, one that extends into digital media's tendency to obscure all that disappears. Strikingly, within the vast body of work on Edison's phonograph, only a few words are dedicated to its reusability, despite this being a singular feature in its contemporaneous technological landscape. It was the first invention of its kind that allowed everyday users not only to record sound but also to control the lifespan of their recordings by rerecording over them several times. Although dictation machines and reusable records remained a success in the eyes of only a few—chiefly Edison—and were ultimately abandoned, they nonetheless introduced a novel mode of interaction between humans and a mechanical device that as yet had no established scripts and, consequently, no instinctive consumer base. Thus, the reusable combination of phonograph shaver and erasable cylinder created a feature the likes of which would only reappear half a century later with writable magnetic recording technologies.

More than simply tracing the rise and fall of reusability, I begin with uncovering operational evanescence in early recording technologies, which are too often assumed to be fixed rather than dynamic entities. This presumed stability typically stems from the propensity to essentialize a particular function or instrument. The following sections, therefore, show how privileging claims of infinity and abundance obscures design decisions that reveal the material conditions of crafting storage technologies in the modern age.

FOREVER AFFIXED: THE GHOSTS OF THE PAST SING

From the technology's inception, fantasies that infinite technical preservation would overcome human finitude played a role in grappling with the phonograph's yet- or soon-to-be-realized potential. Despite the gap between the phonograph's initial performance and what it would later be engineered to accomplish, Edison was quick to proclaim the arrival of "speech capable of indefinite repetition from automatic records."[12] A remainder of the talking or singing (and admittedly finite) subject was to be captured in material form, mechanically conjured to perform again and again for its listeners. This inbuilt juxtaposition between flux and stasis, human and machine, and finiteness and abundance heightens the affective power of sound etched into an inanimate object. Hearing those first attempts to capture human voice was purported to stimulate in the audience "the profoundest of sensations, to arouse the liveliest of human emotions."[13] "Liveliest" is certainly an intriguing choice of words to describe sentiments in response to a moment when it seemed that humanity had potentially come closer to transcending mortality.[14] Storage space seemingly acts as a custodian of life and offers immunity from the finality of death, or, at the very least, gives off the "illusion of a real presence" after passing.[15]

The immortalized moment substantively extends and shapes the voices of the living and their psychological experiences. Various scholars, Friedrich Kittler chief among them, view the transition from writing's symbolic logic to the indexical quality of analog recording (whether through the camera lens or the phonograph stylus) as a decisive, epoch-making event in history, one that reconfigures the human body, the senses, perception, and epistemic regimes more broadly.[16] Just as the audiences of the phonograph became hyperaware of vocal expression, the device, as described by Barbara Engh, also "dissociated the voice and embodied consciousness."[17] The emergent reciprocal and disjunctive relation between machine and body meant that nineteenth-century recording technologies constituted "new archives of consciousness."[18] So momentous was this spatial and temporal reorganization of reality and phenomena that Mark Katz coined the term "phonograph effect."[19]

A crucial element of this effect was the displacement of the fleeting by the ostensibly permanent. The association of wax (a malleable matter from which the recording cylinder was composed) with death is not unique to phonographic production. Jane Eade suggests that the soft composition of wax was central to the fabrication of the phonograph's artistic antecedents, considering the substance's properties as an "ideal medium for the combination of morbid realism with a message of fleshy impermanence."[20] For Eade, the choice of this material to create *memento mori* objects was due precisely to its softness and susceptibility to decay, which would prompt viewers to contemplate the transitory nature of mortal beings. In contrast, Edison's laboratory would offer wax a second chance as a chemically hardened substance that was, in some views, to do the opposite; rather than serving as an analog of the human body that would equally perish, it would take the person's place, in certain respects.

Edison's phonograph, with its relative hardness, has been widely theorized as an adversary of death. Jonathan Sterne rigorously accounts for the breadth of historical sources that alluded to the world beyond as reincarnated through the record.[21] In an exploration of the cultural history surrounding Edison's era, he traces the phonograph's conceptual connection to an array of techniques designed to extend the durability of products, and flesh and bone. These methods range from preserving perishable goods through canning to embalming corpses, indicating a broader social preoccupation with preservation. Under such conditions, the assumed boundlessness of storage defies and solves the problem of humanity's boundedness. Indeed, one of Edison's competitors in the cylinder market responded to such yearnings (or anxieties) for the ever after by branding its celluloid-based products Indestructible and Everlasting. These were said to be unbreakable media that could outdo the comparatively fragile wax cylinder.[22]

Much space has been devoted to how Victorians assuaged their obsessions with mortality by appealing to endurance in engraved form; in light of this emphasis, undoing seldom appears as a relevant practice. John Durham Peters's widely referenced *Speaking into the Air* contemplates the spiritualistic tendencies that informed the reception of the sound recording apparatus in this era. One commentator—possibly parroting Edison—proclaimed: "Death has lost some of its sting since we are able to forever retain the voices of the dead."[23] Severing the link between presence and the living body, the advent of recording via the phonograph evidently ushered in a new auditory market, one built on repositories of sonic (and ghostly) memories. Whether made of wax or shellac, these materials granted a tangible, lasting existence to sounds that, by their very nature, should have vanished the moment they reached the listener's ears. Peters reminds his readers that, as all technological solutions do, it introduced a new predicament involving a type of communication based on the phonograph's immutable simulation of sound. Can a dialogue with the dead, mediated through an iterative process of a machine, truly be deemed a two-way street when all it offers is its vaunted "indefinite repetition"?

This asymmetric incommunicability that began with the phonograph reshaped our understanding of transmission and complicated the very act of memorialization.

Kittler, for his part, follows spectral invocations through the poetic and literary works of Rainer Maria Rilke and others, emphasizing the phonograph's pivotal function in fostering a widespread discourse grounded in analog capture (a direct imprint of sound itself), unlike the arbitrariness of written language. What the phonograph registered was not merely speech but something far deeper—something capable of piercing the protective layers of our psyche, revealing what psychoanalysis calls the Real. The recording needle brings us face to face with reminders of our impermanence, those unsettling echoes of time that resist everyday defenses. Douglas Kahn and Charles Grivel similarly riffle through pages written by poets, critics, and novelists like Auguste Villiers de l'Isle-Adam and Edgar Allan Poe in search of themes that cut across artistic engagements with this piece of hardware.[24] Overwhelmingly, they, too, describe how the machine is positioned alongside death and against it, as the epigraph to this chapter notes; it represents the end of a subject and, at the same time, nothing short of an unattainable wish: "May it last forever!"[25]

Read from this perspective, with the arrival of canned voices, the distinction between affixing the "last words of dying persons," as promised by Edison, and recording the voice of an opera singer for entertainment becomes immaterial; whether one is intentionally capturing a person's last breaths or simply capturing *any* moment is of little importance for such accounts.[26] This context collapse in favor of decontextualized outcomes is not exclusive to studies of the phonograph; parallel assumptions have permeated speculations on the nature of analog image making. Every shot taken is a moment gone, and every face apprehended within the frame will prove to be someone's death mask, so goes the argument.[27] Film theory's yearning for the possibility of continuity beyond the relentless march of time, even if only as a moment preserved on celluloid, has been summarized by Philip Rosen as "the sublimation of this impossible impulse to defeat death."[28] These acts of cinemato-graphy, photo-graphy and phono-graphy thus have something in common when it comes to the existential interpretations of the act of inscription.

At this juncture, I take a cue from Sterne's astute observation that the tension between the promises of eternity and the undeniable realities of impermanence parallels the "difference between the imagination and the practice of sound recording in its early days."[29] Theories that cast wax as a site of memory and as an archive often foreground phonographic preservation, an emphasis closely aligned with that conjured by the Edison company and its branding language at the turn of the century.[30] This kind of disposition upholds the archive as sacrosanct through a process of idealization, arguing that it is the essence of the machine while deemphasizing the importance of praxis as relevant to the ontological debate. To put it plainly, it is a question of what kind of stories we feature at the expense of others. My aim is to sidestep the fancies of the period and its long-lasting hold on theory—the influence of which Andrea Bohlman and Peter McMurray called the "phonographic regime"—to flesh out the analytic potential of undoing adapted to a particular technical configuration.[31]

All in all, promises of infinity presume abundance, a rhetoric that clads the realities of instability, privation, and scarcity that guided the making of this particular and short-lived ephemeral feature. The reusable cylinder's uniqueness is subsumed and dismissed under the generic label "phonography," which means disregarding several constitutive differences between idealized and actual use. The decision to foreground the cylinder aims to challenge the latent suppositions that readily equate a machine's act of capture with the durability of the record that must hypothetically follow. Recording does not equal preservation—at least, not always. We must be careful not to confuse the ability to store with the assumption that such a record will persist over long stretches of time. Finally, the prevailing emphasis on the phonograph's presumed ability to seize something of this mortal world for perpetuity creates a tacit notion of immutability, all while cylinders regularly eroded during use, and only some remain playable today (a fact that created a pricey market for any remaining artifacts in pristine condition). In tandem with unplayability caused by mold and fungi, wear, warping, disintegration, or decay, there is also an ephemerality of a different kind.

The introduction of transiency, in the intentional sense and for purposes of reuse, is a matter regarded almost entirely inconsequential. It is important, therefore, to underscore some critical details that have fallen by the wayside. In technical terms, the makeup of phonographic records fundamentally differs from one talking machine to another. Irrespective of brand names, the phonograph and its circular cylinder and the gramophone with its flat disc represent two distinct modes of sonic production. The gramophone's flat records were created in a single act of stamping or engraving before being delivered to the customer; Edison's reusable objects, by contrast, permitted multiple re-recordings on the same mutable substrate. This innovation effectively shifted a measure of control over a record's lifespan into the hands of users, regardless of their intended purposes. The ability to erase and reuse is a unique feature of the wax cylinder.[32] Unlike shellac, the wax cylinder circulated through a different economy, possessed distinct material properties, and was shaped by an altogether different design philosophy. The next section examines how, early in the development of the cylinder, Edison adopted the practice of shaving as a means of fully harnessing the potential of the material as a re-recordable medium. It was thus not only a vessel for channeling apparitions or disseminating the voices of singers and players; it was also not only a medium used to stockpile voices captured during colonial expeditions and early field recordings in the service of Western science and control;[33] it was also meant for practical uses, a reusable tool for the middle-class laborer.[34]

CYLINDERS UPON CYLINDERS: CAPTURE, OPERATIONAL RECORDINGS, AND DISCARD

How did impermanence enter a domain vehemently associated with artificial immortality? The phonograph's initial (not yet reusable) model was conceived before Edison reached the acme of his worldwide fame and notoriety. In the mid-1870s, he was enlisted by businessmen and corporations alike, tasked with the creation of devices and novelties. During this time, he chanced upon the notion of boxing voices while experimenting with a method to mechanically transcribe telegraph messages onto paraffin paper. His aim was to enable these messages to be read multiple times at different speeds, potentially allowing further telegrams to be transmitted with minimal, or even no, human involvement.[35] He observed that the physical imprints left on the paper tape generated faint, indistinct sounds, sparking within him the suspicion that a similar process could be applied to the recording of human speech. The phonograph came into existence as a means of automating labor, increasing efficiency and productivity, and "saving expensive copper cables."[36] Therefore, the technology's nascent stage was less an exercise in conjuring spirits and had more to do with the earthly concerns of resources, investments, and profit. Casey Cep puts it best: "Edison's gift, here and elsewhere, was not so much inventing as what he called perfecting—finding ways to make things better or cheaper or both. Edison did not look for problems in need of solutions; he looked for solutions in need of modification."[37]

It almost goes without saying that the eponymous naming of Edison's phonograph tends to obscure the contributions of many others. Among them were engineers such as John Kruesi, Jonas Walter Aylsworth, and Walter Miller, who labored in his laboratories to bring this blueprint and countless others to fruition (although not all of the prototypes became commercially successful business and household devices). Edison's enterprise expanded exponentially with the "establishment of history's first industrial research and development facility, at Menlo Park, New Jersey."[38] For some, this achievement remains the most foundational of his inventions, even amid the numerous contenders vying for prominence, from electricity to cinema. In many ways, Edison's public persona serves as a precursor to the archetypal Silicon Valley tech entrepreneur, often compared to figures like Steve Jobs—a charismatic leader portrayed as a solitary genius. The company's promotional materials tend to obscure the army of employees behind him, reinforcing the image of an isolated, singular visionary.[39] Likewise, the technological complex designed for Edison's business is an architectural precursor to start-up spaces where work, innovation, and life commingle.

With the expanded workforce, the once modest workshop evolved into a bustling laboratory that set its sights on the creation of a device capable of capturing and replaying both speech and music. This endeavor soon culminated in the creation of the first phonograph model, which evolved from a mere sketch into a rudimentary yet functional machine capable of imprinting sound waves onto a cylindrical tinfoil roll.[40] The early version of the phonograph garnered significant attention from the press, which recounted its public demonstrations with a sense of awe and wonder. During such events, audience members actively participated in recording their voices and raptly listened as they were replayed, although the audio output left much to be desired. Even for listeners at the time, the low-quality recordings were scratchy, intermittently unintelligible, and noisy, garbling speech and distorting tunes with inaccurate playback speeds and wavering pitch. As such, the traveling exhibitions elicited feelings of both enchantment and dismay. Fueled by the public's yearning to own a tangible piece of an apparatus that had captured the evanescent, licensing companies began peddling tinfoil souvenirs. Lisa Gitelman fittingly describes these as "dead tokens" because the rolls would become unplayable once removed from the machine; with only a precarious receptacle as its storage medium, fleeting sound was lost to time once more.[41] Although the company and its licensors began to tout the phonograph's capabilities for "preservation for all time" on a commercial scale, transience remained a stubborn, unwanted presence.[42]

Ironically, only a decade later, ephemerality would become the fulcrum on which Edison's sound recording business would be relaunched. As public interest in the imperfect tinfoil technology—a mere proof of concept—began to fade, so too did Edison's enthusiasm for the invention. Edison revisited the concept a decade later, in 1887, emboldened by Alexander Graham Bell and Charles Sumner Tainter's graphophone and Emile Berliner's gramophone. The next-generation phonograph players were reputed to deliver a far better experience compared to the original device. The improved phonograph, which was soon selling around fifty machines a day, introduced several new features that drastically altered the production processes and consumption experiences of recorded sounds.[43]

Following in the footsteps of Volta Laboratory, the roll was retired and replaced by a wax cylinder, which proved to be a superior recording substrate and a more durable substance than tinfoil. Suddenly, it was possible to mount and remount the cylinders on different devices, which meant that phonograms could be swapped, and recorded sound could travel across short and long distances. The improvements introduced in the second iteration of the phonograph broadened its applications beyond the realm of popular amusement at fairs and exhibitions. It found new roles in public and domestic musical entertainment, professional use by governments and private businesses, and even as a tool for personal correspondence, transforming the phonograph into an epistolary aid.[44]

The newly developed storage device allowed for a two-minute recording on wax, a notable leap in sound recording capabilities. Initially, the cylinders were composed of an organic mixture of "animal, vegetable and mineral waxes" that were later blended and hardened with "cotton string, tape, or a mesh cloth backing."[45] With their ears to the ground and attuned to the demands of sellers and consumers, Edison's laboratory team continued to refine and change the cylinder's formula and makeup, pivoting from natural wax to organic "metallic soaps" made of salts of fatty acids mixed with metals. Owing to additional alterations to the substrate's composition and the machine's design, the recording time (and thus its storage capacity) doubled to four minutes by 1908. For all the design flaws critics pointed out regarding its fidelity, the improved models boasted better overall audio quality, increased volume, and the ability to produce multiple copies from a single recording.

In addition to this increased storage capacity—and pivotal for this discussion—was the addition of a knife that would shave off a top layer of the wax cylinder, leaving the substrate smooth and ready to capture new sounds. In plain terms, the process of recording and erasing could be repeated until there was no matter left to subtract from, or, more precisely, up to twelve rounds.[46] The enlistment of erasure to optimize and adapt retention was thus hardwired into what was heralded as a crypt of living speech for eternal preservation. It was certainly no accident. A laboratory note from 1888 details experimentation that entangled making with undoing: "Where the process of trimming a layer of wax from a cylinder (literally erasing a recording) had been a distinct operation (requiring a separate adjustment of the cutting depth), Edison now added a narrow trimming knife blade near the recording point so that erasing and recording were carried on simultaneously."[47] The many patents that Edison and others in the company submitted to protect such erasable schemes indicate that the shaver was not an insignificant feature.[48]

Given his historically close relationship with corporate clients, Edison's business plan and marketing strategy primarily appealed to the needs and desires of companies attempting to revolutionize and modernize their workflows. In short, he destined the device to perform rather unremarkable busy work. The taxing tasks of committing speech to paper, including letter writing, court transcriptions, and journalistic reportage, would be eased by introducing voice recording. Wherever there were professionals in need of improving the operation of dictation, there would be the phonograph—a precursor to the myth of the paperless office that would appear some decades later in the 1970s. Soon enough, even the Senate and the House of Representatives each had six phonographs (and a shaving machine) to streamline the day's work.[49] One observer expressed the secret behind this swift adoption in poetic terms, foreshadowing, in many ways, how we discuss artificial intelligence (AI) in the twenty-first century: "The real mission of the phonograph is that of a helper. Its life and greatness among the labor-saving mechanisms of the world will depend on this fact. It is a humanized bunch of iron nerves and sinews that has come among us to relieve the world more or less, of mental strain; to bring the world's workers in closer contact with the means of multiplying their power, saving time, and preserving that which, without it, would escape all record."[50] In this evocative scenario, the phonograph quite clearly amplifies the laboring body, not the dying one.

The maxim of efficiency at the Menlo Park laboratory was thus logically replicated into acts of reuse, which in turn translated into monetary gain. Storage limitations would be addressed by expanding the recording time of a cylinder (a task that proved to be quite the engineering feat); better yet, this problem could be resolved by admitting impermanence into the scene of sound writing. In an effort to reduce the cost of a single record, the improved design drew upon a long tradition of material scarcity, frugality, and recycling.[51] Simply put, the price per recording diminishes if the material is reused multiple times.

This new form of record keeping soon swept through modern offices, prompting a corresponding reorganization of their physical spaces. The phonographic apparatus and its requisite laborers were distributed across the workspace, occupying several different areas. After a recording was made, an office boy would deliver it to a stenographer for transcription onto paper. Once transcribed, he would then delicately remove the cylinder from the machine, shave it clean, and store the blank cylinder in a wooden cabinet for future use. Consequently, the strategy to enhance the cylinder's storage capacity also required bureaus to allocate space specifically for storing cylinders that awaited future operations. While a few cabinets were equipped with pegs to hold the blank cylinders, the more typical arrangement involved meticulously organizing the canisters in drawers. These phonograph-specific furnishings, along with the evolving logistics of interoffice communication, became the newest elements of a burgeoning architecture of modern control and efficiency.[52]

The figure of the box was so entrenched in the corporate lexicon that *The Phonograph and How to Use It*, an Edison-sanctioned publication, begins with an attempt at a brief prehistory of phonography. The opening passage cites a vision from a seventeenth-century speculative satire, which envisions a fantastical box. It is a strange version of a book filled not with pages but with mechanical bits designed to be heard rather than read. Reminiscing about what the phonograph would eventually become, the story describes a movement "straight, as from the mouth of man [after which] proceed all the distinct and different sounds."[53]

Three centuries separate this invocation of a marvelous contraption from the pragmatic day-to-day happenings of the early twentieth century, as captured in an anecdote from October 1, 1910. On that day, a bomb exploded in the *Los Angeles Times* building, killing twenty-one people. In response, the mayor enlisted the help of detective William J. Burns, who was celebrated in the press as "the greatest detective certainly," to track down the perpetrators.[54] During the investigation, one of Burns's colleagues discovered that the suspects owned a dictating machine and proposed retrieving the recordings, hoping they might contain incriminating evidence. However, Burns advised him to focus on finding something else first: "Take a look around the offices of the suspect and see whether there was anywhere a short square black box on legs." Burns explained that the box was a shaving device, "and if the operative found such a device, there would be no need to search further for records made by the suspect."[55] One box generates, while the other erases. (Yet, even though an erasing machine was present, Burns had cracked the case, an achievement for which he received a letter of commendation from the president.) More than an example of media forensics at the turn of the century, this reporting suggests that knowledge of boxes and their operational processes was becoming increasingly common during this period. As these technologies for communication (and not necessarily preservation) were being popularized, domesticated, and mass-produced, they became embedded in everyday life.

A history of these sound storage boxes would be incomplete without addressing why the shaver itself warranted its own dedicated container. In the early 1900s, several personal-use phonograph models produced by the Phonograph Company came equipped with an integrated shaver component. The marketing rhetoric celebrated the promise of reusability. However, the attachment's performance proved less than stellar, as it struggled with erasure. As a result, the machine produced subsequent recordings of inferior quality. By the 1910s, this once-integrated shaving operation had been primarily outsourced to stand-alone devices, leading to the spatial and functional separation of inscription and erasure. Consumers could either purchase a personal shaver or visit dealers to have their home-recorded cylinders undone. Just a few years later, in 1912, Edison introduced a new, more affordable hand-shaving machine, sold for as little as $4.[56] Thus, in just over a decade, what was initially marketed as a built-in feature was swiftly transformed into an additional expense.

The division of capture and cancellation into separate, neat containers was mainly a result of the phonograph's architecture, which it shared with other media. As an anti-residual medium, the phonograph aligns with centuries-old endeavors to protect machines from dust—a concern now mirrored in the pristine conditions of contemporary data centers. Machines, to put it simply, struggle to function when any particles interfere, slipping in between and under their moving parts and disrupting their delicate setup. As the dust generated by the shaving procedure dissipates (in stark contrast to dust settling in an archive, a testimony to time accumulating on top of objects untouched), the likelihood that some particles could remain on the cylinder's surface becomes a major obstacle. Inescapable microscopic remainders of records past had the potential to disrupt proper operations, thus merging the old with the new in an aberrant manner. The box mitigated that threat by featuring a compartment on top for collecting and discarding the residue. Those who performed the shaving over and over again, it was claimed, gained embodied sensuous knowledge of its inner workings and probable failures: "After very little practice, the eye and ear of the operator will become accustomed to the sound and appearance of a proper cut, and will readily detect anything wrong."[57]

The phonograph's box enclosed its guts, shielding them from harm as much as possible.[58] As an entertainment device in the home or as office technology, its cubic form serves as both a tangible, protective structure and, phenomenologically, a design that pushes its technicity to the background. As Thompson theorizes, "in order to efface the machine, the machine had to become inaudible."[59] Containers hide, allowing contents to be heard with clarity. Looking closely at the phonograph, we see that it is rife with acts of self-negation, one of which is embodied in the very process of cutting into the cylinder. The design of the shaving box ensures that the potentially disruptive, audible noise of reproduction—the mechanical hum of undoing—can be pushed aside.[60]

De facto, shaving diminishes the lifespan of the record, which, if left untouched, might otherwise endure for longer, allowed to degrade and oxidize over time. Yet, each cut into its surface removes more material, bringing the record closer to its end. It would be a mistake to regard this process as nothing more than destructive. From an operative perspective, I would even go so far as to argue that shaving as materialized in wax is both a constitutive and a generative process. For Edison, shaving was a crucial element in enabling capture, not merely an action that follows inscription. Negation lies at the very heart of crafting recordable cylinders, a necessary step long before the first sound is even seized or replayed: "I employ a removable phonogram-blank having a recording-surface of a yielding material. I prefer to use a wax or a wax composition. These blanks after being mounted in the machine have their recording surface turned true by a knife which is carried by the rocking holding-arm and the point of which is preferably in close proximity to the recording-point. The blanks used with my machine are also preferably adapted to have their surface turned off by this same cutting-tool for the purpose of using them a number of times, an old record being removed to make place for a new one."[61]

Technically speaking, simply molding the wax into a cylindrical shape was insufficient. Its surface remained uneven, unfit to capture sonic impressions, until a knife delicately carved into the spinning cylinder—penetrating, reshaping, (de)forming, and refining it. Only through this process did the surface become smooth and leveled, a "tabula rasa" of sorts. Through negation, it was ordered to bear imprints ("turning true"). Ergo, the blank record is born out of an act of undoing, one intrinsically tied to its creation. Neither act can exist without the other. Once the surface is rendered inscribable, the shaver may be summoned again, this time to strip away undesired content ("turn off"). This second erasure introduced potentiality rather than permanence. The promise of future recordings in the plural depends on the continuous removal of layers, gradually wearing down the material rather than preserving or petrifying it into a fixed state. In this way, the medium remains open to change, not frozen in place.

Historical accounts of the phonograph's rise and fall often lay the blame squarely on Edison's failure to grasp the true nature of the market he himself had been so instrumental in creating. While Edison had grand aspirations for his invention's potential uses, particularly in office work and dictation, the public, it seemed, simply wanted to listen, nothing more.[62] As a result, the sales of blank cylinders and Ediphones (phonographs designed specifically for dictation) gradually declined, while prepackaged, flat-disc, read-only records—featuring captivating performances by skilled musicians—became the new standard of entertainment during the early twentieth century. Around the same time as the blue Amberol cylinder was introduced to the market in 1912, Edison finally relented and entered the flat record business. In the long run, even though numerous blanks were sold, reusable storage was passed over for the disc, with its comparatively larger storage capacity of seven minutes and lower price. The company gradually phased out musical cylinders throughout the 1920s, while reusable cylinders for dictation continued to be produced in relatively small quantities, sustaining a loyal, albeit shrinking, diehard fan base well into the 1960s.[63]

There is much to learn from the relatively short life of the reusable cylinder format, even as it consisted of spurts of success followed by commercial slumps. The purpose of attending to the branching directions of this inscription-based technology was to examine the open-endedness of an early moment. The cylinder's layered multiplicity holds particular significance for this reason, especially when interrogating the essence of a technological object as something operable, harking back to Ernst's provocation. The voluminosity and circularity of the cylinder enable its recyclability, whereas the flat horizontal record only allows for a sliver of the possibilities offered by such early sound recording techniques.[64] Whether it is a format that never got its due or a brilliant idea that created a hitherto nonexistent market, the reusable element of Edison's phonograph foreshadowed a mode of engaging with recording technology that most users (or inventors, for that matter) had not anticipated. Edison certainly did not know what his device would eventually inspire. The phonograph's reusable successor, the tape recorder, would become a household product almost half a century later, separated from its forebear by two world wars and a multitude of innovations in virtually every aspect of life.

HUMANITY FOUND A WAY TO BOX SOUND: NOW WHAT?

This chapter has tracked scholarly drifts and trajectories over a century and a half of engagement with a device and its maker. Two essential questions remain unanswered. Why has one form of termination—the finitude of life—dominated discussions in media theory to such an extent that it has largely eclipsed another cessation? What can explain the relegation of erasability to little more than a footnote in historiographic debates, even as Edison's phonograph has been so extensively studied? Adding to the latter question, Thomas Levin elucidates, "The reason why it is Edison's cylinder phonograph and not Emil Berliner's flat gramophone record that has been the repeated object of literary fascination is due to no small degree to [. . .] the cylinder's 'read/write' inscriptional capacity—it is both a playback *and* recording device."[65] Levin locates users' agency and ability to initiate an action, let alone capture it on wax, as the point of conceptual and commercial attraction. I concur with this observation, although it, too, glosses over the recursiveness of reuse.

Discussions of a machine that conserves human voices and fixes them onto some physical substance in defiance of time while its recorded subjects edge closer to their demise are certainly enticing. Nevertheless, this is but one implication of what the phonograph can potentially do. When the analytic focus centers solely on the top layer of the cylinder, where inscription and transduction take place, we risk overlooking the unique process of cutting deeper into the substrate and the commercial relations it precipitates. Certain features of these devices came to symbolize the entire category of analog recording technologies in ontological debates on sound. Yet, in its idealized form, the discourse on "phonography" overlooks one type of operationality and an alternative economy of reuse. Inevitably, a certain degree of specificity is sacrificed when an entity is transformed into a category. Yet, that this particular erasure of erasure occurs is hardly surprising, given the mechanism's inherent tendency to efface itself and to be effaced. Neglecting the shaving process, therefore, ignores not only a specific mode of use but also a fundamental aspect of what the phonograph is. Its uses, after all, entail impermanence—some due to the laws of biology and physics, and others according to the currents of the market.

The absence of erasure in much of the literature might best be understood as a discursive emphasis on the nature of *re*-production, which spotlights the relentless repetition of a recording. By shifting attention to re-*production*, one begins to grasp the cyclical process of creation and unmaking, where making becomes undoing, and negation gives rise to generation once more. In the realm of *re*-production, the technical object is assumed to be stable, providing a sense of temporal continuity, material permanence, and the comfort of infinite life—until such time as decay sets in. With re-*production*, the only certainty is operationality, with no assurances as to what content, if any, will endure. One approach is concerned with the *what*, while the other focuses very much on the *how*. We need to think both at once.

If, as Charles Grivel suggests, "man only invents in his own image," might the absence of a discussion about the erasable element be read as symptomatic?[66] Despite frequent references to records capturing the final words of the dying and other macabre relics, Edison staked much of his recording business on the steadfast conviction that the phonograph was integral, rather than antithetical, to everyday dealings. Operational erasure in office settings or for personal use in the home certainly seems a trivial area of inquiry compared to mortality. Perhaps explaining why it has largely been overlooked, save for the work of the few scholars mentioned above, may offer a compelling opportunity to engage with the device's technicity as bound by scarcity. To traverse the cylinder's surface and delve into its deeper layers is, paradoxically, to confront the denial of what this technology was meant to overcome: finitude and finiteness.

The depth of the layers also invites consideration of the real, rather than imagined, conditions of production and consumption. Edison began to craft this technology during and throughout the Gilded Age, a period demarcated by commercial growth, emerging big business, and ever-widening inequality between the haves and have-nots. Against this end-of-the-nineteenth-century background, American economists like Simon Nelson Patten endorsed the goal of production as achieving a state of surplus. Patten is just one example of a thinker who—contra Malthusian theories of scarcity, deficit, and natural diminution—believed that progress bolstered by innovations in technological production and social reform would herald abundance for all.[67] Although storage may be stretched and its capacity enlarged, it is nevertheless worth noting that theories of boundlessness, as we have seen, share this capitalist optimism, in which a seemingly inexhaustible product cancels out the depletion of a body. Immortality was discovered not in the afterlife but in this world made of flesh, chemical compounds, and mechanical parts. For his part, although he was fascinated with the spirit world, Edison created a different kind of abundance despite and through the material properties of the exhaustible resources at his disposal.

Bernard Stiegler had long attended to the constitutive relation between humans and their tools. Translating his critique into material terms, the promise of the eternal misapprehends the reality of technology, which, by his account, "is itself finite. As a supplement, it opens out a gap that can be seen as in-finite, but that is not infinite but rather, more precisely, indefinite (the principle of indetermination), and, relative to retentional finitude, quasi-infinite."[68] In accepting wholesale that the phonograph's legacy is chiefly about preservation without also considering other less frequent types of operations, what recedes is that there is no boundless storage capacity, limitless growth, infinite resources, eternal life, indestructible matter, or ever-enduring boxes.

Two

CINEMATOGRAPHY IN A TIME OF MATERIAL CRISIS

Cutting is more essential than presence—not only through the effect of editing, but already, from the start, both by framing and by the controlled purge of the visible.[1]

• • • To think with erasure means to navigate between what is and what is no longer, to seek meaning in the physical spaces where records are undone and continuously remade. Where the previous chapter traced an adaptive recourse wrought by the phonogram's selectively ephemeral design, here I shift attention to the moving image, to a cinema built not only from what was captured but from what was cut away in the process. In contrast to the capitalist-driven model of entertainment that began to coalesce around Edison's time in the United States, the Soviet film industry of the early twentieth century was bound by an entirely different set of circumstances, in which dearth sculpted the trajectory of its emergence.

In the immediate aftermath of the revolution, the pages of various publications became arenas of combat, with practitioners and theorists of the period clashing over cinema's ontological and ideological stakes. Among the most incendiary exchanges—and a personal favorite—was the caustic polemic between the celebrated director Sergei Eisenstein and Béla Balázs, a Hungarian critic. Balázs sought to demonstrate that the cameraperson, the photograph, and the lens were essential in film's ascendancy to an art form, using the recently released *Battleship Potemkin* (1925) as his example.[2] Eisenstein's rebuttal arrived in print within weeks in an essay titled "Bela Forgets the Scissors."[3] In this dispute over the primacy of vision in film, he derided and summarily denounced lens-centered arguments. Eisenstein positioned his counterattack against what he saw as a Western insistence on individual authorship, the ennoblement of the camera operator, and the sanctification of the single shot as cinema's irreducible unit. No, Eisenstein insisted, it was not the lone eye or one man behind the apparatus that dictated meaning but the synergistic toil of negative cutters, their relentless shears excising and reconstituting filmic fragments into a whole through montage. Eventually, Balázs capitulated.[4] And yet, for all this fervor surrounding the act of cutting, the meaning of negative mediality remained conspicuously underdeveloped even in such deliberations on montage. This theoretical lacuna, this refusal to interrogate operative erasure as a material fact, becomes a leitmotif.

Admittedly, the creative charge and lasting influence of early Soviet cinema far exceed what any brief summary of illustrious biographies could capture here, and no single account could fully do justice to the breadth of scholarship the films have engendered.[5] The sheer scope of manifestos, treatises, and books on the subject attests to the dual existence of montage: a foundational principle of cinema, and a fault line where theory unraveled into the finest of aesthetic and political distinctions. Whatever tensions flared among filmmakers such as Eisenstein, Dziga Vertov, Vsevolod Pudovkin, Lev Kuleshov, Esfir Shub, and many others—and however unbridgeable their disagreements may have seemed—they converged on at least one fundamental tenet: the significance of the cutting shears. Yet, while the act of severing celluloid contributed greatly to cinema's materialization, they saw the scissors as a means, never as an end.[6] Throughout their many discussions of cinema's essence, its presumed ontology rarely seemed to meet the cutting tool or, by extension, the material conditions that prompt its use. Therein lies the core of this chapter.

Film historians have long observed that the chronic shortage of raw film stock constituted a material condition of Soviet cinema's (im)possibility. This constraint, integral to production, is mostly unremarked in the directors' well-trodden theories of montage.[7] As key figures who were simultaneously history-defining artists, early adopters, and influential critics, they solidified various presumptions about what film is. To echo David Bordwell, they were the "most eloquent theoreticians, all of whose theories assumed that filmic meaning is built out of an assemblage of shots which creates a new synthesis, an overall meaning that lies not within each part but in the very fact of juxtaposition."[8] This emphasis on generation eclipses any reckoning with what is discarded in that it obscures where the negative terrains of production are most incisive. Although storage (consisting of emulsion, base, reel, and canister) was a primary exigency for young communist directors navigating a new professional reality, their discourse, outlined in the following section, instead prioritizes images inscribed upon the surface of film and their perceptual effects.

Film is many things, certainly an aesthetic artifact and a conduit of ideological expression. It is also, fundamentally, a storage medium, a materiality. As much as Soviet directors wrote and operated with an acute awareness of social conflict and the means of production, as exemplified by Eisenstein's pious screeds, they also bracketed quotidian concerns from their rigorous theorizing of the craft and its function within the Soviet Union. Alla Gadassik puts it aptly: they built "a cinema that gave rise to influential theories of montage aesthetics, yet had surprisingly little to say on record about the actual work of *doing* montage."[9] The task of revising this glaring omission in film theory consists of interrogating how film's technological affordances, namely, its recombinatory potential, prompted routinized operations, strategies of optimization, and unrealized propositions for the large-scale reuse and recycling of moving images.

A THEORY FOR THE ART OF THE PRESENT/FUTURE: MONTAGE

The young "creative workers," as some of the directors called themselves, aspired above all to formulate a new grammar of action and a representational logic aligned with the plenitude they assumed would instantiate itself under socialism—but which never actualized.[10] As early as 1919, the Bolshevik leader Vladimir Lenin declared cinema to be "the most important" of the arts (or at least this is how the story was repeated).[11] The visual medium, still in its embryonic phase, had been assigned a privileged role in heralding a new spatiotemporal order across the republic's vast territories. In practice, Lenin's nationalization decree, which sought to consolidate the film industry and its ancillary trades under the People's Commissariat of Education, remained largely aspirational as a regulatory schema. Nevertheless, the nation was primed for a process of "cinefication" (*kinofikatsiya*), with grand plans to extend political influence on Russia's peripheries by circulating films outside the cultural center of Moscow.[12] This redistribution was conceived as a means for propagating ideology and recalibrating the very field of perception. Class struggle was to become more than an abstract topic of conversation confined to elite forums of the well-off and educated, as moving pictures were tasked with encoding Leninist doctrine into an audiovisual vernacular legible to (largely) illiterate rural audiences. Soon, the agitational train initiative (*agitpoezda*)—a mobile infrastructure for the distribution and exhibition of propaganda films to the peasantry—was set in motion.[13] The expectation was that railroad networks would function not merely as vehicles of spatial connectivity but also as vectors of ideological unification across long distances and social strata. That is, cinema was positioned as one apparatus through which the contradictions generated by the revolution's aftermath and the miseries that followed could somehow be explained away.[14] Given this strategic emphasis on motion pictures, the New Economic Policy designated film as key in the transition from a war economy and instituted a centralized governmental mechanism to regulate film imports and exports: Sovkino. The film industry in turn donned the clothes of mass production, as an ever expanding and unwieldy institutional apparatus was erected, consisting of bureaus, studios (*kinofabriki,* or "film factories"), laboratories, workshops, unions, and committees.

Disentangling the threshold at which historical context transitions into aesthetic theory presents a complex challenge. Lenin, as has been tirelessly cited in the literature, maintained a particular affinity for cinema, construing it as one privileged technique out of many for reorienting the sensorium and capturing the hearts and minds of the new regime's citizenry. The young directors who commenced their work either on the cusp of or immediately after the revolutions unreservedly promoted motion pictures as an instrument, unambiguously advocating for film's propagandistic function in both their theoretical tracts and cinematic practice. Their impassioned spirit for political change, coupled with the early institutional legitimation they received from the establishment, attests to the fact that artists were never merely ancillary to the broader sociopolitical upheaval in a society teetering on the edge of radical change. Soviet cinema was almost never an autonomous aesthetic project, even prior to the consolidation of the Stalinist iron grip and the subsequent tightening of ideological oversight that would come to regiment artistic production in the 1930s and beyond.

In theories of montage, the "Kuleshov effect," as it retrospectively came to be known, was perhaps the foremost demonstration of the principle underlying the process of editing.[15] Trained in fine arts, Lev Kuleshov entered the movie business as a set designer shortly before the October Revolution, although in his own admission, he did not fully comprehend its nature at first.[16] In this tumultuous period, he was invited to manipulate foreign and prerevolutionary films. The resourceful reediting task codified as "remontage" (*peremontazh*) exemplifies the ideological plasticity of the cinematic image achieved through physical rearrangement, wherein the same fragments could articulate wholly different political horizons for spectators, many of whom were encountering moving images for the first time.[17] (Admittedly, the Soviets were not the only ones to censor films, though they did formalize the practice. For one, Eisenstein's own film received a similar welcome in Scandinavia.)[18] At this division, Kuleshov learned the art of fast-paced editing, or "American montage," as he called it, and had a chance to admire the works of Western filmmakers like D. W. Griffith and Charlie Chaplin.[19] Quickly emerging as a linchpin of Moscow's cinematic milieu, he established a workshop in the 1920s, where he worked and collaborated with a group of enthusiastic and aspiring like-minded compatriots. His best-known feature, *The Extraordinary Adventures of Mr. West in the Land of the Bolsheviks* (1924), introduced techniques developed under his leadership, reflecting and communicating to the masses the radical spirit of the era through comedy.

In the experiment leading to the eponymous effect, identical close-ups and shots elicited multiple and diverging readings when they were embedded in different sequencing structures, thus revealing the intricate relationship between an edited segment and viewers' tendencies to construct a coherent narrative where there was none to begin with. Kuleshov's demonstration of the contingencies of perception rendered explicit mechanisms of signification and interpretations through this physical rearrangement of film. His conclusion, grounded in the experience of reediting preexisting footage, spelled out a "theory of editing" that oscillated between the tactile and the hermeneutic: "miraculously [the film comes] into being in my own hands [. . .] Two shots gave rise to a new notion, a new image that neither of them contained: a different third [. . .] At the director's will montage infused a different meaning into the content."[20] Importantly, this differential relation could precipitate an emotional experience irrespective of an actor's actual performance. As a leading pedagogical figure, Kuleshov had an influence on the consolidation of a distinctly Soviet school of filmmaking that was as profound as his legacy, both domestically and worldwide. Although he had fallen out of critical favor by the end of the 1920s, his ideas persisted through his students, who built on these theoretical and practical foundations. His former student Pudovkin, for one, advanced a parallel conception of dynamic montage in writings that were translated and disseminated across Europe; it was through one of his public appearances that the term "Kuleshov effect" gained formal recognition.[21]

As opposed to Kuleshov, whose body of work was a concoction of newsreel and scripted performances in a variety of genres, including melodrama, Dziga Vertov insisted on using "non-acted" materials and derided film dramas as the "opium of the masses."[22] In his view, documentary's raw immediacy, when paired with the propulsive rhythm of rapid montage, jarred the spectator's consciousness so that it could be reconstituted. He first entered the film studio in 1917 as an office employee before slipping into the world of newsreels, where his path briefly overlapped with Kuleshov's. Soon thereafter, he founded his own collective, Cinema-Eye (Kinoks), in the hope of igniting a new wave of passionate visionaries who would spurn their predecessors' reliance on theatrical and literary inheritances. In manifestos and other publications, he issued an excoriating call to arms, decrying the "junk-dealers" of fiction films and demanding not just new modes of depiction but a wholesale reconsideration of the objects seen on screen.[23] Appropriately, Vertov's first directorial outing was the *Kino-Pravda* (1922–25) newsreel series. Intended as a cinematic analog to a newspaper, these "film-truth" newsreels were inexpensive to produce and functioned as a kind of optical percussion, reverberating with the pulse of proletarian life as they mirrored struggles and relentless efforts for renewal. Regardless of his political fervor, the Sovkino studio severed ties with the director in 1926, forcing his departure from Moscow and his shift to shooting projects elsewhere, in places such as Kiev and Odessa, where he also captured scenes for *Man with a Movie Camera* (1929). By the 1930s, he had returned to the scene, but his career had failed to regain its former momentum, as once innovative formalist tendencies had curdled into aesthetic liabilities, out of step with the prevailing demands of socialist realism.

Widely considered a documentary milestone, *Man with a Movie Camera* struggled to captivate moviegoers and had lackluster ticket sales at the time of its release. Its avant-garde approach, shaped by constructivist principles, dispensed with leading characters and traditional narrative structure. Instead, two types of film workers take center stage. The first, a cameraman—Vertov's brother—rushes to capture a world in flux. In a rhythmic ode to technique, the mechanical eye of his device is positioned as the ideal means for registering the pervasive mechanization of the metropolis and the seamless integration of workers into production machinery (and, by extension, of the photographer into his own apparatus).[24] The second, a cutter—Elizaveta Svilova, both collaborator and wife—is shown hunched over the editing table, excising and suturing pieces of celluloid of the very film in which she will later appear. Foregrounding the assembly-line logic of film production, *Man with a Movie Camera* at once exposes the labor behind cinematic construction and evokes a kinship between the weight of heavy labor, infrastructural revival, and the speed of cultural creation. Fueled by his signature rapid montage juxtaposing representations of base and superstructure, the film touts its display of "real" facts. This emphasis is best understood through the spirit of the de facto media philosophy of "factography" and its "rigorous referentiality," which dictates what is captured and how it is ultimately structured for the viewer.[25] Vertov curtly described this ethos as "shooting facts. Sorting facts. Spreading facts. Agitation with facts. Propaganda with facts. Fistsful of facts."[26]

In contrast to Vertov, Sergei Eisenstein envisioned an entirely different direction for Soviet productions. The global recognition of his ("acted") masterpiece *Battleship Potemkin* (1925) solidified his status as the most celebrated and contentious figure of his generation. Its international success propelled him into a precarious position, as he was lionized as a cinematic innovator yet increasingly ensnared in the contradictions of a system that demanded both radicalism and political obedience. It would also place him, along with other artists, in the line of fire during the purges of intellectuals in the 1930s, from which he barely escaped.[27] By the time he returned in 1932 from a largely fruitless world tour through Europe, the United States, and Mexico, artistic autonomy had been subsumed under stringent state control. Sovkino was nationalized, the first Five-Year Plan completed, and an ever more rigid ideological apparatus for the arts had consolidated. With the space for experimentation closing, Eisenstein was forced to carefully navigate his artistic convictions and personal life. As the master of Mosfilm and the supposed standard-bearer of Soviet cinema, he became a visible target, vociferously assailed by rivals and colleagues, his projects languishing under bureaucratic inertia as he awaited state approval. Even those that made it to the screen did so under increasingly circumscribed terms. *Alexander Nevsky* (1938), one of the few to secure ideological sanction, not only reflected shifting tastes but was also a symptom of the subordination of film to the demands of the Communist Party.

Amid these twists and turns punctuated by political intrigue, the kernel of the cinematic vocation remained, for Eisenstein, inextricably bound to montage and its built-in dialectic. “Film strips [. . .] engendered a ‘third something’ and became correlated when juxtaposed according to the will of an editor.”[28] The objective of this “third something” was to forge an intellectual cinema that sought not just to depict but to incite. It was, in his terms, a true “cine-fist!”—a cinematic strike designed to shock the spectator into a state of political clarity, a pointed rejection of what he perceived as Vertov’s merely contemplative “cine-eye” proposition.[29] For Kino to function at its most potent, it had to produce a visceral response that would awaken workers from their docile state. From his earliest writings to the final stages of his career, Eisenstein refined a taxonomy of montage, including “intellectual,” “metric,” and “rhythmic,” transforming what might otherwise be a technical practice into a system of thought.

If Eisenstein’s montage sought meaning in collision, Esfir Shub’s intervention lay in excavation, in an archaeology of moving images that repurposed the past to serve the imperatives of the present. Shub occupied a singular position among those who sought to reimagine the sociopolitical potential of film. Emerging from the crucible of postrevolutionary theater and steeped in constructivist experimentation, she envisioned cinematography as nothing less than “the art of the future.”[30] This horizon could only be summoned through a meticulous engagement with the past, materialized in the historical and factographic assemblage of images. What might appear as a conflict of tenses—the paradox of looking forward through the lens of the past—was, for her, a self-evident axiom, an intuitive act rather than an epistemological contradiction. She refined her brand of cinematic praxis in the early 1920s within Goskino’s reediting division (montage bureau), the so-called *motalka* (editing table), where she assumed the role of cutter (*montazhnitsa*), quickly transforming an ostensibly technical position into the locus of interventionist artistry in service of political realignment. Between two hundred and three hundred prerevolutionary films—some commissioned at the behest of Nicholas II, alongside imported Western fiction films laden with unbefitting values—passed through her hands and were subjected to her editorial scalpel.[31] Scenes were eliminated, their order inverted, and the intertitles rewritten or altered. Shub’s method of calculated intervention subjected film objects to profound transmutation, granting them a second life within the Soviet cinematic sphere. The discarded remnants, whether strips of celluloid or ideological excess, were left—both literally and figuratively—on the cutting room floor, casualties of a process she articulated in explicitly Marxist terms: "[Ideological montage] is a remarkable application of the dialectical change from quantity to quality."[32]

The depths of warehouses and dimly lit basements and the chaotic labyrinths of haphazardly assembled libraries concealed reels of footage that had been scattered across time and space, parts of which had been auctioned off to private collectors overseas. Sifting through tens of thousands of meters of film—dramatic productions, private recordings, and newsreels alike—Shub commenced an exhaustive search in pursuit of materials of historical consequence. Some reels remained intact, some were partially disfigured by time, and many had succumbed to decay, leaving behind nothing but residue. From this vast archival debris, Shub extracted just 1,500 meters and reconstituted them into *The Fall of the Romanov Dynasty* (1927), a directorial debut that would become her most renowned feature.[33] Such compilation documentaries operated on a different register than the resourceful refashioning of popular imports, recalibrated to serve a new spirit. Rather than merely constructing sequences out of bits, they forged an armature, a historical retelling sharpened into an "ideological weapon."[34] History did not simply unfold in this reconfiguring of found footage; it was unveiled and restructured to articulate its latent truth. Downplaying the director's will and the editor's intervention, the assembled historical documents, in Shub's formulation, "determined the film form" themselves.[35] Cutting and splicing were not acts of distortion but methods of revelation, binding disparate fragments into a coherent, politically charged cinematic argument.

Like Vertov, Shub celebrated the power of unstaged, authentic images as an instrument of nation-building. Yet while Vertov's montage thrived on the intercutting of shots, hers derived meaning from the juxtaposition of salvaged fragments from the same historical moment. A conviction she shared with Eisenstein, who briefly worked alongside her shortly before his debut, reinforced the primacy of editing: "montage is a key skill for cinema workers. A person who cannot edit should not make films at all."[36] However, unlike him, she rejected the authority of the fiction film, dismissing its appeal to mere emotion, and opted instead to unearth and exhibit nonfiction documentation of historical facts in ways that spoke to the intellect via alienation—for instance, cutting from dainty aristocrats to the laboring peasants who sustained their luxurious standards of living. This method was meant to visualize the history of class struggle as an inexorable force whose contradictions would inevitably resolve in an uprising in the name of equity. The Left Front of the Arts group (LEF) used Shub's favorable reception as a director to castigate and isolate Vertov, accusing him, by comparison, of being enamored with abstractions, formalism, and subjective construction over the objective reality that Shub's work and its longer and slower sequences best embodied.[37] To some degree, by the mid-1930s, Vertov had little choice but to follow in Shub's footsteps and alter his methods of work somewhat, adopting a similar disposition toward the ready-made film.[38] Yet gradually, like many of these avant-garde artists, her work fared worse under Stalin's rule. Denied the ability to realize their proposed projects, both Shub's and Vertov's attempts to regain favor were met only with silence.

To the Party's disappointment, early postrevolutionary cinema revealed a doggedly defiant divergence between official aspirations and popular taste. Revenue from Soviet experimental productions remained meager as audiences gravitated toward the escapist pleasures of capitalist amusements. The Buster Keatons and Mary Pickfords of the world proved more compelling than the masterpieces cinephiles now revere; the Odessa Steps sequence of *Battleship Potemkin,* for example, resonated far less than slapstick and melodrama. Lauded within intellectual circles, avant-garde cinema risked being eclipsed by mass entertainment. The commercial stagnation of Soviet directors' works, irrespective of their technical virtuosity, contributed to the USSR's decision to reestablish international film trade agreements and licensing deals in the early to mid-1920s.[39] As a result, more than three-quarters of programming consisted of imported productions. Despite a desire to cultivate a film industry independent from those of other countries, in-house productions struggled, undermined by financial constraints, corruption, and the affordability of Western acquisitions.[40] For a brief period, before Stalin's adoration of a different aesthetic took hold, montage represented the apogee of a certain moment, an intellectual commitment rather than a profitable enterprise. However, an account of film form alone cannot fully address all the factors involved in manipulating film strips in the editing room. At this juncture, the discussion must switch gears from the intricate interplay between politics and artistic choices to the economic dimensions of the era, given that the act of cutting had much to do with matter or, more precisely, the lack thereof.

USSR (UNDERSUPPLY, SHORTAGE, SCARCITY, AND REUSE)

Whereas idealistic aspirations were a driving force behind selecting subject matter and determining how it would be portrayed on the silver screen, the principles of montage and their mobilization existed in a more immediate context: the material basis of cinematic production. The turbulent final days of tsarist Russia, the February and October Revolutions, the ensuing civil war, and the devastation of World War I had already strained supply and distribution chains. The severing of diplomatic ties with the Western alliance and the trade embargo it imposed only deepened the crisis.[41] The incoming administration also suffered growing pains as it had to swiftly assume all responsibilities and care for a fractured, war-torn country. Reforming institutions, implementing model procedures, and delivering on promises of a just future and better practices collided with a chaotic reality that affected nearly every facet of daily life. Cinema, like every other industry, was swept up in the turmoil.

A significant share of the professional workforce had fled the country, taking with them films and essential equipment such as cameras and projectors (much of which originated from Pathé's and Gaumont's substantial pre-Soviet presence in the region).[42] What was left had fallen into a state of disarray, with no spare parts to fix decommissioned devices and few specialists capable of repairing them. Basic provisions, including food, heating, and electricity, were heavily rationed, making the theaters, however ideologically imperative for this new era, a negligible concern for the Party. When screenings did take place, the Allied blockade asphyxiated foreign relations, which in turn forced theaters and exhibitors to circulate the same worn-out reels and whatever foreign film managed to enter the country, with the most degraded copies often making their way to rural areas.[43] The ordeal was most acutely felt in the peripheries, where film distribution lagged, and prints arrived frayed and tattered, to the dismay of the villagers. Meanwhile, exhibition revenues from local productions were projected to sustain an industry that, since 1921, had been expected to achieve financial self-sufficiency. In practice, however, this goal remained aspirational.[44]

Plagued by material constraints, Soviet productions trailed behind imported films. The formation of a domestic cinema faced a critical setback as the available stock of raw film and liquid reagents for developing dwindled at an alarming rate. In overthrowing the monarchy, the revolutionaries also dismantled an infrastructure reliant on international relations and imports to sustain production. The depletion of resources was at least officially attributed to individuals and private firms that stockpiled tsarist-era assets in the fog of war, accelerating shortages at a moment when the country had yet to establish its own manufacturing system.[45] Scrambling to compensate for severed trade ties, the new regime introduced emergency measures. A 1918 decree mandated the registration of all remaining stock, followed by a nationalization order the next year that sought to expropriate private studios and seize their materials.[46] These efforts met with only partial success as private firms continued to operate and, in many cases, outperformed the struggling state-run studios.

After 1918, a patchwork of organizational structures (committees, departments, divisions) was erected, leaving studios to wrestle with a bureaucratic maze and forcing directors to formally petition for available inventory. Studios were subsumed into a regulatory framework that dictated the distribution of scarce resources. The process of securing film stock became an exercise in administrative navigation, requiring formal petitions for inventory that remained perpetually insufficient. The supply chain itself reflected the paradoxes of the revolutionary project. Despite hostilities, raw stock was either smuggled in via Latvia or would be acquired over time from German companies.[47] The intervention of the German communist organization Workers International Relief (Internationale Arbeiterhilfe) would later mitigate shortages, procuring essential supplies.[48] The situation, however, varied across the Soviet Union. Despite a façade of centralization, regional disparities persisted, with outlying territories having varying degrees of latitude in circumventing official channels. Ukraine, for instance, maintained separate negotiations with Western companies, highlighting the uneven application of economic control within the so-called unified Soviet sphere.[49]

At this early juncture, one newly formed technical department entertained an audacious and undeniably resourceful idea. Given the improbability of stumbling upon a cache of usable raw material, they considered mitigating the shortage by repurposing the substrate of previously developed and screened films. The initiative was led by Nikolai Minervin, a photographer, documentarian, and technician, whose proposal was as radical as it was precarious: stripping the chemical layer from the existing celluloid base and re-emulsifying it with a fresh photosensitive emulsion layer composed of silver, salts, and gelatin. The intent was clear: to erase the old impressions of unwanted motion pictures for the sake of creating new ones that would celebrate the political enterprise Moscow so urgently sought to exalt. In essence, the project aimed to "revive" already exposed films into new storage containers, but the process proved untenable. As one recalled, "such work proved to be not only awfully labor-intensive but also cost a pretty penny, and the resulting product was measured literally in meters. Moreover, Minervin's renewed film had exceptionally low sensitivity. Granted, during the acute 'film crisis,' even this was worth its weight in gold."[50] The boldness of the plan to reclaim and repurpose film stock was constrained by the lack of technical expertise necessary to execute it at scale. A source noted that the re-emulsification project ultimately stalled due to "our limited knowledge at the time of how to properly clean the substrate."[51] In other words, they had not found a way to perfect film reuse, precisely because film, like the wax cylinder, was anti-residual in nature. However much the technicians may have wished to strip the base by hand, their attempts were circumscribed by severe understaffing, insufficient funding, and the absence of the logistic infrastructure that might have resolved the problem with skill and time.

Minervin remains a marginal, if not entirely forgotten, figure in Soviet cinema scholarship.[52] His earliest known footage dates to 1908. As a man of means, he turned his camera first toward the world of the nobility, capturing their refined diversions—dining, sailing, and even early aviation. But his lens did not linger exclusively on aristocratic indulgence. He also filmed rare glimpses of the Kuban Region, shadowing locals through slippery, ice-laden mountain passes, all while maneuvering the hefty apparatus. His final film was made, perhaps inevitably, in 1917, marking the abrupt conclusion of a cinematic vocation that unfolded on the threshold of the revolution.

With his attempts to reuse the film's raw substrate unsuccessful, Minervin's "laboratory" only partially fulfilled his promises to yield an adequate quantity of positives and negatives, as stipulated in a contract with the Film Committee dated November 18, 1918.[53] Kuleshov later recalled Minervin's makeshift approach to crafting positive stock in a modest laboratory in 1920: "Developed film would be hung up to dry on the trees in the courtyard: there was no question of purified air, clean overalls, or white gloves. Nevertheless, the film *On the Red Front* was well printed."[54] The anecdote encapsulates a moment in which cinematic production persisted under conditions of scarcity, where production standards were dictated not by proper protocols but by sheer necessity. Sometime during the 1920s, Minervin was arrested. Upon release, his focus shifted exclusively to the technical dimensions of the industry.[55] Throughout the decade, he filed multiple patent applications concerning the treatment of film strips. A 1928 advertisement in the magazine *Kinofot* announced that his studio developed negatives and, among other services, acquired old reels and fragments.[56] Whether such acquisitions served production, restoration, or experimental re-emulsification remains an open question.

Having previously failed to contract with laboratories that possessed the technical ability to mass-produce stock, the authorities dispatched technicians and filmmakers abroad, including to the United States, in a series of fruitless expeditions that yielded little beyond confirming their own dependency.[57] More than a decade into a substantial shortage, procuring raw stock had become as pressing an issue as the ideological message it was meant to carry. Without an adequate storage medium, the state was unable to widely disseminate its principles. With little recourse, committee officials secured permission to import negative stock and chemical compounds from commercial firms in Germany (a transaction said to have supported the production of Kuleshov's and Vertov's films in 1924). This arrangement was by no means satisfactory. Even in the metropole, the material deficit exerted a gravitational force on the industry's most prominent figures, with Vertov's dismissal from Sovkino in 1926 ascribed to his excessive depletion of reels during the making of *One Sixth of the World*.[58] Beginning in the wake of the revolution and extending into the early 1930s, administrators, directors (including Kuleshov), and professional associations actively and consistently advocated for bolstering the manufacturing of national film stock by passing resolutions and appealing to the administration to address this dire need.[59] Even as domestic stock production accelerated, making it possible to distribute hundreds of copies of a film, its uneven quality and quantity ensured that reliance on foreign goods still persisted.[60]

I dwell on Minervin's overlooked project not for what he accomplished but for its conceptual potential, a project suspended in the embryonic phase of cinema's material history. It serves here a purpose other than "an instructive example of the desperate measures that were being taken."[61] What if he had succeeded? Could the film base itself have become an endlessly reconfigurable substrate, its surface stripped and reinscribed in an infinite cycle of reuse? If so, what could film productions and the motion picture industry have evolved into? What alternate economies might have emerged had the raw base of cinema been conceived not as a finite resource but as a regenerative medium? Minervin's experiments against scarcity situate him not alongside the theoretician-directors but within another order altogether—that of engineers, for whom technical composition was neither a given nor a necessary impediment. Unfortunately, unlike phonogram records, film resisted such a recursive practice. That Minervin's process never scaled beyond the workshop is less an individual failure or consequence of film's material intransigence than a reflection of the specific conditions that circumscribed his endeavor.

The Soviet industry nearly collapsed under the weight of its own shortages, but similar pressures of material finiteness extended beyond national borders. Michelle Aubert notes that in France in the 1920s, re-emulsification emerged as a direct consequence of strained access to Eastman Kodak stock, a condition that dictated the tempo of title releases.[62] These short-lived handcrafted procedures, however futile, illustrate a broader media logic in which inscription and operative erasure coexisted as codependent operations. Positioned between Edison's shaving of wax cylinders and the later development of rewritable magnetic tapes, this type of intervention suggests that film, too, might have belonged to a lineage of media subject to cycles of reuse. The illusion of permanence, so often upheld in commercial discourse, has always frayed at the edges when met with the design of the medium and its retentional limits. This genealogical link suggests that incorporating adaptive forms of retention is not incidental but essential to mitigating resource expenditure at the points of both manufacture and consumption. The prospect of generating and freeing up storage capacity by effacing and coating the old film never solidified into an industry standard, instead surfacing intermittently in the domain of artistic practice, where figures such as Barbara Hammer and Bill Morris played with the temporality and physicality of celluloid. And so, the problem has persisted, with disparities between commercial demand and material availability rendering salvage methods ever more pressing. And although used substrates never found their way back into film manufacturing, silver recovery—the act of chemically dissolving emulsion to extract its residual silver grain—became an industry fixture, a stopgap measure performed by Kodak and others to mitigate the steady attrition of depleting materials.[63]

A MATERIAL (NOT A THEORETICAL) CONSTRAINT

As Minervin's vision of adaptive retention remained unfulfilled, the industry pursued another route to self-sufficiency under mounting pressure to supply an abundance of crowd-pleasing visual propaganda. Mobilizing erasure by other means, recycling footage emerged in parallel, offering an alternative to his subtractive process. Factography, as Devin Fore observes, prioritized the immediacy of the present over any distant horizon. More than a tendency, it operated as a code spanning journalism, art, literature, and film, which helps explain why reuse and nonlinear montage resonated so seamlessly with the period's conceptual currents and sensibilities. This disposition toward the momentary, he explains, encouraged efficiency, ephemerality, and rapid circulation, embedding film production within a broader system that valued dissemination over permanence.[64]

This brings us back to reediting departments and their instantiation of a practice whereby the disassembly of found footage itself becomes a form of construction. Spaces such as these were where Shub and others first learned about film by dismantling it. In 1919, Vladimir Gardin, co-founder of VGIK (the first film school), delivered his appeal to "montage as a practical means for making do in the face of material privation."[65] Recutting meant turning insufficiency into a formal and logistic system of production that worked *through* rather than *despite* resource deprivation. Put another way, negation became a productive force rather than a mere subtraction. The widespread realization of Gardin's scheme, however, was not always seamless. The effort to mobilize cinematic undoing for communist values had fallen short in the eyes of some contemporary critics, a point emphasized by Yuri Tsivian.[66] Some altered versions failed to convincingly recut films into credible new cinematic units, they claimed. Notwithstanding their adaptive potential, secondhand movies, it seems, remained bound by the limits of material possibilities, which could not always be sutured away.

Setting her apart from contemporaries—and in implicit contrast to Minervin's abandoned path—Shub's compilation method responded to the dearth of resources by theorizing it as a political, aesthetic, and historical condition of filmmaking. During this time, she developed a focus on "factual material" that would become a major aspect of her approach.[67] Calling attention to the dire need for institutional moving image libraries, she advocated for erecting film archives in Moscow and across the republics. The work of locating, dating, sorting, cataloging, and finally formulating standards for the safekeeping of such valuable resources would be an indispensable part of their operations, she claimed, as she herself undertook the task. Shub made the case for establishing an archival system for future generations and years to come, sounding the alarm already in the 1920s that valuable documentary footage was under precarious conditions of neglect. Available negatives, duplicates, and positive prints were in states of disrepair, mishandled, left to decay, or siphoned off through illicit channels, many lost abroad, including to the Soviet Union's ideological adversary, the United States. If archival rigor appears at odds with the logic of recycling, Shub's method maintained a crucial distinction: for her, such preservation techniques avoided tampering with original negatives and restricted alteration and recutting to duplicates. In this sense, her archival ethos aligned with, rather than disavowed, her editorial practice. As Joshua Malitsky contends, her plea redefined the discourse surrounding the film-factory, repositioning it as a *factory-archive*. Yet despite its intellectual resonance, this conceptual shift was only partially realized.[68] As the industry faced recurrent inventory crises, the deficit metastasized. Over time, plunder extended beyond foreign films and newsreels to Shub's own body of work, her negatives ransacked, dismantled, and repurposed elsewhere.[69]

Renewed scholarly attention to Shub's practice reflects a broader shift in cinema and media studies toward materiality, a focus that makes her exclusion from lists that celebrate the "greats" of Russian-speaking cinema all the more revealing. The omission signals two key issues: the persistent marginalization of women's contributions and the views governing her intellectual milieu at the time.[70] Women were particularly overrepresented in the cutting rooms of the silent era, in both Soviet and Western industries. Prior to the clear delineation between the roles of "editor" and "cutter," cutting departments were overwhelmingly staffed by a female workforce. Their responsibilities included cleaning film, making repairs, removing and trimming unnecessary sequences from dailies and rushes, and splicing negatives and prints with glue or cement.

Despite the precision required, this was predominantly menial labor: taxing, physical, and tedious. In this vein, of the aforementioned depiction of one of the most renowned editors of her day in *Man with a Movie Camera*, one critic wrote: "Bending her large strong body over the film, with scissors in her hand, Svilova is at work [. . .] Vertov's assistant. She cuts and glues what then seems to be life [. . .] She doesn't know how to answer, to explain, or to speak. She only knows how to work."[71] Svilova's function is articulated as pure labor, an agent whose presence affirms process rather than authorship, a mute body within a collective of workers.[72] Feminist film scholarship identifies the advent of sound as a historical tipping point in this gendered division of labor. Editing, once conceptually aligned with domestic craftwork such as sewing and weaving, as seen in the intercut scene of Svilova, increasingly acquired the status of a specialized, technical operation.[73] As industry discourse elevated the editor's creative agency, the workforce was restructured, gradually displacing women from their seat at the cutting table and thus from the profession. Bluntly put, it was easy to cut out the erasers.

Shub's intellectual environment, as Bill Nichols delineates, was marked by a tension between her approach and that of her compatriot documentarians.[74] Working within the confines of the used resources they already had in their possession was no match for the prevailing artistic fixation with shooting the "new" on a finite resource. The reigning theory of film, at the very least, disregarded material necessity and instead considered film an "accumulating resource."[75] Conversely, Shub carefully and meticulously handled the contents of boxes upon boxes containing abandoned canisters and fragments, using even the shortest of trimmings. Recycling was significantly less costly to produce. Assembling fragments, scraps, and pieces into films was a feasible panacea that was nevertheless ambiguously received by the others. Such hands-on knowledge entered her directorial work and set her apart from others, yet ultimately, she, too, intended editing for the purpose of agitation. Cutting was a material means to an ideological end.

What, then, was this material? Cinematic "material" colloquially referred to anything already captured on celluloid and awaiting assembly. In a cursory nod to the film's "body," it was labeled mere "raw material." Yet even the designation "raw" only intermittently referred to the storage medium. More often, the term "raw material" designated pre-reassembled footage, not the film base or the substances used to compose it.[76] The raw was the shot, frame, and scene before it had been placed in its proper place in a sequence. Not until these severed pieces of captured images—scripted, documentary, or newsreel footage—were combined would they become "cooked."[77] Without the cutting hand guiding production, raw material was simply unrealized potentiality, an unprepared meal. In Pudovkin's writing, even the human was raw. "The man photographed," he wrote, "is only raw material for the future composition of his image in the film, arranged in editing."[78] Everything is and is not matter.

The collapse of the distinction between "material" and "raw material" is not incidental. Rather, it is symptomatic of the moment's missed opportunity, when theory averted its eyes from matters of daily concern. The paucity of raw stock was so endemic that Kuleshov's workshop instituted the practice of "films without film." Actors rehearsed before an unloaded camera and simulated shots, enacting scenes in accordance with how they would have been composed. It was a movie realized sans its substrate.[79] A quintessential paradox, film without film crystallizes the idea that matter is an obstacle that can be surmounted, however briefly, through disregard. Even though Kuleshov, who as a director and former re-editor operated under the constraints of the period, had to officially request stock for the workshop's experiments (even as little as 90 meters), such irksome restrictions remain external to his theory of montage. When he did finally come by available stock, he praised the resulting "effect [which] was achieved solely by the organization of raw materials and cinematographic method [. . .] We learned from this scene that the chief strength of cinema lies in montage because with montage one can destroy, repair, or completely recast material."[80] In such descriptions, we see how plain ol' material and raw material become interchangeable. Even as the technical (re)arrangement of film's constitutive parts is acknowledged, destruction and repair refer not to the physical element but to the generation of a believable whole for the viewer.

Within this context of acute lack, negation performed for the sake of generation—such as Shub's—is underrepresented in debates about montage. The issue of excision is, then, a delicate one, fraught with complexity, present on one hand and veiled on the other. When Kuleshov searched for the meaning of cinema, he opted to perform the cutting. "We took one strip of film, cut it apart into its separate shots, and then discussed where the very 'filmness' which is the essence of filmic construction lay."[81] The ontology of film is said to reside elsewhere; swiftly moving from this splayed mise-en-scène, the celebrated teacher of montage steers away from the intrinsic properties of the technology and devotes much space to what editing facilitates. By turning toward effective communication, Kuleshov downplays cutting out and foregrounds the power of the splice: "We went to various motion picture theaters and began to observe which films produced the greatest effect on the viewer [. . .] The content of the shots in itself is not so important as is the joining of two shots."[82]

It is rather curious, then, that a movement that dedicated much of its energy to praising the overhaul of the means of production paid comparatively less attention to its own methods of making as intrinsic to "filmness." The adulation of the shears, cited earlier, was perhaps a momentary lapse. Or rather, the drive shifted toward conceiving of cinema as a meeting between the biological and the machinic (à la Vertov's "aided eye") and its site, the film theater, not the editing table.[83] However justified Bordwell is in his reasoning that "a shortage of raw film stock is itself hardly a precondition for the creation of the montage style," it was undoubtedly one of its immediate circumstances.[84] My point is not to argue that scarcity necessarily begets this particular manner of handling film. Rather, insofar as montage represents the conceptual expression of physical editing, most of these theorists were able to blur its connections with material concerns. In the long run, the move away from materiality toward psychotechnics laid the foundations for a categorical omission of *cutting* in theories of film form in the next decades.[85]

CUTTING STORAGE

The disavowal of the technicity of cinema is rooted in its alignment with the illusion of "living pictures," from optical toys that create motion from still images to audiences' suspension of disbelief and critics' description of film as effervescent and magical. In this regard, such disposition also extends to theories that sideline production processes in favor of emphasizing perception and representation. And on screen, self-reflexive moments that pierce this illusion are few and far between. I conclude this chapter by casting a wider historical net around the absence of the relation between materiality and cutting.

Before they came to deliberately splice film strips together, early filmmakers did not conceive of images as fragments in need of reordering. Instead, the affordances of the apparatus dictated a linear unfolding of one uninterrupted event. Pioneering cinematographers, such as the Lumière brothers, considered film stock as one unit. The camera, initially immobile, was set in a single location and captured an occurrence, more or less preplanned, that played out in front of its lens. The brevity of actuality films, seldom exceeding two minutes, was less an artistic choice than a direct consequence of the roll's storage capacity. The camera ran until it could run no longer. For a time, shooting practices followed the dictates of the raw material, unfolding in strict alignment. As productions grew in complexity, it became increasingly improbable that the entire length of the film would be used in a continuous manner.[86] The pursuit of longer run times spurred experimentation with joining rolls end to end, rendering duration itself as pliable. Cutting, in this sense, evolved as a means of circumventing limited retention by reorganizing matter.

With much of silent-era motion pictures lost to time, mishandling, or deliberate destruction, film historians point to Edwin S. Porter's *The Great Train Robbery* (1903) as one of the earliest surviving instances of post-production editing.[87] Before long, scissors and adhesive agents eclipsed the popularity of in-camera techniques such as the trick film. The latter, pioneered by Georges Méliès, relied on halting the camera mid-action, rearranging the scene, and then resuming the shoot, thereby producing seemingly impossible occurrences using a single roll. Alternatively, in a directorial decision that would resonate with many of the Soviets, Porter crosscut a shot of firefighters racing to rescue hapless victims with newsreel footage of a fire. This manipulation of time and space with a simple gesture broke from convention and became a defining moment for cinema history. The Soviet directors would also acknowledge D. W. Griffith's editing as an influence (what would eventually come to be called "invisible" or "continuity editing"). As discussed in this chapter, the Soviet intervention turned away from the seamlessness the American system would come to canonize, though it began by learning to see through Hollywood's cuts.

Compared to Russia, the US film industry was rich in raw resources, with Eastman Kodak establishing its dominance in the stock industry and becoming a leading global manufacturer. Those who worked in film in the United States in the opening decades of the twentieth century would presumably have done so in a *relative* state of abundance. Scarcity surfaced instead when it came to storing motion pictures, whose value depreciated with rapidly changing tastes and print quality. This is why film scholar Jay Leyda, who painstakingly chronicled the birth of the Soviet industry, critically describes how "The American Film has always been plagued by an industrial compulsion to junk the past—'Sell next week's film.' The need to ridicule the used to make room for current product reached its heights with the introduction of sound-film, when it was made almost unthinkable to pay admission to see a silent film."[88] Previously screened movies were considered expendable, their value deemed less than the cost of their retention. Ironically, in the Soviet Union, films were made ephemeral because their substrate was valuable. But, as it turns out, diminishing supplies were not an affliction unique to the USSR in the 1920s. Material adversities confronted the US entertainment business during World War II, as Kodak increasingly redirected its business to support military needs and drastically diminished its exports, leading to fewer raw materials imported into Britain and other countries.[89]

From every conceivable standpoint, film is a finite storage medium; its physical design was adapted to lengthening, remaking, censoring, and salvaging by way of cutting and splicing. These deformations of the malleable substrate were performed by editors, directors, exhibitors, and distributors worldwide, presumably to meet popular demand and aesthetic sensibilities, and to avoid local governmental pressure.[90] Ultimately, negation was part of a process that helped produce various versions of the same film to be shown in different places and times, meaning that the scissors were, like the phonograph shaver, a tool for generating by undoing the unwanted. "It turned out that you could alter the film endlessly."[91]

Film is, then, an object in constant flux: composed, decomposing, and recomposable. Each cut and subsequent splice leaves a mark, one that necessarily weakens the integrity of the physical print. Cutting should ideally—though not without exception—be performed carefully and thoughtfully so as not to prematurely destroy a work print or even an exhibition copy.[92] Glue (eventually replaced by cement and tape) added the possibility of structural modulation by relocating a frame outside its original position. Later, light boxes eased the work by facilitating close examination of the captured images. The Moviola, a breakthrough technology, streamlined post-production.[93] The upright device was released to market in 1924, practically by chance. Its inventor, Iwan Serrurier, meant to invent a projector instead. Using a magnifying glass, the Moviola previewed images in motion, offering editors a chance to see the footage before deciding where and what to cast out. (In lieu of such advanced mechanical aids, the rapid Soviet montage style relied on the "eyes and scissors [. . .] since [they] still have no devices for reviewing negatives, nor machines for splicing. Industrious organization, sharpness of vision, formidable visual memory, an agility and quickness of the hands.")[94] By the 1960s, dual-screen flatbed systems like the Steenbeck and KEM, which demanded less specialized skill than the Moviola, dominated post-production workflows. This trajectory—from manual handling to increasingly mechanized precision—ultimately culminated in the arrival of Avid software, which heralded the era of nonlinear digital editing.

Such technological transformations are marginalized in, if not entirely missing from, film theory (which has, since the 1990s, concentrated on a principal technological distinction between the digital and the looming death of the analog). Soviet auteurs serve as a focal point in this chapter for their artful elaboration of complex techniques in tandem with the increasing abstraction of the craft itself. Yet the gap between praxis and theory—and the resulting neglect of materiality—is not confined to this specific time or place or to a single school of thought. Consider apparatus theory, which emerged in the 1970s with scholars such as Laura Mulvey, Christian Metz, and Jean-Louis Baudry, among others, and soon became a cornerstone of film studies.[95] Although its name suggests that, at its core, it would situate technology like projection, sound, and the theater at the heart of cinema, these theories effectively investigated how film as a perceptual medium influences the mental activity and subjectivity of the viewer. In this way, it is possible, for instance, to discuss not the camera itself but its perceived gaze. Apparatus theory introduced textual methodologies that stimulated critical and psychoanalytic readings of projected images, narratives, and ideologies. Production and technicity proper remained outside the scope of their immediate interests, which prioritized the human over the inanimate elements within the apparatus.

The psychoanalytically and phenomenologically inspired suture theory that unraveled a decade later in a series of debates between Jean-Pierre Oudart, Kaja Silverman, Jacques-Alain Miller, Stephen Heath, and others is also not without relevance.[96] It metaphorized the viewer's relation to the film's content as an act of "stitching." Linguistically rooted in the physical splice, the theory nevertheless gravitated toward the realm of interpretation and experience. The act was replaced by its theoretical counterpart, the experience of suture. While Oudart, for instance, maintained that the spectator always faces absence, he meant not the void created by the missing frame but the film's rearrangement of signifiers and their relation to the psychoanalytic imaginary. It was about presence and absence on and with film, not of film. As long as the cinematic text was considered a form of syntax or "speech," theory rendered the *body* of film and ostensible technical minutiae like cutting inconsequential to moviegoers as such. In the same vein as exchanges about montage, notwithstanding some notable differences, suture was the theoretical doppelgänger of the splice, which overshadowed the abyss pried open by the shears. When it comes down to it, negation is easily ignored precisely because it hides in plain sight. And yet, it remains the scaffolding upon which cinematic creation most commonly takes shape.

Three

RANDOMIZING MAGNETIC PARTICLES INTO TELEVISUAL OBLIVION

The tool is tending to vanish from consciousness. We commonly say that its function has become automatic. What we should make of this is the new equation: consciousness only survives now as awareness of accidents.[1]

• • • So far, I have explored the introduction of erasability at the turn of the twentieth century in the United States and in the early twentieth century in the Soviet Union. This chapter turns to the mid-twentieth century and looks out into the space between Earth and the moon. It is in this expanse that issues of storage and shortage dramatically came to a head. If this sounds cryptic, let me explain.

Phonography and cinematography have been extensively examined from every angle, with writings on their technical features, industry structures, ontologies, and aesthetics cramming shelves and library stacks. This is less the case with magnetic recording. The philosopher Vilém Flusser celebrated video as "an epistemological tool: it presents, speculates, and philosophizes."[2] Notwithstanding these innate capabilities, the relative under-theorization of magnetic recording may very well be a result of its ambiguous standing as a hybrid object of study.[3] Although it was first conceived in the early 1900s—around the time the reusable phonograph was garnering attention—its first major application came nearly half a century later when it was used to record radio and television broadcasts. It was not until the 1970s that it became a ubiquitous personal medium and a distribution system that ran parallel to cinema. This chapter limits itself to considering the technology's protracted emergence and subsequent adoption. In this context, magnetic recording functions as both a substrate involved in the production of live programming for television and, at the same time, a temporal extension that undercuts synchronous and immediate consumption. Differently put, transmission and magnetic recording, two braided technical systems, constitute the televisual apparatus, even if each of their mandates is ostensibly contradictory: the one disseminating, the other hypothetically safekeeping.

This bifurcation presents an ontological conundrum. Is television an ephemeral medium whose signals disappear as soon as they air, or does its capacity to be stored on tape render it a medium of permanence? My claim is that neither of these options exclusively holds and that there is, in fact, a third element at play. Historically speaking, the commercial sphere had vested interests in promoting television's live quality by valorizing the distinction between immediate and prerecorded, all while concealing the industry's growing reliance on storage devices. Meanwhile, theories of television had, in much the same way, lauded "liveness" and instantaneity as a distinguishing characteristic from film, likening it instead to telegraphy and telephony.[4] Video recording was adopted under the radar, and by the time it was finally incorporated en masse by the entertainment industry, transiency had already become ingrained in commonly held views about the nature of television. As a result, the question of what signals become after they are dispatched through the ether was suppressed.

Simply put, signals were recorded, although they were not necessarily retained for long. As recording and storage were conceptually devalued, so too was the primary subject of this book: erasure. Undoing, a generative and operable process—but also a self-effacing one—slips through these cracks. Today, streaming services create an expectation of automatic retention, accessibility, and retrievability of content. However, this is not entirely true now, nor was it at all conceivable until well into the 1970s. Archiving audiovisual materials was, in reality, a concept slow to emerge.[5] Magnetic tapes were kept less for their content and more for their value as a reusable medium that enabled further production. By the time the practice of storing broadcasts became somewhat standardized in commercial and other contexts, deletion was already an integral part of working with magnetic reels.

Now, back to the moon business as a case in point. In 2006, news of the possible disappearance of the original footage of the Apollo 11 moon landing spread in the media, alerting the public that the tapes that had captured those extraordinary scenes in 1969 were nowhere to be found. At the time, NASA maintained that "despite the challenges of the search," it did "not consider the tapes to be lost."[6] Only three years later, in a press conference held just days before the fortieth anniversary of this momentous event, did the space agency admit that the search for the missing records had been completed, unsuccessfully.[7] It concluded that the materials had likely been degaussed and their contents irrevocably erased.[8] The capture of a moment's incredible potentiality—when it seemed a question of when and not if humanity could set sail on its extraterrestrial futures—had been undone by earthly concerns. In technical terms, degaussing means they went through a process of demagnetization that jolts particles and neutralizes them into a random order. This results in the irrevocable annihilation of previous traces. In plain terms, Neil A. Armstrong and Edwin "Buzz" Aldrin Jr.'s first steps on the dusty surface of Earth's satellite had been wiped out from official governmental holdings.

I keep with this story throughout the chapter for two reasons. First, the moon landing is a meaningful event for the theorization of television. Second, little attention had been granted to the revelation of the loss of the original recordings, even though this was a moment when undoing finally made headlines, for a change. Quite a few factors are at play here. To begin with, while broadcast is often perceived as synonymous with transiency, most would assume that an epoch-defining moment would have been met with a different fate. An astounding achievement such as three individuals crossing Earth's orbit, with two of them safely setting foot on an arid celestial body, surely merits a place in the history books, to say nothing of our audiovisual collections. But things have not quite turned out as expected for NASA's moon landing. The loss of the tapes provides an opportunity, perhaps a belated one, to reconsider *operative erasure*. The startling displacement, which would only later be revealed as the inadvertent disposal of materials of import, reveals a truth about retention. NASA had evidently experienced a scarcity of storage space; its solution was to resort to the affordances of magnetic tape. Negation, however counterintuitively, enables production before, during, and after use. The tangled history of the moon landing's videographic capture is more than a mere instructional tale. This unexpected incident highlights the habituality of reuse. It also unravels a set of generally accepted attitudes regarding the meaning of television, demonstrating that erasure has been largely absent from both popular and scholarly deliberations about what constitutes the televisual.

HOW TELEVISION BECAME OSTENSIBLY EPHEMERAL

True to the "tele-" in "television," the 1969 space walk was a global experience that brought people together across vast distances and deeply entrenched divides, all at the height of the Cold War. This highly planned and choreographed on-screen celebration briefly brought about a shared sense of unity here on Earth. It was, therefore, hailed—at least at the time—as a universal achievement, a turning point after which human history would be forever changed.[9]

Arguably, the lunar exploration is also to television what the 1938 broadcast of "The War of the Worlds" was to radio: a seminal episode that cemented a kind of originary medium specificity. Merging myth and television, Lorenz Engell maintains that the event radically altered its medium of delivery. "We can almost speak of pre-Apollonian and post-Apollonian television," so much so that "it is the basic model for all television events since then [. . .] measured and described in relation to the expedition to the moon."[10] The landing in the Sea of Tranquility became a quintessential example of a "media event," as theorized by communication scholars, one not initiated by the press yet inherently grounded in television's expansive reach.[11] Particularly, as Lynn Spigel reminds us, "by 1960, almost 90 percent of American households had at least one receiver."[12] As a major event, it encompassed an array of temporal dimensions: first, it prompted meticulous preparations; then, the programming began to unfold (a moment filled with anticipation of either success or disastrous failure); third, the event materialized in near-perfect synchronicity on countless screens across the globe.[13] The most intriguing stage for me, however, is what took place after, out of the sight of its observers.

Overall, the theoretical reception of the landing tended to concentrate on the synchronous element of the experience. Marshall McLuhan touched on this issue when he described watching the Apollo 8 broadcast from space in 1968 in the following manner: "We were on Earth and the moon simultaneously [. . .] The true action in the event was not on Earth or the moon, but rather in the airless void between."[14] McLuhan later appeared on an expert panel broadcast on ABC in the lead-up to the moon landing. One can only imagine how his earlier reflections on the compression of space-time resonated all the more when Armstrong first descended from the American craft. His rumination on the event underscores the collapse of difference. From another viewpoint, Paul Virilio conceives of the landing (and, coincidentally, cyberspace) as offering a window into "'telepresence' without consistency and, more particularly, without a true spatial position, since the remote interaction of a being at once absent and acting (teleacting) redefines the very notion of *being there*."[15] Televisual logic became entrenched in human experience, and the latter, in turn, was fundamentally disoriented by these developments of the twentieth century. Such was the magnitude of the moment.

These observations obviously touch on the planetary scale and its representation as it was disseminated by earthly technical infrastructure and communication technologies. But it was the simultaneity of the live event, fusing the gazes of the astronauts, NASA employees, the press, and audiences, that captivated most commentators. Rarely, however, is the enormous extent of the technical effort involved in airing the moon landing mentioned, nor is its afterlife in recorded form seriously debated. The near-total silence surrounding the taping of the materials is related to an often employed heuristic division between recording technologies, such as cinema and phonography, and those of transmission (telegraph, radio, and television included). The emergence of this techno-aesthetic binary is illustrated in Rudolf Arnheim's thoughts on television as early as 1935, not much different from McLuhan's aforementioned remark: "Emission and reception become practically simultaneous. Space and time are annihilated [. . .] For the first time in the history of man's striving for understanding, simultaneity can be experienced as such, not merely as translated into a succession in time."[16] Decades before venturing into space and years before television had become a household device, immediacy had already been praised as its essential feature.

These perspectives portray only half the picture, oblivious to historical episodes that point to a more complex reality. Early on, before television became a mass medium, engineers worked to solve the problem of transmission in tandem with retention. It is, therefore, not without irony that, as Siegfried Zielinski points out, early attempts to affix ephemeral signals took place "before the images even moved or appeared to be alive."[17] One prominent example is John Logie Baird's pioneering early experiments with a mechanical system capable of simultaneously sending and receiving moving pictures. While his work on transatlantic transmission is widely recognized, his attempts to develop a method for recording said signals onto a gramophone record have been largely forgotten.[18]

Television recording also drew on the legacy of prerecorded radio broadcasts. By the late 1920s, even the major radio networks that dominated airwaves could no longer keep up with the demand for regular live programming. During the following decade, they consequently allowed partial prerecording of shows using acetate discs and transcription services.[19] At the same time, independent and local stations that were gaining popularity filled their airtime with prerecorded music and shows. The networks thus had to set themselves apart, and they did so by using the seemingly impervious rhetoric of "liveness" (regardless of their own hybrid production practices). The label "live" was used to signify "quality programming," which would then—and not coincidentally—be syndicated in recorded form to those very same small stations the networks sought to stifle. This marketing move was backed by the Federal Radio Commission, which established strict standards and regulations for obtaining broadcasting licenses that gradually pushed local live broadcasts to the margins by the 1940s.[20]

The stage was set for the eventual integration of magnetic recording for later viewing or distribution. Prior to its introduction in the pre–World War II era, various celluloid-based methods were attempted, including the intermediate film system, which allows near-instant replay for broadcast; telefilms, which appeared irregularly starting in the 1940s; and kinescopes, which were shot by a motion picture camera filming a live broadcast as it was displayed on a video screen.[21] These last records, shortened to "kines," were the primary method of recording for time-shifting purposes; that is, they were a technical solution to the challenge of transmitting "live" content at the same time of day across the various US time zones. In short, within the scope of the televisual, broadly construed, recording was unevenly but persistently tested well before magnetic recording entered the scene. (This is not to say that when it did arrive, magnetic recording was necessarily used as an archival technology, merely that it was utilized, at the very least, for temporary storage.)[22]

The networks opted to promote live programming with higher production costs as aesthetically superior to films made for television and other prerecorded shows. Glorified by executives during television's golden age, liveness was celebrated as a hallmark of immediacy, spontaneity, and novelty. In the words of a prominent critic, "the essence of television techniques" is that they take place "in the present and therefore more real than anything taken and cut and dried which had the feel of the past."[23] As it happens, such discursive favoring of ontological immediacy and presence veiled commercial interests. This reverence for real-time broadcast served to attract the attention of audiences, advertisers, and sponsors; to shape regulations; and to fend off competition from the smaller stations and other entertainment industries. Liveness as a value was "a strategy of business practice fashioned by a confluence of network, local, sponsor and governmental interests."[24] This was a rather clever ploy, given the growing number of prerecorded shows already being broadcast by these same networks.

Although television is, in fact, the product of various technical manipulations that destabilize the idea of transparent flow, it has enjoyed a reputation as precisely the opposite. Long after most content was recorded in some way by the networks, theoretical approaches continued to celebrate the simultaneous and live. As Andrew Crisell would have it, television resembles or approximates an "ideal" and unmediated form of communication.[25] In his foray into media ontology, for instance, Herbert Zettl argues that television is "a temporal, ephemeral experience whose only record is memory."[26] Somewhat differently, but concluding on a similar note, Samuel Weber's reconsideration of television as "seeing at a distance" (how appropriate for the theme of space exploration examined here) focuses on transmission. Simultaneity, by Weber's account, is therefore constitutive of the definition of television as a "semblance of presentation."[27] His extensive ontological and phenomenological analysis pays no particular attention to processes of production, postproduction, and handling. It is simply a matter of what we see on screen.

One ought to be careful not to succumb to the allure of liveness, particularly when the relationship between historical materials and historiography is troubled, as in the case of Apollo 11. In 1973, just four years after the landing, historian Pierre Nora observed that the significance of this event extended beyond the mere exploration of uncharted territories. What made it exceptional, he argued, was that it was a televised event—live, no less. "It takes place on an immediately public stage. There is no event without its reporter-spectator or spectator-reporter," he remarked.[28] From a surprising angle, Nora goes on to propose that the landing exemplified "the model of the modern event."[29] In his view, such events no longer require scholars to interpret them; he laments the obviation of the raison d'être of historical work, given that meaning is constantly being reshaped by journalists on the spot. "Now, however, the intermediaries [that is, historians] are cut out of the loop, a sort of telescoping of event and report takes place, and in the incandescence of multiple meanings, we are blinded."[30] In the bright light of such a highly televised moment, what Nora and the others overlooked was not so much the erosion of scholarly authority in the public sphere as the complex mediating processes that materially sustained the moon landing as a piece of history.

Omissions such as these overlook not only the medium's multifaceted technical history but also its innate negative condition. Ever a thinker of things obscure, Jacques Derrida aptly conveys this tension: "Television always involves a protest against television; television pretends to efface itself, to deny television. It is expected to show you the thing itself, 'live,' directly. Such 'direct,' 'live' presentation, translated into the Christian code is the 'real presence,' the 'transubstantiation' or the 'Eucharist,' and in a more general way, a phenomenon of incarnation: deictic and sensible *immediacy* of the mediator."[31] Derrida lays bare television's projection of idealized communication, which is, in itself, a trap. To sustain the illusion of immediacy, the technical recedes from view. If we look carefully, however, behind the veil are all sorts of tools and systems, including storage. The insistence on the meaning of television as singularly derived from "presentness" therefore excludes the fact of recording.

Applying this insight to our model event, the fascination with the moon landing as an epitome of the "live" meets the unintended legacy of a sustained disavowal of the "supplement," to use Derrida's term, in much of the writings on broadcast. With these overlooked aspects unraveled, understanding the significance of the tapes begins by examining both their creation and their eventual undoing, an accident uncovered only decades after the fact.

LIVE FROM THE MOON! (BUT NOT QUITE)

The astronaut Michael Collins, who remained in the command module of Apollo 11 while Armstrong and Aldrin reconnoitered the area around their small lunar module, unknowingly foreshadowed the quiet vanishing of these sought-after tapes. During the lunar walk, he lightheartedly joked with mission control: "I'd like to point out [. . .] that I have no TV set on board, and therefore, I'm going to be one of the few Americans who is not going to be able to see the EVA [extra-vehicular activity]. So I'd like you to save the tapes for me, please."[32]

While Collins was waiting for his fellow astronauts to return to the craft, around 600 million viewers worldwide gathered in front of television sets. On July 20, 1969, they watched remarkable images of the first extraterrestrial walk in the history of humankind. Armstrong and Aldrin roamed the face of the moon for about two hours and thirty minutes. The entire mission lasted eight days. The major networks, vying for audience attention, provided a prolonged mediation of the launch, landing, and, finally, the journey home, ending with the victorious splashdown.

Despite the intricate interplay between receiving and transmitting signals, as well as retaining them, neither the live broadcast nor the recorded footage was essential to the space mission. Although the telecast was vital in cementing the American spectacle of technical superiority over the Soviets in the race for the new frontier, it was not, as NASA's video engineer Richard Nafzger recalls, a vital aspect of the scientific mission itself. Indeed, "it was almost an afterthought."[33] In other words, the broadcast was produced for geopolitical and social considerations as a reaction to the launch of the Sputnik satellite in 1957 and to fears of the "red" domination of the cosmos. By 1969, when Apollo 11's mission was successfully completed, the space program had cost American taxpayers upwards of $24 billion.[34] In the face of philosophical, political, and social oppositions to such expenditure, as well as pushback from scientists who did not consider the camera a crucial part of the mission, it was nevertheless decided that "the taxpayers have a right to *see* what they pay for."[35] And so, the camera mediated between individuals and masses on two heavenly bodies in a charade of optical equity.[36]

Viewers who tuned in on that eventful evening were inundated with black-and-white images as eerie as one could previously only have imagined space to be. Impressions of muddled quality, ghostlike by some accounts, produced an unearthly aesthetic that demarcated the importance of the event by appearing distinctly unlike any other viewing experience. Amid an array of photographic equipment that included several Hasselblad still cameras and a stereoscopic camera, a portable black-and-white Westinghouse unit was stowed in the lunar module (LM) and deployed shortly after landing to capture the astronauts' first steps. Meanwhile, two 16 mm Maurer data acquisition film cameras were placed inside the command and service module (CSM) and the LM to capture mission-specific data, onboard activity, and the descent of "The Eagle." Signals from the moon were transmitted to Earth, received by tracking stations including Goldstone (US) and Honeysuckle Creek and Parkes (Australia), and relayed via satellite and landline to NASA's Mission Control in Houston.

From there, they were distributed to broadcasters and ultimately materialized on screens across the world.

Topping the ratings, CBS planned a thirty-two-hour continuous broadcast filled with live interviews with experts, anchored by Walter Cronkite in the studio, and mixed with prerecorded programming of everything from sci-fi movies to miscellaneous space-related segments.[37] The network used a staggering 142 cameras in its studio. Douglas Trumbull, who had previously worked on *2001: A Space Odyssey*, crafted a system containing multiple projectors—playfully named HAL 10,000—to support the incorporation of graphics as well as other types of content. This setup maintained the semblance of live broadcasting but was not entirely live, as reporting on the unfolding mission was visually accompanied by simulations and animations of the docking (created by Ralph McQuarrie, who later designed for *Star Wars*). Through approximations, these speculative means granted visual concreteness to what the transmitted audio from space could only attest to in sound: that the moon landing was, in fact, progressing. When the astronauts touched down, Cronkite rejoiced and exclaimed: "The date is now indelible. It's going to be remembered as long as man survives."[38] All in all, CBS News director Joel Banow estimated the network spent nearly $1 million on the coverage of this event.[39] The president of CBS News later boasted, "It was one of man's greatest achievements, it was one of television's great achievements."[40]

As exhilarating as the synchronous broadcast may have been, its transformation into a historical artifact and resource was almost instantaneous. Once rendered material, the recording became something to be filed, shelved, forgotten, and ultimately erased. Unconcerned with questions of the ontological kind (but generally aligned with the previously mentioned discourses of scholars and industry professionals), NASA's engineers were also taken by the allure of the immediate. After the widespread reporting that a search was underway for the tapes—and therefore that they had been lost—Nafzger maintained that first and foremost, "the goal was live TV."[41] The tapes in question were, admittedly, a byproduct of broadcasting efforts, with long-term retention never having been a primary goal. Liveness was, then, an essential aspect of crafting the experience and collective memory of the moon landing event. The temporal structure of this media event neatly tied the state of "awaiting the arrival of history" with watching history "as it happens."[42] For NASA, as well as the viewers at home, it was the *now* that counted.[43]

To make the miraculous possible and enable the masses on Earth to witness the walk in real time, certain sacrifices had to be made for the sake of show business. Compared to the sharp stereoscopic images and vivid photographs the astronauts took during the mission using the Hasselblad cameras, the transmission had a distinctly blurry quality. This aesthetic was not an intentional choice made to fit an imagined far-flung planet. At just 500 kilohertz, the Apollo 11 video transmission from the moon used a narrowband signal, which was only a sliver of regular broadcasting standards.[44] By contrast, at the end of the 1960s, US television broadcasts allocated 4.5 megahertz of bandwidth to video signals. To comply with the alloted bandwidth for sending signals from the moon, NASA engineers chose to pursue a strategy of compression, minimization, and segmentation. The slow scan method they used decreased the overall number of scan lines and reduced the ratio from thirty to ten frames per second. Once received on the ground, signals had to be converted to fit broadcasting. In effect, this meant reversing compression using duplication. Each captured frame was repeated several more times, stretching the ten captured frames per second back to thirty. Thus, the blurriness of the broadcast was a product not just of communication woes across roughly 250,000 miles of space but of a repetition that compensated for format disparities. Along the way, additional noise was also introduced in the process of converting and transmitting signals on the ground, adding to the uncanniness of the eventual images.[45] Although the slow scan format, which debuted in the Apollo 7 Earth-orbiting mission, was never used after Apollo 11, its structuring of the visuality of the event remains iconic.

Meanwhile, the downlink from the moon was also recorded on kinescopes and magnetic reels, not because of its historical significance but because of the fear of malfunction. "It was taped so that we could play it back through the converter *if we had to.* It wouldn't be live anymore, but it would still be video from the moon."[46] Once the call was made to allow television broadcast, ensuring live transmission from the moon was of utmost importance, and tapes were a mere contingency. Still, quite a few of them were produced. "You had tons of tapes being made at every site, prime and backup recorders, and on and on." Notably, these were not created solely for the sake of audiences, as moving images represented just one type of data the agency was interested in acquiring; the extravehicular activity "was one track out of 14 other tracks that had telemetry data, voice data, biomedical data, tracking data, so mainly, those recorders weren't for TV."[47]

The relatively low quality of the eventual broadcast, which had nevertheless produced a memorable expression of this techno-scientific landmark, was the catalyst for initiating a search for the tapes some forty years after the recordings were first made. John Sarkissian, a scientist at one of the tracking stations, wondered whether it was time to digitize and unveil high-definition images and sounds of the 1969 mission to viewers at the turn of the twenty-first century.[48] To this end, he had to find the slow scan tapes that contained the raw feed from the stations. These, he assumed, would be of better quality than the ones shown on television because they had recorded the data prior to its conversion. Presumably, there were forty-five Ampex reels buried amid hundreds of thousands of boxes somewhere in an archive waiting to be rediscovered. As though from a popular mystery plot, a team of former and current NASA employees and enthusiasts assembled to track the materials that would soon be labeled "the missing tapes." The search spanned various locations and continents. After several years, they finally determined that the reels had likely been degaussed.

ARCHAEOLOGIES OF ERASABILITY

So, how can this curious deletion be explained? Addressing this question first calls for delving into the early history of magnetic recording. Practices involving demagnetizing entire tapes and eliminating specific segments (editing) have followed discontinuous paths within the development of this recording substrate.

In the standard tale of the medium's evolutionary arc, the experimental phase begins with Valdemar Poulsen, who sought to inscribe sound onto magnetic wire at the dawn of the twentieth century.[49] This inaugural apparatus for capturing sound was displayed at the 1900 Paris Exposition, producing the oldest magnetic recording to have survived to this day. The major commercial development of the then-new medium took place not in Denmark but in Germany, with the Magnetophon unveiled in 1934. Fritz Pfleumer, its maker, touted the device's mutually destructive capabilities: to inscribe and to obliterate.[50] Unlike previous substrates, such as wire, Pfleumer's machine employed magnetic paper. Within a mere three years, the Magnetophon and its portable model had become the backbone of

German radio broadcast, outperforming other technologies in functionality and market dominance.

The next major chapter unfolded in postwar California, next to the vibrant circuits of the entertainment industry. Ampex, the company that produced the first American magnetic recorder, got its break by modifying the design of two Magnetophons. These had been obtained by a soldier and engineer, Jack Mullin, during the war and shipped across the Atlantic. By 1946, barely a year after the war's end, Mullin had already demonstrated the apparatus to the members of the Institute of Electrical and Electronics Engineers (IEEE). In April 1948, the fledgling Ampex company secured its first significant order from ABC: twenty units of the Model 200 sound recording machine, financially backed by Bing Crosby, a radio and entertainment magnate. Less than a decade later, the growing company unveiled the VR-1000 video tape recorder (VTR) in 1956. CBS—the winner of the live moon landing broadcast wars—was the first to use the VTR machines. Ampex's magnetic technology soon became a cornerstone of American television production, enabling time-shifting, prerecording, and post-production editing. Although kinescopes were intermittently used alongside magnetic recording, they were deemed expendable and typically tossed after airtime, their brief utility outweighed by an industry largely indifferent to preservation.[51] Kinescopes, then, initially a budgetary footnote, represented the predicaments of single-use storage, while reusable magnetic tapes established themselves as indispensable to ongoing production cycles. The VTR machine enabled an "economy of being able to erase and rerecord a tape whenever desired."[52] Negation, it turns out, functions as an engine for the continuous generation of value.

Although the implications of erasability seldom feature in the histories of magnetic recording, which so often amount to recounting technical details, Peter McMurray offers a significant counterpoint to this prevailing lack of interest.[53] He proposes three intersecting categories that encompass the periods, locations, and functions of the varied attempts to affix sound onto tape. First, he highlights experiments involving the stretching and looping of tape conducted in Nazi Germany. Next, he points out that during the postwar era and following the seizure of Magnetophons, the Soviet Union also appropriated the technology. In a manner reminiscent of their use of film (discussed in chapter 2), habitual demagnetization, according to McMurray, was a condition of possibility because the Soviets lacked access to sufficient tape blanks. This resulted in a greater focus on the potential of reusing recording substrates for as long as possible. Finally, he claims that the United States refined the techniques of cutting and splicing magnetic tape for editing.[54]

My main concern with this account is that erasability was not a contingent addition or a feature introduced as an afterthought several decades later. From the outset, it was a process, technique, and solution integral to the necessities of the medium, as revealed in early experiments and initiatives. Media archaeology's proposition to uncover overlooked and undeveloped loose ends reveals a subterranean logic not immediately apparent at first glance. As an adaptive strategy for probing the possibilities of retention, erasure was embedded from the very beginning, as evidenced by Poulsen himself. In his initial trials, Poulsen adhered to the procedure: "Each time, a brief message was recorded, replayed to assess quality, and then erased with a strong magnet."[55] I rehash this to underscore that scarcity was already a fundamental condition when magnetic methods first produced audible traces—around the same time Edison was transducing sound waves into grooves and making those, too, erasable.

Moreover, in 1921, long before the mobilization of the German star device across the Atlantic, someone at the US Bureau of Standards already envisioned a groundbreaking camera "with self-sensitizing plates on which not separate pictures but a continuously changing image is formed and erased after being telegraphed to a storage room."[56] Remarkably, this outlines an early vision of a reusable analog medium that separates transmission from capture, with the latter distinct from long-term storage. This speculative configuration reiterates one of the core reminders of this book: retention does not inherently imply permanence. Possibility and its actualization are not one and the same. Or, more precisely, in that era, the two functions were not as closely intertwined as they are today.

Around the same time, Ludwig Blattner wagered his fortunes on a different kind of future, convinced that magnetic recording would soon overtake the clunky sound-on-disc and sound-on-film techniques that dominated the British film industry. It did not. The Blattnerphone, bearing the name of its passionate promoter, never quite transformed cinema but instead found a place in a different though related domain. At the BBC Empire Service, where it lent itself to the prerecording of content for time-shifting across Britain's far-flung colonized territories, the Blattnerphone found its most prominent application.[57] These resulting records were routinely erased, spliced with scissors, and stored without care, symptomatic of an ideological and economic drive that favored circulation over preservation and discard over maintenance.

The final specimen unearthed in this excavation is the work of Semi Joseph Begun, an engineer who contributed to the development of several devices during the 1930s in Germany and went on to patent many of his ideas in the early 1950s after immigrating to the United States. His contributions include crucial advancements in degaussing, a process that, like many of Begun's insights, remains underexplored.[58] Central to his work is the realization that no viable process of recording, of high or low fidelity, can exist without undoing. For the machine to function as intended, each press of a button moves the tape first through the erasing head (where the magnetic field is neutralized) before ever arriving at the recording head. In this meticulously engineered choreography of capture and erasure, we see the persistence of a logic already familiar from reusable wax cylinders. Negation is not the opposite of inscription but its precondition. Failure to fully erase prior traces and lingering residual impressions contaminates the fidelity of any new recording, which could only partially overwrite the remains of the past. To unravel this seemingly paradoxical relationship, we might look to the following wartime anecdote, both amusing and unsettling in its effects: "One of the Allied war chiefs, probably Eisenhower, had to make a broadcast from Radio Luxembourg shortly after its capture and chose to make a tape recording prior to the occasion which would then be transmitted. This was done, and then transmission was well under way, when to everyone's horror Hitler's voice suddenly broke in on the recording. The tape was an old one which had been inadequately erased!"[59] In light of such incidents, it is no surprise that Begun sought to develop more effective methods to ensure flawless demagnetization. Operative erasure is, in effect, an anti-residual strategy mobilized against interference.

While engineered to impose order, the operation carries within it the possibility of veering off course. In doing so, it introduces an unintended element to the human-machine interaction, revealing a fissure between intentionality and execution. If preemptive erasure is crucial for minimizing noise, it also opens the door for accidents to become an all-too-likely consequence (that is, deletion that is neither voluntary nor well timed). Long before the aforementioned lunar erasure, Begun had already foreshadowed that "the ease of making magnetic recordings or of erasing prior magnetic recordings may often be disastrous to commercial recording which can easily be run through such prior recorders with the control switch inadvertently set to 'erase' or 'record,' and in a few minutes erase an expensive recording to nothing but a blank magnetic track."[60] Thus, a technology designed to repeatedly capture carries within it the seeds of its own unraveling. A single misstep can turn priceless footage into irreversible nothingness.

In this pre-concretized phase of magnetic recording during the early twentieth century, a kaleidoscope of successful, failed, and unrealized ventures closely intertwined retention with elimination and elimination with accidentality. This ephemeral design made erasure not only auxiliary and necessary to recording, but also materially and economically advantageous. Acts of erasure became woven into every stage of production and postproduction, from recording to editing and reuse. Thus, engineers and dealers of magnetic storage understood erasability as a prerequisite for operability from the very beginning. The root of the loss of the lunar tapes, therefore, lies not in the act of demagnetizing itself but in the misrecognition of the historical value of the tapes (one precious track hidden between thirteen others). It is a misstep within a convoluted administrative web, but not an accident in the purest sense—a claim that seems provocative only when considered in isolation and disconnected from the broader technological context just outlined.

LUNAR HISTORY IN THE ARCHIVES

In truth, by the late 1960s, when the moon landing tapes were produced, degaussing was already a mundane aspect of recording, replaying, and managing tapes. During the press conference announcing the conclusion of the search for these tapes, Nafzger expressed his regret, stating, "We should have had a historian running around saying, 'I don't care if you are ever going to use them—we are going to keep them.'"[61] He lamented the lack of a guiding principle that could reconcile archival pragmatism with the imperative to protect culturally significant materials.

In the years after the 1969 lunar expedition, tapes were routinely demagnetized to free up storage space for new projects and information. Typically, materials like the Apollo tapes were retained at the ground sites only for the duration of a mission, after which they were sent to NASA's Goddard Space Flight Center. The report detailing the possible fate of the missing records clearly lays out the process. If the telemetry data they contained was of no immediate concern, the tapes would continue their journey to the Washington National Records Center (WNRC), where they would be ultimately stored. In the event that tapes were required, "Goddard recalled them and either reused the one-inch tapes [. . .] or disposed of them because of the high cost of storing them."[62] Hence, tapes were regularly withdrawn from the archives and reviewed, and those deemed to lack scientific value were sent for degaussing. If the substrate's quality held up after multiple uses, the tapes were repurposed and used to record new data.[63] Dolly Perkins, deputy director-technical at NASA's Goddard Space Flight Center, referred to this as part of a standard "procedure."[64]

In other words, after signals from the moon reentered Earth, they encountered something entirely opposed to the vastness of the galaxy they had just crossed: a lack of physical space. At NASA, a severe shortage of materials fueled a major wave of recalls. The final report, under the subsection "Motivation for Recycling," highlighted the considerable shortage of blank tapes the organization experienced in the 1980s.[65] Ampex, as it turns out, had altered its tape composition, switching from an organic substance to a synthetic binding material a decade earlier, unaware that this substitution would cause rapid degradation. Due to what professionals refer to as "sticky-shed syndrome," these tapes would last only a few short years.[66] The agency's data production soared, aggravating the situation, and with it, the need for storage space grew rapidly. NASA reached a point where hundreds of thousands of tapes were required to maintain proper operations.

The narrative surrounding the introduction of this artificial binding material remains rather vague. Some attribute the redesign to an environmental campaign in the 1970s that rallied around the slogan "save the whales" and sought to end the commercial use of whale oil products in manufacturing.[67] Indeed, in 1972, the United States finally signed the Marine Mammal Protection Act, imposing a moratorium on hunting marine mammals. There are no direct sources acknowledging the use of this specific ingredient to make magnetic tapes, except for a remark made by an Ampex employee, a former director of advanced development.[68] If early recording substrates did indeed draw from such biological sources, it casts a grim shadow over the history of magnetic recording. Regardless, what followed was a pronounced shortage of blanks, compelling the widespread adoption of reuse practices.

In the absence of comprehensive archival records tracing the precise movements and locations of the lunar tapes throughout the decades, the research team concluded that the most plausible scenario is that the legendary declaration, "One small step for [a] man . . . ," along with Apollo 11's telemetry data, was recycled. This archival bind revealed that the more an institution has to preserve, the more it may confront its own storage limitations. As NASA continued to accumulate vast amounts of data, it was compelled to devise strategies for selectively discarding information so it could retain more of what was crucial to its ongoing endeavors. Excess breeds scarcity, which is then mitigated by reusability. This episode is therefore illustrative of how the affordances of a medium may simultaneously enable and obstruct its overt goals.

While degaussing is, on its face, a routine and unexceptional operation, it proves monumental in terms of the technical, economic, and bureaucratic relations it reveals through the loss of invaluable records. In other words, the unexpected erasure of one-of-a-kind footage reflects a chain of events shaped by intersecting assumptions about "liveness," the materiality of magnetic recording, engineered recycling, and institutional protocols of preservation and recall. A scathing report from the Government Accountability Office in 1990, most likely composed after the tapes had already been erased, reviewed NASA's storage facilities and archival practices. The report highlighted many shortcomings in the agency's repositories, which at the time housed approximately 1 million reels. Among the issues it cited were the limited number of locations that provided adequate conditions for long-term preservation, the neglect of inventory checks across NASA's distributed facilities, and the agency's "failure to maintain backup tapes of original data so they could be restored if the originals were stolen, lost, or accidentally destroyed."[69] Thus, while Perkins's assertion that "as far as [Goddard Space Flight Center employees] know, all the tapes were handled properly from a mission perspective" may be sincere and accurate, it is a strictly procedural description.[70]

Commenting on the contradictory but complementary roles of scarcity and plenty in twentieth-century media ecology, Nora draws a distinction between governmental and commercial repositories. Whereas professional archivists, as he claims, are charged with executing "controlled destruction," a necessity born of institutional constraints, their commercial and amateur counterparts, unburdened by such limitations, indiscriminately preserve any and all recordings.[71] This account is not entirely precise. TV networks, for their part, made their own copies of the moon landing on tapes, kinescope recordings, and 8 mm films—albeit in degraded quality compared to the original tapes NASA sought. Still, in contrast to the commercial archives Nora imagines, these networks also routinely reused their broadcast reels.[72] However expansive their storage facilities or deep their financial pockets, even private companies cannot escape the economic realities of limited storage. Those scavenging for historic missteps might also point out that "Douglas Edwards and the News," the first CBS show to use the Ampex videotape recorder (VTR) for prerecording content, "was not considered eventful in itself (cost conscious CBS recycled the original 2-inch videotape)."[73]

Overall, the history of broadcast archiving in the United States is anything but straightforward.[74] An archive dedicated to television broadcast was not established until the year before the moon landing, with the creation of the Vanderbilt Television News Archive. Lucas Hilderbrand illustrates how this project, initially a private endeavor, was conceived to address what was, at best, the unsystematic archiving practices of governmental bodies and, at worst, a widespread indifference to preservation and the value of such records.[75] Notably, it was not until the passage of the American Television and Radio Act in 1976 that the Library of Congress was directed to create a repository for broadcast materials and television programs. That any recordings of the moon landing exist at all, in any quality, is thus rather fortunate. Current amazement at the news of the loss of the original footage likely stems from present-day assumptions about the omnipresence of digital capture, where the "archive" is often assumed to expand its reach automatically rather than through intentional selection processes—a problematic conjecture to say the least, as I argue in chapter 5.

Just a few years ago, Sotheby's auctioned three deaccessioned Ampex Quadruplex tapes, labeled as "Original, first-generation NASA videotape recordings of the Apollo 11 lunar EVA," for $1.82 million on the fiftieth anniversary of the moon landing.[76] These tapes had been purchased in the 1970s by a NASA intern, along with more than a thousand others, with the intent to resell them to TV stations for reuse. Although they were not the high-quality recordings the search party had been seeking, their unexpected resurfacing illustrates the life cycle of lunar records.

In much the same way that the processes of recording and demagnetizing were overlooked in theoretical discussions praising television's "liveness," the removal of large quantities of materials from collections often "barely registers within the archival profession."[77] This parallels "accession denial" in curatorial debates.[78] From nearly every vantage point, deliberate negation persists as a tacit, unspoken but essential issue, not only in media studies but also in fields directly concerned with preservation, such as museology and archival studies. Deaccessioning, while certainly practiced, is rarely openly addressed. Mark Greene suggests that the reluctance to discuss it publicly stems from the fear of tarnishing a collection's reputation among donors, stakeholders, and the public.[79] This near taboo, as Martin Gammon speculates, is also a product of a particular undercurrent in the way institutions that offer a resting place for records and objects of the past are conceptualized.[80] According to him, a museum collection stands in for the utopian Enlightenment project: a stable, comprehensive microcosm of the world. How, then, can we reconcile this ideal legacy with the hurdles faced by collections, which are so far removed from notions of wholeness and totality?

In this context, my approach is to confront negative mediality and production head-on. Instead of being deaccessioned and gifted or sold to other collections, the slow scan footage was repurposed in-house out of sheer necessity during a period when the protection of televised content was rarely performed, even by the producers themselves. At some indeterminate moment, someone at NASA made an ontological incision into the repository, irrevocably altering it. This was an act deeply entangled in the hastiness of presentism.

> It probably wasn't until the 25th and even 40th anniversary, it became more and more apparent to me [Nafzger] how historical this event really was. I knew it was historical, but how many people watched it and what it meant, since we never went back again, became more and more important in the eyes of many [. . .] *we didn't have a historic perspective and that's probably one of the reasons we don't have those tapes!* No one had a historic perspective. They had a perspective of, "what's the next mission? *Let's get going.*"[81]

When the tapes were degaussed, the materials both of and for history vanished along with any illusion of long-term completeness. Their significance seems to have been recognized only in hindsight once they failed to reappear on command. It seemed reasonable to believe that anything aired to millions of people would earn its place in the historical record to become a stable, cherished audiovisual resource for the future. And yet, such conviction collided with the stark finality of the tapes' disappearance.

The aporia introduced by reuse and made all the more vivid through the search for this missing artifact is consequential. It exposes an entire system of mediatic structures and relations that govern data transmission and retention. In the shadow of the moon, the premature erasure of these storing objects problematizes some of the fundamental ontological assumptions about broadcast technologies and calls into question the archival dream of total retention. In the end, the moon landing telecast and its simultaneous recording represent an extraordinary feat of overcoming previously uncharted distances, only for this content to confront the enduring finiteness of Earthly matter and everyday budgetary constraints.

Four

TYPOLOGY OF PURGE AND THE ORDERING OF ERRATIC TYPEWRITING

"work" (writing, yes, sitting down at the table and writing, sitting at the typewriter and writing, writing right through the day, or right through the night, roughing out a plan, putting down capital ls *and small* as, *drawing sketches, putting one word next to another, looking in a dictionary, recopying, rereading, crossing-out, throwing away, rewriting, sorting, rediscovering, waiting for it to come, trying to extract something that might resemble a text.*[1]

• • • A single sheet laid upon another soon forms a pile. One pile alone seems harmless, but when it is placed atop another, and another, it begins to resemble a tower. And papers have a habit of multiplying. Inevitably, one searches for places to contain this growing multitude: a shelf, a drawer, a filing cabinet, or perhaps even an entire room. And with each new space filled, the problem of storage becomes ever more pressing, as the pursuit of safekeeping demands solutions that always seem just out of reach. This chapter engages the technology of the typewriter, which, no doubt, contributed to the sudden proliferation of paper in the latter half of the twentieth century. Picking up where the previous discussion left off—with the accidental erasure of magnetic tapes—here, operative erasure is resolutely intentional. I therefore trace a repertoire of gestures devised to stave off the unruly surfeit of office work.

Marshall McLuhan, a perceptive commentator on media across all their forms from print to the electronic era, engaged with the explosive abundance triggered by the typewriter, a machine whose many inventors and origins remain hard to pinpoint and are the subject of contentious debates. The typewriter, he theorized, "carried the Gutenberg technology into every nook and cranny of our culture and economy."[2] It dissolved the temporal gap between writing and publication, making the two occur simultaneously; this acceleration led to what McLuhan likens to pyramids of paper and files that eventually drove the emergence of a new kind of business: file-cleaning services. Around the same time when *Understanding Media: The Extensions of Man* appeared in print, the phrase "information explosion" likewise entered popular vernacular. Each, in its way, reverberated the shifting conditions of the postwar market. McLuhan recognized that this surge in productivity also initiated various spatial and conceptual constrictions. For instance, the popularization of the typewriter reinforced stricter norms and expectations of correctness and standardization.[3] Expansion and contraction, then, are two faces of the same technical phenomenon.

The idea of a sudden eruption proves to be more than a passing thought, and indeed became the backdrop to the shared anxieties of workers and businesses. Just a few short years after McLuhan's observations, IBM released a peculiar, somewhat eerily toned and by now seminal corporate film for those writing of the typewriter. Released in 1967, *The Paperwork Explosion* was directed by none other than Jim Henson. With a run time of under five minutes, it promises that every word and letter dictated and processed through IBM's devices would free workers from the tedious task of composing, sorting, and handling paper. The fast-paced editing conjures a sense of impending doom as it depicts workers buckling under the stress of keeping pace with "progress" and the pressures of the industry. The elimination of laborious tasks feeds into a phantasm of control through standardization, which quickly collides with the grim reality of market conditions. Production demands far exceed the capabilities of available employees. The workers' recitation, "People should think, machines should work," echoes at the end of the film. It is a disquieting reflection of a frustrated midcentury workforce, encapsulating the mood of those living through the explosion that would morph into a utopian dream of the paperless office, a vision that would gain traction a decade later, although it has yet to be realized even today.[4]

Just as IBM's corporate hallucination drums on with "not enough time" and "not enough people" to manage the load, those attempting to do too much with too few resources are bound to fail. Although mechanized writing was intended to provide a technical fix, it unleashed a different burden: entropy. Typographical errors, as we all know, tend to proliferate rapidly, slipping into even the most carefully written texts. Whether caused by human oversight, mechanical glitches, or the inherent imperfections of the writing process, errors are a persistent setback. Precisely for these reasons, this vulnerability creates an opportunity to study writing, documents, and paper not just for their content, but for their material form, as Lisa Gitelman has proposed.[5]

What we find on the page is "operative writing," a concept introduced by Sybille Krämer to highlight the range of actions that signs enable once they are no longer viewed simply as graphic representations.[6] I suggest here that operative unwriting is equally essential. Errors and the eradication thereof have been part of the writing process for millennia, long before the use of paper, and persisting after paper had been, supposedly, declared redundant. Over time, they became so routine that they were often treated as a commonplace fact of composing any document. The latent presence of error renders its remediation and correction imperative to technological design. In this light, John Durham Peters remarks that "the historiography of writing has been biased towards literature and away from bureaucracy, towards pens and away from pencils."[7] His assessment calls attention to less glamorous but equally important aspects of writing. The daily dealings of the bureau, its tools, and, as this book insists, its erasing techniques are integral to understanding paper as more than a decontextualized surface that withdraws from apprehension. Jacques Derrida, an eminent philosopher of paper, has not tired of reminding us that the " 'What is?' question—'What is paper?'—is almost bound to go astray the minutes it is raised."[8] To loosen the grip of the complexity of the ontological "what," this inquiry takes up the "how" of paper.

Cornelia Vismann's work stands out for offering a theory of the history of administrative media practices. Vismann identifies a paradigmatic shift that was underway long before the typewriter dramatically accelerated the creation and circulation of printed materials: beginning in the 1500s, medieval chanceries moved away from the practice of discarding canceled originals after legitimizing copies and began to embrace an archival ethos that emphasized preserving drafts and versions of a given document.[9] As Vismann explains, the ensuing institutionalization of this archival impulse led to the amassing of an overwhelming number of originals and copies, creating a scarcity of available space. By the late nineteenth century, a hierarchy emerged to process the overflow, such that all documents were sorted into the sanctioned, the discardable, and the not-yet-either of these two states (that is, those still awaiting classification).[10]

In this chapter, my emphasis shifts from the document proper to the engineering of error correction, particularly in the twentieth-century realm of the ubiquitous typewriter and "messy" typewriting. Here, paper is also a mass-produced storage container integral to the production and circulation of business communication. Media theorists have primarily and justifiably viewed the machine as a tool designed to train and conform the body to this new mechanical rhythm (ergonomics aside) while regulating its output on paper. Few, however, have considered how the automation of undoing both echoed and instituted standards of correctability before the prodigious arrival of autocorrect. The goal was to achieve frictionless production, although perfection remained ever elusive. Given the inevitability of errors, scientists, office workers, and typewriter manufacturers proposed various strategies to reduce the proliferation of drafts that would be discarded, but the history and meaning of which have yet to be examined in depth. These techniques for correcting mistakes included rubbing out, overlaying, evaporating, and dislodging. Some of these innovations have endured, while others have faded into obscurity. Together, they represent varied approaches to rendering errors less disruptive, transforming the typewritten page into a reusable surface and its inscriptions revisable.

TYPERIGHT: THE INTERPLAY BETWEEN HAND AND KEY

Although there were many forerunners, including the now lost 1808 model engineered by Pellegrino Turri, the typewriter that first appeared on the market in 1874 was the brainchild of Christopher Latham Sholes, Carlos Glidden, and Samuel W. Soule.[11] It was made and sold by Remington, a gun-manufacturing company. Over the following decades, the Remington typewriter became immensely popular in the United States, transforming how writing was produced by authors, clerks, and everyday users. One of its major flaws, however, was the lack of instant feedback.[12] The first model, which introduced the "QWERTY" keyboard, did not allow users to review their work until the document was typed. It was a typewriter without visibility, with no "screen interface." By contrast, Underwood's machine, launched at the end of the nineteenth century, was the first to allow users to read what they typed as they typed it.

The whirlwind of papers being created, passed along, dispatched, and received in the office provided a vibrant backdrop for the typewriter—a machine that fused anonymization and amplification.[13] My focus in this chapter is on the growing body of literature that examines the role of technical innovations in exercising control as a business practice. Although data management has posed complex logistic challenges since the days of ancient empires, sociologist Max Weber differentiates the form it took in the modern era. Rationalization proceeded via an "apparatus of material implements" that subtly but profoundly reconfigured the very foundations of modern state organization.[14] The files and papers Weber referenced were integral to a "bureaucratic principle," which was effectively "a bureau-technological one."[15] Catalyzed by the Industrial Revolution, private offices in the nineteenth century eagerly adopted new tools to streamline work processes and manage the mounting flow of information, as James Beniger demonstrates.[16] JoAnne Yates further underscores the often invisible role played by technologies as they transformed internal communications into standardized operations and objects in the quest for efficiency.[17] Yates notes that the typewriter, along with paper-based technologies such as duplicators and filing cabinets, shaped and was shaped by power dynamics in the office, reflecting managerial practices that first took root in the railroad industry and later spread to manufacturing companies.[18]

The number of "typists, stenographers [. . .], and secretaries" employed in the United States skyrocketed from over a hundred thousand in 1900 to an astonishing three-quarters of a million by 1920.[19] This remarkable growth was indicative of a radical overhaul in labor roles. The term "typewriter" took on an ambiguous techno-gendered meaning, referring both to the machine and the women who commanded it. As Kittler details, the convergence of machine and feminized labor in the office did not occur in isolation but entailed displacing the male stenographer, who had once taken dictation by hand. "[The typewriter] inverts the material basis of literature."[20] By the dawn of the twentieth century, office work had rapidly become a feminized domain, with the "typewriter girl" emerging as a desirable figure and trope. This feminized operator became, in Kittler's terms, part of a ciphered mechanism, her hands transmitting the author's vocal commands into text. But in this newly established scenario, the secretary retained almost no autonomy over the content she produced: relaying information, she was a near-perfect channel, a body within the apparatus, a "woman employed in processing discourses."[21] Yet the frequent failure of inscription remains understated in his lengthy analysis. Human hands faltering at the keys is an entirely different phenomenon from the mechanical breakdown Nietzsche experienced with his writing ball, which so fascinated Kittler. In practice, office work meant confronting the inevitability of human error: accidents, miscommunications, misplaced documents, misunderstandings, misspellings, and a host of other recurring mishaps.

There is much to consider when it comes to the less-than-perfect execution of orders committed to the page. As Gitelman astutely writes, "Documents are epistemic objects."[22] Even a brief glance at the literature surveying the history of printed matter reveals that "error" has been cast as the antithesis of the proper, the good, the perfect, and the correct. The invention of the printing press introduced an entirely new breed of typographical errors, distinct from the occasional misspellings or idiosyncratic blunders of scribes and clerks. Elizabeth Eisenstein fittingly names this phenomenon the "standardized error."[23] Here, the result of a momentary lapse of attention became visible and permanently fixed in the multiple copies that were disseminated, reproducing the original blunder. The wider the distribution of an error, the more urgent its correction becomes. As Lothar Müller suggests, printing and error correction became deeply intertwined with a discourse of "truth."[24] In the age of print, when a mistake could no longer be scraped off a scroll, the error's relative permanence shifted the stakes of accuracy and amendment practices.

Errors could be intercepted at two junctures: caught in the act during editing or addressed retrospectively through various remedial techniques. The appearance of the role of the professional corrector in the bustling print shops of Renaissance and early modern Europe operationalized preemptive control.[25] Errata came after the fact, typically attached at the end of a book, where readers would find a catalog and an admission of the printer's or author's missteps.[26] Some of these forms did not just provide elucidations and reformulation, though; they included instructions for the reader, such as cutting out and gluing emendations into the book. This required the "user" to interact with the text—to physically engage with the printed words of others. Adam Smyth offers a nuanced typology of error corrections whose spatial and temporal relations between author, text, and user were rather distinct. Other than the errata list, one would have also encountered "the handwritten annotation, the pasted insert-slip and the cancel page."[27] By the late eighteenth century, the imperfections of print culture had become so widespread that satirists cleverly repurposed these corrective practices for their own aims.[28]

This legacy stands in direct contrast to the idealized image of the office of the nineteenth and twentieth centuries as a well-oiled, optimized machine, where every component—human and mechanical—dutifully played its part in a Taylorist vision of productivity. In such a system, avoiding errors is paramount and precision venerated; however, speed, its twin ambition, renders typographical errors all the more likely. "So obsessed were early office managers with the pernicious influence of error on efficiency that entire studies were commissioned," writes Matthew Kirschenbaum, and "the habits of typists were scrutinized at the most minute levels [. . .] it was known how much this all cost—in paper, in carbons, in erasers, and above all, in time."[29] Thus, the 1936 introduction to *Improvement of Instruction in Typewriting* flags errors as a central concern: "A large section of the text is devoted to problems of determining how to discover what errors a student habitually makes, to trying to discover the causes of such errors."[30] The authors speculate that oversight stems from a general unawareness of the root causes of these mistakes and a lack of knowledge about how to address them once identified. "It is hoped that this diagnostic and remedial section," they promise, "will be at least the beginning of a movement to determine with ever greater accuracy the causes of and remedies for individual errors."[31] Under the rubric of "error analysis," the authors delve into discussing the contributing factors, including issues like posture, that presumably interfere with the production of legible documents. Ostensibly, detecting and systematizing the identification of errors and optimizing the body that produced them could minimize or even entirely preempt them.

Yet no perfect solution was ever found, and secretaries were left to correct their mistakes as best they could. One common method was to type an X over the unwanted character. This gesture, X-ing, obscured the original letter just enough to make it at least partially illegible. X-ing, however, was often frowned upon and criticized as a "failure to appreciate the need for neatness in work."[32] If there was a hierarchy of error correction, X-ing ranked lower than erasing.[33] The latter was performed with a small circular rubber—immortalized in Claes Oldenburg's statue *Typewriter Eraser, Scale X*—although it, too, had its drawbacks. The eraser's remnants could clog the machine and hinder its smooth operation. A quick reflection on other storage technologies that have already been discussed (the wax cylinder, magnetic tape) reminds us that such media are, by design, anti-residual. Their function hinges on principles of order and cleanliness.

In the frenzy of dictation schools, typing classes, and competitions that followed the successful launch of the Remington, any lapse in grammar or breach of etiquette was labeled "faulty automatization."[34] So the question remains: was the machinery or the human operator at fault? The prevailing spirit of the time assumed it was the gendered, undisciplined body, which could not be expected to focus or function with the precision of an artificial mechanism and which thus squandered energy, time, and resources.[35] The typist's labor was frequently hyper-visible and overlooked, her skills undervalued, and her fallibility always presumed. This perception took root early on; one typewriting guide from 1893 went so far as to cast errors as a reflection of character, claiming that "slovenliness is often manifest in excessive and dirty erasure."[36]

While the manual advised avoiding errors to prevent costly and time-consuming corrections, this very flaw soon became a business opportunity. Error, once cast as a disruption, was recontextualized as a productive and lucrative interruption. Take, for instance, the promotional material for Eberhard Faber's Typewriter Eraser, playfully titled "The Sudden Disappearance of Miss Take." After all, an error is, naturally, a "Miss," not a "Mr.":

> Scene: A Modern Business Office
>
> Time: A very busy morning
>
> Characters:
>
> Mr. BOSS, of A Modern Business
>
> Office Miss DOE
>
> Secretary to Mr. Boss
>
> Miss TAKE, the inevitable error
>
> Mr. Boss finished dictation with the usual "please, Miss Doe, hurry that air mail letter." In the typing, Miss Take appeared—discouragingly bold. "Now" thought Miss Doe, "if only this eraser will remove you cleanly without injuring the paper." Miss Doe erased carefully but deliberately, and quick as a flash Miss Take disappeared. The letter was completed and Mr. Boss was delighted—thanks to the superb quality of the Eberhard Faber Typewriter Eraser.[37]

Feminist critique diagnoses the female body as an epistemological and ontological interruption within, and as a challenge to, philosophical and scientific traditions.[38] The so-called errant that confounds logos is thrown into sharp relief in this very example. Error may be endemic to the act of writing, but here gender is coded as the glitch and the patch. The burden of correctness was, admittedly, not equally shared. Men were neither trapped by the confines of the office nor subjected to similarly harsh judgment; their gaffes were easily forgiven. Rachel Plotnick revisits this often overlooked chapter in the typewriter's spatial pre–World War II history when men were encouraged to roam freely and travel for work with the device.[39] Typing on the go often resulted in less-than-pristine drafts, although these imperfections were inconsequential and certainly did not invite scrutiny of the typists' professionalism or morals as those of a "Miss."

There is also the matter of literature, which I have yet to address. Many renowned authors—including luminaries like Nikolai Gogol, Herman Melville, Franz Kafka, Jorge Luis Borges, and David Foster Wallace, to name a few—have used the modern office as a backdrop to explore the human condition in their works. While the typewriter often appears in seminal literary texts, it also serves as the preferred tool for composing prose and poetry for writers such as Henry James and William Burroughs. In *Track Changes: A Literary History of Word Processing*, Kirschenbaum explores the complex relationship between technological innovation and artistic creation, showing how shifts in instruments for composition, revision, and publication reshape not just the physical act but also how authors conceive of and execute their craft.[40] As Kirschenbaum suggests, the tool is not merely a simple conduit but fundamental to the process and its final result. For Hannah Sullivan, alterations and corrections to typescripts and proofs are an inevitable part of bringing a manuscript to publication.[41] This also plays out in Georges Perec's own writing about writing, as cited in the epigraph of this chapter, where "crossing-out, throwing away, rewriting" are every bit as integral as writing itself.[42] The excisions, erasures, and deletions between one draft and another are thus essential to seeing a work through to its final form. In attending to the experimental, literary scholars Craig Dworkin and Paul Benzon probe the avant-garde's repurposing of typewritten errors into an aesthetic strategy of subversion.[43] "Each error on the page, each mark left unremoved, unerased, and uncorrected, opens up a media-historical detour in miniature."[44] In some cases, then, the error can itself become poetic. Whereas Dworkin's and Benzon's interests center on the aesthetization of error, mine revolve around the design of what allows error to be removed from sight (preferably before it ever registers as legible) and within a realm far less beguiling than the arts.

CORRECTABLE, CORRASABLE, INDELIBLE

A thought experiment: imagine a device in which every keystroke is consigned irreversibly to the page. Any idea, however fleeting or errant, materializes in black and white, inscribed, fixed, and unalterable. No mechanism for revision exists, and what enters the machine becomes a record. In 1714, Henry Mill envisioned just such a contraption. He was granted a patent for "an artificial machine or method for the impressing or transcribing of letters," although no available documents show evidence of his design ever being constructed.[45] Mill's invention promised one thing above all: that its impressions would be "more lasting than any other writing, and not to be erased or counterfeited without manifest discovery."[46] It was the possibility of deliberate deceit, not errant keystroke, that haunted him; even so, the hypothetical is proactive. What might a world without erasure, where nothing can be retracted, look like? In a reality where mistakes cannot be negated and the capacity for revisions is limited, we would soon find ourselves drowning in a sea of abandoned drafts. Paper filling every corner, each failed attempt jostling for space with the next, a testament not only to work but also to our imperfections. What is gained in permanence is lost to abundance.

An entirely different approach to managing typewritten errors was already underway in the 1920s and 1930s. In an effort to preempt the explosion McLuhan would later invoke, Harvard Business School professor John G. Callan devised a novel method he dubbed "deferred indelibility." This curious phrase referred to a coating that offered flexibility in an increasingly rigid administrative world. The word "indelibility," rooted in the Latin *dēlēbilis* ("able to be destroyed"), is an oddity in itself, hinting at something impervious yet fleeting. Callan, not one to settle for the obvious, explored a host of names for his invention, some catchier than others: Tabula Rasa, Oblitera, Erado, Eradico, Deleo, Deletus, Rasable, Easirasable, Quickoff.[47] All these contenders hyped its key feature: mistakes could simply be wiped away. Eventually, he patented his idea and collaborated with several American paper manufacturers to produce "Corrasable Bond."[48] The chosen brand name, likely derived from the Latin *corrādere*, meaning "to scrape off," speaks more to the act of erasure than to the quality of the paper itself. With this, Callan bridged the medieval practice of scraping errors with the bureaucratic demands of his contemporary world, bringing the past and present together under the rapid stroke of a typewriter key. As promised in an ad for the bond in the 1930s, one could remove the error "without leaving the slightest trace of erasure on the paper—no dulling or 'roughing' of the surface, no 'cloudy' gray drabs, no smear or smudges."[49]

Callan's idea embraced the ephemeral: a smooth, adhesive surface held ink at bay, preventing the typo from being absorbed into the paper and allowing mistakes to be wiped away without effort. But such a reprieve was short-lived. Once the ink penetrated "the paper's fibers," it became permanent, and "any erasure would require a sand rubber, as with ordinary typewriter paper."[50] Callan's vision was not of a blackboard-like medium on which marks could be endlessly erased at will. Instead, he designed for practicality—a mechanism of built-in delay and a short grace period for revisions.

This window spanned a single business day, functioning as an administrative interstice that permitted limited revisions while ensuring that, once finalized, the record would remain unaltered. By the time a document left the office, its contents had congealed into an authorized artifact, impervious to amendment, reliable, and resistant to tampering. In August 1934, anxious about potential patent infringements, a collaborator lamented, "Apparently everyone is coming out with an easy erasing paper."[51] There was, indeed, a growing market for the budget-conscious consumer eager to curb unnecessary waste. Advertisements rather hyperbolically proclaimed an "all time low" in rewrites, promising a more efficient typing experience that saved money by eliminating the need for a fresh sheet of paper with each oversight.[52] In the spirit of gendering the machine, Corrasable's promotional materials took aim at the unpredictable nature of the human body. "Some office men think their typists are so good that they never have to erase—well, look at their erasers—or ask them. Delible will save a respectful percentage of its cost, and more than the small difference in cost, on any busy day."[53] Here, it was the typewriter (woman, not machine) who was cast in doubt. However well and diligently she performed, a lingering suspicion persisted, as if every mark on the page might mask an error surreptitiously effaced. Correction signaled inefficiency and was framed as a misallocation of labor that diverted energy from ostensibly more productive tasks, unless it could itself be optimized.

The company codified a hierarchy of correction, ranking interventions by intensity: the less effort expended, the more desirable the method. The ideal correction, naturally, would be the one that left no evidence, achieved so seamlessly it evaded detection altogether. "[Inscriptions] can be removed with soft rubber, leaving little to no trace," as long as they remained on the surface of the protective film.[54] By lessening the need for harsh friction typically required for removal, the coating's design simultaneously curtailed particulate dispersion. Let it be repeated: these storage media, in their very constitution, are structured to resist any remainder (even when, as we shall soon see, overlaying remains the sole procedural option). Unresolved marks, eraser shavings, dust, and other particles often lead to compromised, if not entirely corrupted, new impressions. That said, the introduction of Corrasable Bond did not make the rubber eraser obsolete. Once the ink penetrated through the coating and into the depths of the substrate, there was no alternative but to revert to the tried-and-true yet destructive method of abrasion, even though its correction was unmistakably visible and inferior. Erase too vigorously and the resulting residue could clog the typewriter—a wrench in the machine and a veritable disaster for productivity.[55]

Although rubber found its place atop the pencil in the late nineteenth century, "Indian rubber," as Joseph Priestley mistakenly named it, had been recognized for its ability to remove unwanted traces as early as the eighteenth century.[56] Rubber soon became indispensable for fixing typewritten errors, most notably with the iconic Van Dyke Eberhard Faber eraser. Its design, circular and narrow, allowed precision, erasing one character at a time, while the attached brush efficiently swept away the remnants of the correction; it could "clean while it erases," a dual ordering gesture.[57] These techniques, though widely adopted, were far from flawless and rarely achieved the seamless finish they promised, often betraying their intervention through telltale smudges and traces. Callan, however, deftly refigured the shortcomings of such methods into a promotional advantage. Their failure to rub away cleanly was only proof of the superiority of his invention.

While his goal was to enhance office work and streamline typing, the invention faced significant issues in the eyes of consumers, who questioned the effectiveness of the very features he had carefully designed. First, they noted faint traces and ghostly effects left behind on the page after erasure. The bond's dual promise of reusability and indelibility had cultivated the expectation that a single sheet might sustain iterative inscription without degradation throughout the paper's lifespan. As a result, much of Callan's correspondence with paper manufacturers centered on this problem of persistent and visible signs of removal. Second, and paradoxically in opposition to the first complaint, the paper was deemed too ephemeral. The core issue was that even after the surface coating had been disturbed and the paper was presumed to have transitioned into its indelible phase, it remained susceptible to further effacement. A range of publication guidelines forbade the use of this bond and its ilk, such as onion skin paper, for manuscripts and official documentation, prompted by the concern that such materials might not endure.

Faced with these opposing criticisms (not erasable enough, too erasable), Callan responded by challenging the notions of absolute permanence and complete erasability. Although inscriptions could still be removed even during the indelible phase, he argued that such corrections should not happen without effort. He defended the appearance of gray traces, claiming them essential for revealing unsanctioned actions. These "ghosts"—apparitions of what once was but no longer resembled its original form—served as a countermeasure against forgery and tampering. A ghost, belonging neither to the inscription nor the substrate, attested only to its existence as a generative negation. All in all, despite these seemingly contradictory complaints and Callan's nuanced but not entirely satisfactory response, erasable bonds sold by companies like Eaton's gradually became a staple by the mid-twentieth century.[58]

THE LIQUID SUPPLEMENT AND WOMEN'S WORK

Where abrasion (even as subtle as required by the Corrasable Bond) operates through subtraction, Bette Nesmith Graham turned instead to a counter-logic of addition for negative correction.[59] Historically, the palimpsest, a technique of layering records one atop the other, had long offered extra storage for scribes, scholars, artists, and writers grappling with the pressures and costs of scarce materials.[60] Graham's correcting fluid followed a similar yet modernized and mass-produced principle. First concocted in her kitchen in 1956, Liquid Paper quickly became a household name, synonymous with easy, efficient revisions.[61] It circulated across contexts, from office desks to schoolrooms, where even children came to depend on it for its retroactive mitigation capabilities. Of the various innovations surveyed in this chapter, Liquid Paper is perhaps the most recognizable and persistent artifact of office life. In the latter half of the twentieth century, this typographic principle was commodified by various brand names such as Wite-Out, Tipp-Ex, and many others.

Liquid Paper also represents one of the most iconic entrepreneurial stories in the history of office supplies. Once Graham, a former typist, gradually broke free from the traditionally feminized realm of clerical work and the domestic space of the kitchen, she rose to become a stationery mogul and owner of a multimillion-dollar corporation. The product perfectly blended a familiarity with the administrative industry's needs with the artistic sensibility of an amateur painter. Composed of an opaque tempera-based pigment, the solution was designed to mimic the appearance of paper, not by erasing mistakes but by ingeniously concealing them. In essence, it offered a simple solution to the irritations of paperwork: paint over the mistakes, banish them from view, and start (almost) anew.

As its inventor admitted, Liquid Paper was "a feminine product."[62] Dubbed "the answer to a secretary's prayers" by one trade publication, the correcting fluid was directly and unmistakably aimed at women.[63] "I knew what the secretary needed, and I just needed to tell her that I had it," Graham explained.[64] Her knowledge came from personal experience. Graham began working as a typist at the age of seventeen. After attending a local business college, she became an executive secretary at a bank. "I was a secretary and had a need myself, and this was really the reason that I invented Liquid Paper—so that I could type on that electric typewriter, which had been brought into most offices about 1950." Most likely, she was referring to IBM's electric typewriters, which used a carbon ribbon instead of the cloth used by earlier models, making unnoticeable erasure nearly impossible. When errors occurred, rubbing the surface left visible marks due to the carbon film. "My fingers would hang heavy on the keyboard," she recalled, "and the first thing I'd know, I'd have a mistake with a deposit of carbon which I simply could not erase."[65] The imperfections of abrasion and the often flawed promise of traceless erasure pushed Graham to seek a "better method."[66] Liquid Paper nestled itself between the original substrate and the new inscription, offering a seamless way to mask errors without the need for removal. Instead of relying on the subtraction of errors, she devised a quick-drying formula that would act as an intermediary, forming a new layer on top of the original. This supplemental layer was to match the paper it had covered, whether blue, green, yellow, or white.[67]

Given the strong stigma associated with errors, Graham faced reprimand at the bank not only for her mistakes as a typist but also for using "that white stuff" she had invented.[68] In dismissing her brilliant technical solution for a common problem, such reprobation highlights the prevailing normative judgment that equated errors with a lack of discipline. Prevention was viewed as more virtuous than correction, which was considered merely a concealment of incompetence. Despite her manager's scorn, word of her invention began to spread, and soon enough, everyone wanted the material, which she aptly named "Mistake Out" in those early days. Later, it was rebranded as "Liquid Paper," and the product was pitched to IBM, which declined. In a fitting twist of irony, Graham was purportedly dismissed from the bank for mistakenly signing a letter with "Liquid Paper Company" instead of her employer's name.[69] Yet this misstep hardly mattered, as the company quickly evolved from a loosely kept office secret into a global phenomenon.

By 1960, just a few years after her initial home experiments, Graham hired a chemist to help refine the formula for Liquid Paper. Within two years, around a thousand bottles of the correcting liquid were being sold each week, and her then fifteen-year-old son, along with his friends, began working full time to produce and market the magic substance. In 1964, automation finally took over, and production moved from her home to a proper manufacturing facility. What began as a modest operation, with virtually no advertising except for a simple brochure handed out to secretaries, had by 1968 made its first million. Under Graham's leadership, the Liquid Paper Company embraced a distinct philosophy "dedicated to changing the concept that profit is primary to all business" and actively created opportunities for women, incorporating them into higher management roles.[70] As the 1970s drew to a close, the office workaround was lucrative enough to be acquired by the Gillette Corporation for the remarkable sum of $47.5 million.

LASER BEAMS FOR TRACELESS EVAPORATION

Whereas Corrasable Bond's promise to "erase without a trace" was born from the minds of marketing professionals eager to promote (in)delible paper, it was not until the invention of a physicist that this hope approached reality. Both the twentieth-century office and laboratory were spaces preoccupied with standardizing the processes of documentation and recording.[71] Against the backdrop of Liquid Paper's meteoric rise in popularity among office workers, Arthur L. Schawlow began experimenting with lasers to efface mistakes on the page, aiming to restructure the work he oversaw in the lab. Reflecting on his scientific writing process, Schawlow admitted, "I do struggle. I used to think I could write pretty fast, but I couldn't. And when I do a draft or something I tend to cross about every second or third word and keep struggling with it."[72] One likeminded engineer expressed his own frustration as someone who had "always been involved in 'paper work'" and, in a letter to the inventor, recognized the invention's true value, emphasizing "how expensive mistakes in typing really are."[73]

The idea of a laser eraser first occurred to Schawlow in 1963. After a decade at Bell Labs, Schawlow accepted a position at Stanford University's Department of Physics in 1961, where he began his groundbreaking research into lasers and spectroscopy—work that would later earn him the Nobel Prize in physics in 1981 alongside Nicolaas Bloembergen. As a side project, Schawlow explored unconventional uses of lasers, one of which was the laser eraser.[74] Schawlow applied for a patent in 1965, stating that the need for such an invention stemmed from a specific challenge: "Most individuals and secretaries, in particular, are aware of the troublesome nature of making erasures of a typewritten letter or other character from the paper," he noted in the application.[75]

The professor sought to harness his expertise with lasers to create a tool that would not just conceal errors but dissolve them altogether.[76] The same frustrations that had spurred Graham's invention were also on his mind. He insisted that previous methods had not truly addressed the issue of correction being more laborious than typing itself, even with Liquid Paper at hand, for correction demanded a different kind of attention and action. He also noted that abrasion-based solutions were harmful to machines due to the buildup of residue.[77] The laser eraser, by contrast, could obliterate misplaced letters with remarkable speed, seemingly leaving behind no material trace.

Neither subtraction nor addition, the laser eraser operated according to the principle of absorbability. The dark carbon pigment absorbed short pulses of radiation, causing the generated heat to vaporize the characters.[78] The standard white paper, by contrast, being relatively nonabsorptive, remained unharmed. In his patent application, Schawlow suggested that the laser could be mounted on a typewriter and fully integrated into the apparatus, with a dedicated key to activate the negative function. "If it had ever gone into mass production [. . .] you make a mistake, you bring it back to where it was typed, press the zap key, and off it would go."[79] He further speculated that, in the future, the laser could be tailored to different fonts by adjusting the size of the targeted area. Furthermore, Schawlow envisioned that the strength of the laser beam could be adjusted, allowing it to work on a wider range of inks and papers.[80]

The commercial potential for the laser eraser was considerable. Schawlow estimated that around 3.5 million secretaries in the United States were caught in the endless cycle of typing, erasing, and retyping.[81] Like the earlier promises of an immaculate writing space, the laser was hailed as a "future boon for secretaries."[82] But the invention's potential did not stop at the office. Niels J. Reimer, a licensing officer, suggested in 1971 that it could also be used to "cancel errors in expensive printed material, correct printed circuit board errors, or even serve as a hand-held tool for draftsmen."[83] That same year, a paper company wrote to Schawlow, proposing that the laser eraser could also be employed for paper recycling, a clever repurposing of the technology. In a 1973 draft proposal to the National Science Foundation, Schawlow and his team outlined even more areas into which the laser eraser could be integrated. Among these was the possibility of manipulating and editing various substrates, including celluloid—a development that would have had a fascinating impact on the film industry had it ever been implemented on a large scale.[84]

The laser eraser had clearly struck a chord in the ongoing, though futile, struggle to conquer unintentionality. In a 1967 CBS special, *The 21st Century: The Laser: A Light Fantastic*, Walter Cronkite excitedly exclaimed, "By golly, it works!"[85] Over the course of a decade, Schawlow's office was inundated with letters from places as far-flung as Sweden, France, England, New Zealand, South Africa, Switzerland, and Australia.[86] The laser eraser captured the public's curiosity and imagination, with feature articles appearing in outlets like *National Geographic*, *Time Magazine*, *Reader's Digest*, and various professional journals. Soon, inquiries came flooding in from all walks of life—schoolchildren, students, paper companies, artists, doctors, clerks, and librarians—all eager to know how it worked, when it would be available, and how much it would cost. One enthusiastic secretarial instructor even proclaimed, "I do know that when you have [the lasers] placed on the market, all other typewriters will become obsolete overnight."[87]

Even after the patent was granted in 1971, Schawlow still found it difficult, if not impossible, to convince companies to fund the commercial development of the laser after previously failing to secure investments from the likes of Xerox, IBM, and, unsurprisingly, Liquid Paper.[88] The following year, Schawlow created a large laser he put to use in his classroom and several smaller models to demonstrate the technology to potential financiers and users.[89] Nevertheless, despite the considerable media exposure, Schawlow was ultimately unsuccessful in mass-producing the device, and the "erasing market" (if I can call it that) beat him to it. The device's high production cost, compared to that of the IBM Correcting Selectric II which appeared in 1973, caused Schawlow to finally abandon the project. By coincidence, around the same time, Xerox PARC was working on a concept for the laser printer, applying lasers to a purpose opposite to negation.[90]

Although Schawlow's laser-based erasure method never reached the point of manufacturing, it stands as one of many technologies developed to address the challenge of undoing in the pursuit of operationalizing unwriting and the inventive spirit that sought to make paper a more adaptive retentional surface. Its significance lies not in a failure to gain commercial traction but in the sociotechnical imagination it tapped into and revealed. When considering these technologies in succession, it becomes quite clear that integrating the erasing function directly into the typewriter to vaporize letters foreshadowed the desire for an interface capable of perfect cancellation. Even the laser's inventor later conceded, "I think computers were invented for me because I can make my mistakes and fix them."[91] This stubborn slippage drives the technological world, which, in turn, races to capitalize on a remedy for something that is almost certain: human error. The laser eraser is another instance (and a creative one) of the long-standing aspiration for faultless production, elements of which have become so integrated into contemporary workflows that they are now all but taken for granted.

A DISLODGING X

As Schawlow's laser eraser struggled to find investors, other breakthroughs in typewriting technology were rapidly reshaping the landscape. In 1961, IBM unveiled its first Selectric typewriter, a machine that would come to define an era of modern efficiency. Designed by architect Eliot Noyes, the

Selectric swapped out the conventional typebar for a typing ball, drastically reducing mechanical issues like key jams. Paired with a fixed carriage system, this new configuration promised smoother and significantly faster typing.[92] The dream of speed, however, was inseparable from the quest for perfect control that would yield error-free drafts. At the 1964 World Trade Fair in New York, IBM invited visitors to test the Selectric by typing postcards, offering them a hands-on introduction to its innovative capabilities.[93] Just four years later, IBM sold its millionth machine, and the Selectric's popularity only continued to soar.[94] Until 1980, these machines had made up an astounding 94 percent of electronic typewriter sales, before slipping from their once-dominant position as the decade unfolded.[95]

The Correcting Selectric II came along in 1973. An advertisement boldly declared that it eliminated "time wasted in correction." Crucially, this updated Selectric typewriter featured a built-in mechanism that internalized correction, allowing typographic error to be addressed from within the very apparatus that made it possible. A 1980 television commercial dramatized the invention. Two secretaries sat side by side, not as individuals but as personifications of distinct epochs. The first, dressed conservatively in a fully buttoned shirt, wearing large glasses and her hair in a taut bun, signified stagnation, her sartorial cues chosen to register obsolescence. She was plainly out of step with the present. The second, sleekly styled and visibly in sync with her machine, indexed the streamlined futurity promised by office automation. The commercial choreographed the ideological optics of progress through optimization. The contrast was not subtle. One figure breezed through her tasks with poise, aided by a built-in correcting mechanism. Her counterpart, the secretary of the past, lagged behind, fumbled with correction fluid, and paused mid-action to blow gently on the page. The correcting typewriter was not merely faster; it was superior in making its user meet the demands of a new office rhythm. If this was an office race, this typewriter was the clear winner.

Errors were presented as trivial, thanks to a technology that allowed users to "simply backspace to the incorrect character (or characters) by depressing the correcting key. It activates a special tape which removes the error when the incorrect character is struck again."[96] At the press of just one key, a thin layer of tape was applied to the desired area, making the error nearly invisible. Correction was achieved in different ways depending on the ribbon used: one utilized a tape that "lifted off" the ink from the page, while the other covered the mistake. In either case, the Correcting Selectric II offered a speedy intervention to handle typographical errors, reinforcing the idea of pristine documents produced with minimal effort.

The correctable ribbon was made from a film-forming resin that transferred ink to the paper but prevented it from fully penetrating the substrate—echoing Callan's "delible" technique. Instead, the ink adhered to the film, allowing the tackiness of the correction tape to cleanly lift the characters. The Correcting Selectric II also offered a palimpsestic route with correction tape (inspired by Liquid Paper's success): the typing ball would cover up the mistake by punching the tape into the exact shape of the unwanted character. It was a small yet powerful act of negative re-tracing. Unlike previous methods, this system automated erasure, integrating the ribbon tape and erasing key, an achievement Schawlow had only envisioned but never realized.[97] With this device, "error correction became just another typing function."[98] Doing and undoing are produced by the same action. The new feature marked a technological milestone: it eliminated any direct contact between the hand and the surface during the process. Curiously, the old manual practice of X-ing out errors, now supposedly old-fashioned, was symbolically preserved in the Correcting Selectric typewriter, where the erasing key was marked with an X.

As the pace of innovations raced forward and erasing tools became ever more sophisticated, it was only a matter of time before a new technology would eclipse even the most advanced correcting typewriters. In fact, this future arrived sooner than expected. In 1964, IBM combined the Selectric typewriter with a magnetic tape console (100 feet of 16 mm tape), creating the Magnetic Tape Selectric Typewriter (MT/ST).[99] The logic behind this invention was clear: "Our mission was to capture the keystroke on a correctable medium that could produce multiple clean copies because copying technology in those days was crude," explained Leon Cooper, a member of IBM's team working to solve the endless quest for invisible correction.[100] With the MT/ST, typists could generate up to 150 words per minute, once again linking speed to the elusive ideal of an unmarred surface. To correct an error, users simply backspaced to where the mistake occurred or used the FEED CODE function to move the tape if the error was not caught immediately. The correction took place in the memory stored on magnetic tape, not on the already typed-out page; the tape was a correctable substrate, and the original page became only an insignificant draft. Combining automation and analog programming was the first step in crafting the basic functions of word-processing software. Suddenly, insertions, deletions, and rearrangements were possible, not through painstaking retyping, cutting with scissors, or manually pasting and Xeroxing, but with the push of a button.[101] Overwriting became granular, working at the level of lines, words, or even individual characters.[102]

The techniques of subtraction, addition, evaporation, and dislodging are now relics, clung to by only a few steadfast typewriter devotees. They nonetheless testify to the persistence of error, the perennial desire to restore things to their original or intended form, and the pragmatic need to reduce papers by eliminating unwanted marks. Even in the contemporary digital sphere, typographical errors stubbornly persist and drain finite storage space, refusing to vanish entirely. Perfection remains tantalizingly beyond reach, hinting that the issue lies less in the tool itself and more in the nature of the human interaction with it. The earliest effort to introduce the undo command ("revert") took place in 1969 with the File Retrieval Editing System (FRESS), when typewriters were still the dominant production instrument.[103] Once again, storage and erasure were intertwined: "every edit to a file was saved in a shadow version of the data structure, allowing for both 'autosave' and an undo."[104] The undo function—once hailed as the typist's magic bullet—has since become so thoroughly integrated into the writing process that its repetitive use channels the mechanical characteristics and compulsions of the typewriter era.

MUNDANITIES OF USE

The writer Perec introduced the neologism "infraordinary" to define the unnoticed, the overlooked, those details that cancel themselves out in the monotony of daily life.[105] Media technologies, too, follow this path, losing their aura as cutting-edge innovations with time. The sparse acknowledgment of corrective technologies in the media scholarship on twentieth-century typewriting may stem from these tendencies. The innovations, from Corrasable paper to correctable tape, are perhaps more than just quotidian (a term Kittler uses to describe the typewriter); they are extra-infraordinary. Undoing became so commonplace that its appearance or disappearance barely registered as significant. Thus, in response to Bruno Latour's playful question about the limits of the study of technological objects that underpin mental, cognitive, scientific, and office work—"How mundane is mundane?"—this chapter asserts there is no such thing as too dull.[106] According to negative media theory, it is within invisibility and habituality that we find the nuts and bolts of production processes that escape scrutiny and their commercial driving mechanisms.

On most occasions, the typewritten page serves as a space of simmering activity; its constant cycles of writing, erasing, redrafting, crumpling, and discarding rarely transfer to the final draft. Beneath the (admittedly) soporific quality of paperwork lies an inherent messiness that points to the various social, cultural, and economic expectations embedded within this storage medium. Such revelations need not be cataclysmic; they often manifest as unremarkable, irksome interruptions. The act of correction, even more overlooked and dismissed than the error, wields power. It further normalizes and standardizes the process.

The typewriter has historically been a locus of various anxieties. Darren Wershler-Henry opens his book by recounting literary representations of the machine as a haunted device.[107] This portrayal is quite understandable; the mechanization of writing—an act so intimately tied to the body—via the rigid iron box evokes specters that lie beyond the user's immediate control. Error, however, introduces another dimension of concern regarding the body. Plotnick explores discourses of "cleanliness" that emphasize the desire to eliminate residual traces of the human from different media objects, from CDs to digital interfaces.[108] Error correction exists in a state of tension between the unattainable fantasy of clean copies and their sullied and intrusive material realities. When the inevitable traces of the erring body materialize as slips, and their correction fails to achieve perfection, the text is read, per Plotnick, as unhygienic.

All of this unfolds within the broader context of office economies and the uncompromising rhythm and demands of capitalist production, paradoxically making the creation of a flawless object nearly impossible. While paper is less costly and more abundant than vellum and parchment, which once prevailed as writing substrates, the sheer volume that is used is exponentially higher. The storage and retention of paper, too, have evolved into an expensive enterprise, one that the operational unwriting processes outlined in this chapter can only attempt to mitigate.

Five

AN IMPERFECT WEB

Electronic memories forget more efficiently than do human memories.[1]

• • • During the first two decades of the twenty-first century, companies such as Google (subsumed under Alphabet in 2015) solidified standards around gathering personal data, as retention by default came to be regarded as the reigning law of cyberspace. Deletion was supposedly nowhere to be found. Against this background, in 2013, then Google CEO Eric Schmidt acknowledged that "the lack of a delete button on the internet is a significant issue [. . .] There is a time when erasure is a right thing."[2] Such an admission is rather astounding when uttered by a leading figure of a company that made its fortune by doing the opposite—indiscriminately keeping information. It is even more unexpected given Schmidt's former position on privacy. Just four years earlier, he had stated, "If you have something that you don't want anyone to know, maybe you shouldn't be doing it in the first place."[3] Whatever the cause of this change of heart, it transpired precisely when a discourse critical of data retention, popularized under the slogan "the Internet Never Forgets" (INF), was beginning to gain traction.

Emerging from academic and tech-savvy circles, Viktor Mayer-Schönberger's widely cited book, *Delete: The Virtue of Forgetting in the Digital Age*, argued that in its current state, the internet eliminates the possibility of completely deleting information, favoring a commercially driven "total recall."[4] Around this time, the popular media amplified the phrase "the internet never forgets," with major news outlets cautioning readers that their digital footprints could be preserved indefinitely. This conjured a haunting return of the repressed, ever poised to resurface and exact its toll. At any moment, a forgotten detail could re-emerge and be thrust into the public eye, from adult users on the job market grappling with indiscretions captured in old photographs to private videos spiraling into viral sensations. Such a historical trajectory gave rise, for some, to a new malaise, where constant remembrance overwhelms the techno-biological, leading us to search for a (technical) cure to a problem of our own making.

These cautionary tales struck a chord with the public, and as Mayer-Schönberger himself noted, this idea was "quickly picked up by the media, somewhat to my surprise. My idea seemed to have hit a nerve."[5] He subsequently contended that future resistance must involve the reintroduction of forgetting to counteract this phenomenon. "In the two years since my argument evolved [in 2007], my idea has spread, and to my delight, many others have advocated it or proposed something similar."[6] And indeed, a broad coalition of professionals—ranging from academics, artists, and activists to government representatives—began calling for a reversal of the tech industry's entrenched standards around pervasive digital capture. One scholar, for instance, observed, "As we move into a world where memory is perfect and permanent, we should consider whether we need some mechanism to replace the ability to forget."[7] A decade ago, it was clear that both tech companies and their critics agreed on at least one thing: the internet remembers all too well.[8] In this chapter, I delve into the short evolution of discourses and societal imaginaries surrounding digital memory and forgetting. My goal is to outline how this critical call to not abandon forgetting has not only gained traction but also has been subsumed into the dominant ideological frameworks of financialization, mainly by overselling the notion of complete and unalterable digital memory.

The phrase "never forgets" implies that the internet holds onto, or can hold onto, everything, "remembering" every action, word, and image. Julian Stallabrass exemplifies this variant of wishful thinking, reasoning that "there is no trash in cyberspace because there is nothing material to be disposed of and indeed because everything may be kept."[9] And if there is no pile-up, then it is only logically feasible that, as Anita Allen adds, "technologies are making the past easily and eternally present."[10] Their words, and those of others, channel the early assertions (discussed in chapter 1) at the inception of the phonograph that it promised an "ever after" for recorded sound and, by extension, for those who produced it.

The steadfast conviction of the internet's ability to keep all traces "alive" equates capture with long-term retention and effectively nullifies erasure. These portrayals of the internet as a vast, comprehensive repository undergirding social memory are rooted in an unwavering conviction in the nature and profusion of disembodied data sans its storage considerations. By this logic, at least, everything can be captured, and permanence is the inevitable teleological corollary.

What comes next is a discussion of a familiar yet slippery premise, as I unpack how INF equates the concept of artificial memory with the impossibility of forgetting, which effectively (although perhaps not intentionally) black-boxes the operations and processes of deletion that do occur; necessity dictates the obfuscation of some of these processes, while the pursuit of profit prompts that of others. Far from novel, the vision of rampant data accumulation in the 2000s intensified as storage further transcended its local confines of computer hard drives and was dispersed across vast networks and clusters of servers. Relentless extraction, commodification, and consumption pushed data demand to new heights, leading to the proliferation of data centers across the globe and intensifying their strain on Earth's resources. With little regard for its environmental cost, the insatiable thirst for data in the twenty-first century continues unabated, with abundance seen not merely as profitable but as the lifeblood needed to keep everything running. Thus, both the celebration and condemnation of the end of forgetting center on a key feature of the digital economy: the promise of overcoming retentional constraints is propelled by and further fuels the commodification of data.

Whereas the first part of this book explored how the privation of storage media—such as dire shortages of celluloid and magnetic tape—necessitated erasure so as to allow the generation of new records, in this context, I shift to search for the negative within supposed plenty and excess. Attending to deletion is crucial when we recognize the extent to which cutting-edge and emerging storage solutions are marketed as limitless. The drive to store as much as possible, under the assumption of infinite capacity, has become a central tenet of the neoliberal race to accumulate and exploit personal data. My argument is this: although advocates of digital "forgetting" sought to challenge Big Tech's grip on data, they inadvertently offered a totalizing phrase that met an industry eager to exploit its rhetorical resonance. Rather than fostering concern, it became a commonplace assumption that the web and its services may sustain data indefinitely. At first, the narrative provoked alarm. Over time, it settled into the illusion of permanence as a public good—one that only corporations could guarantee. Let me be clear: this is not to argue that concerns about perpetual retention are without merit; surveillance critiques are, in fact, vital. Rather, my aim is to map the decades-long development of this quasi-biological discourse as it morphs into a brand of commercial rhetoric. What, then, are the consequences of generally overlooking those moments when the internet is *made* to undo? The stakes of neglecting deletion are not merely symbolic; they are foundational. By too readily accepting the idea that nothing can be erased, we lose sight of the frequent and deliberate purging that occurs within the "infosphere."[11] I am, of course, referring to the routine discarding and scrubbing of data to make room for more and more.[12]

Digital negation, like other negative medialities, resists easy legibility. Even though various leaks have provided glimpses of the clandestine world of pervasive tapping and data collection practices of governments and private entities, they barely scratch the surface of the actual scale of retention. Likewise, the examples of deletion discussed in this chapter represent only the tip of the iceberg. Commercial and institutional bodies seldom disclose the precise lifespan of users' data, and terms of service and privacy policies often obscure the shelf life of information. This uncertainty cuts both ways. Although these bodies make it clear that data will be sold, the fate of these expanding collections remains far more opaque. Recent leaks from Meta and testimony from a former Twitter (renamed X) employee before the US Senate revealed that even the platforms themselves may not fully understand where or for how long data flows and bleeds.[13] In other words, these systems veil both retention and its undoing. Verification is, therefore, challenging, especially when shielded by nondisclosure agreements.

Moreover, given the challenges of grasping erasure, it is crucial to consider the wide array of actions, motivations, and actors involved in these types of negations, each contributing to dynamics in which undoing manifests in multiple forms at once. This is largely because "the internet" is far too vast an object, too sprawling a material network, and too complex a social space and metaphor to be considered in any singular way. "The digital" now encompasses far more than just the binary representation of data as ones and zeros; it has become a catchall term that does little to elucidate the opacity of contemporary technologies. John Durham Peters observes with acuity that "the internet is an ocean, a graveyard, a market, a brothel, a zoo, a waste dump, and an archive."[14] It is an ambiguous, fragmented space, best approached through an accumulation of perspectives rather than the impossible goal of comprehensiveness. Therefore, no single theory or isolated case study can fully capture what deletion is or what it accomplishes online. This is my humble contribution to the effort.

THE ROAD TO ETERNAL MEMORY

The outstanding relation between the inner workings of the human mind and externalized technological systems has never been static; it is continually reconstituted under emergent media ecologies. Although the exact moment when internal memory and external storage became interchangeable remains impossible to determine, classical texts already wrestle with the tension of this entanglement. Today, "memory" refers not just to neural processes or the capacity of a single hard drive to store digital files, but also to planetary-scale infrastructures that regulate access to data. In an attempt to come to terms with this fusion, media scholars and philosophers frequently invoke Plato's rendering of writing as *technē,* treating it as a quasi-originary moment from which the reciprocity between cognition and inscription can be retroactively traced.[15] The oft-invoked myth recounts Theuth offering the gift of writing (*graphē*) to King Thamus, who repudiates it as a synthetic artifice that erodes true recollection (as the mortal's pathway to the realm of the perfect and the endless) and undermines the very conditions of learning. External storage, he warns, does not generate genuine knowledge but instead simulates it. This carefully orchestrated exchange presents memory and inscription as, at best, complementary and supplementary, and, at worst, as mutually canceling forces.

Prying open the space between remembering and storing only to uncover forgetfulness hidden within, Jacques Derrida, Bernard Stiegler, and Paul Ricœur each offered theoretical reflections on this ancient critique of writing as a memory aid.[16] The compulsive return to this parable underscores its resonance: individuals and societies simultaneously gain and lose something when adopting new technologies of retention that contour possible forms of being. The tradeoff thesis continues to reverberate in present-day debates about digital memory and its near and far futures. Worth noting here is the almost instinctive connection between memory and storage, or, as Derrida observed, the "irreducible link between thought as memory and the technical dimensions of memorialization."[17] For him, as well as for Stiegler, human retention is not divorced from technique but intrinsically tied to it. Plainly, the supplement is at once an addition and a necessity (precondition) for memory. Stiegler, in particular, constructs a chain binding memory and tool, theorizing technicity as compensating for a primordial condition of forgetting by default. Vilém Flusser contributed to the denunciation of this classical distinction by suggesting that it is through genetic and cultural memory, the latter encoded in "hard objects," that humanity negates the entropic pull of nature.[18] Ergo, there is no recourse to the human without tools and external containers, no way to think human cognition without its prosthetic extensions.

Decentering the individual, sociologist Elena Esposito traces the shifts and fractures of social memory as it expands, offloads, and transforms across history. Some scholars point to a rupture, particularly in the early modern period, when spatial mnemonic techniques such as the Memory Palace were supplanted by a vast network of notes, prints, records, and archives.[19] In this view, as the responsibility for retention shifted from active memorialization to external objects, the balance tilted toward forgetting. Socrates had anticipated such anxieties millennia earlier, and INF has only recast them in relation to the internet. Esposito, however, resists the impulse to frame these reorganizations and reformations as a pendulum swinging predictably back and forth. Memory has not withered, nor has forgetting receded; if anything, both have intensified in the post-digital age. She warns against what she calls a "reductive notion of forgetting and therefore also of memory."[20] In order to illustrate this point, she offers in passing an analogy that carries particular weight for the present discussion:

> As long as forgetting is understood in negative terms—as the denial (loss, corruption, or deletion) of remembering—attempts to refer to it inevitably produce a paradoxical situation in which one attempts to see what is *invisible* or refers to a content to deny its presence: first you remember, then you try to forget the recalled content. From this perspective, forgetting is a passive effect of memorization, and memory is understood as a kind of data storage in a warehouse with limited capacity. With the passage of time or accumulation of data (interference), content is lost.[21]

The validity of this critique of reductionism notwithstanding, why the warehouse? The figure of the repository appears briefly, treated as conceptual shorthand, and its actual workings are left unexamined. This reflects a tendency to treat storage and its operationality as secondary, as if the mechanics of retention and deletion require no further interrogation. Whereas systems theory examines how societies construct and regulate memory, negative media theory, by contrast, engages with what Esposito labels paradoxical ("to see what is invisible") to reveal what is obscured beneath discourses of forgetting. What I am resisting here is a flattened reading of unmaking.

Among philosophers and social and cognitive scientists, memory is rarely understood as a fixed entity reducible to the strictly biological, social, or technical. Instead, it resides in a lattice of overlapping dimensions, each informing and affected by the others. Yet fuzziness is not equivalence, and the forces that propel innovation and adaptation may operate in tension with, or entirely apart from, the assumed interests of the social body as a whole. With industrialization, Stiegler maintained, memory underwent a historic mutation, modulating biological function in service of industrial production.[22] Industrialization framed abundance and plenty as its inevitable outcome, and engaging with the present moment thus requires tracing the conceptual pathways that have long nurtured reveries of technological boundlessness, as these frameworks continue to inform prevailing narratives about the internet (in which deletion is conspicuously absent).

The warehouse, when read anew through a critical lens, ceases to be a passive, monolithic container and becomes a reactive node in a network of contingent retentions. In *Programmed Visions: Software and Memory*, Wendy Chun revisits the suture of scientific, theoretical, and ideological currents of the mid-twentieth century that would come to underwrite computational thought: "biology and computer technology have been reduced to complementary strands of a double helix [. . .] Both are a return to a reductionist, mechanistic understanding of life, in which the human body becomes an archive. Both are the basis of a biopolitics that seeks to rationalize and optimize human populations and capital."[23] Chun reconstructs John von Neumann's audacious intellectual maneuvers that made computation and biology loop and refract through one another: computer as brain, nervous system as computational memory. In a move as curious as it was consequential, he managed, as Chun shows, to recast biological memory as a fixed and finite file system, unerasable and ultimately insufficient, thereby legitimizing and even necessitating supplementation by technics—more precisely, by his groundbreaking computer architecture.[24] Far from emerging ex nihilo, sweeping pronouncements such as "the internet never forgets" are thus but a step within a certain genealogy.

Expansiveness animated the surge of such imaginaries in this period, even as many ran counter to or inverted von Neumann's model of the biological. From H. G. Wells's speculative overtures on a "world brain," a phrase that anticipates contemporary debates on singularity, to the designs, prototypes, and unpublished manuscripts of the era's most inventive minds, references to terms such as "memory organs" abounded in relation to machines.[25] Alan Turing, for his part, explicitly invoked an "analogy with the human brain [. . .] as a guiding principle" to engineer intelligent machines modeled on human learning.[26] Recognizing that the brain not only computes but retains, he imagined an "infinite memory" as an endless tape—a concept yet to find its material counterpart. Norbert Wiener further blurred the line between the firing synapses and computational logics. He contrasted short-term memory that "should record quickly, be read quickly, and be erased quickly" with "memory which is intended to be part of the files, the permanent record, of the machine or the brain." He then allows for a distinction between the organic and the mechanical, given that the latter "is intended for many successive runs [that is, reusable], while the brain, in the course of nature, never even approximately clears out its past records."[27] Another instance often retold in the annals of internet history is the concept of the Memex. A few months before World War II ended, Vannevar Bush published a piece forecasting tools that could become "intimate supplements to his memory" for research purposes.[28] A table-sized device, housing a film roll as its storage medium, would arrange information into "trails" of thought, closer to the mind's associative pathways than the rigid order imposed by library systems. Two decades later, Bush returned to the Memex, his rethinking precipitated by the technical advances of the intervening years and the ensuing overflow of information. Drawn to magnetic tape's compression capabilities and access speed, he also emphasized the medium's inherent mutability and erasability, poetically commenting that "the moving finger writes, but its record is not here irrevocable."[29]

Herein lies the conceptual myopia I aim to unpack. Why is negation as tied to capacity (whether material, imagined, financial, or spatial) so rarely acknowledged outside technical manuals and professional discourse, whereas forgetting and unforgetting continue to command disproportionate, often moralized, attention? It could be argued that, given the tethering of tool and mind, an account of the latter might stand in for understanding the whole. I believe a two-part answer offers a compelling explanation for this lack. Chun's work demonstrates how the abstraction of the materialities of hardware and software misapprehends the ephemeral parts of digital media and reduces their complexities to a projection of permanence. This move, as she shows, serves neoliberal interests, where "memory" functions as a pliable asset, strategically redeployed across shifting orders of value.

Working through these patterns across sources, I begin with some reflections on new media that echo conventional wisdom concerning the shift to digital storage and its impacts. French intellectual Maël Renouard, in his memoir, *Fragments of an Infinite Memory*, draws a provisional map of an internet that never forgets, weaving together dreams, visions, and meditations on how digital technology is profoundly reshaping experience.[30] As the title suggests, the book casts the digital realm as an endless, eternal library of the collective mind. Building on the philosophical legacy of *Phaedrus*, he asserts, "With the internet—which fulfills to a supreme degree the externalization of memory first initiated by writing—we might get the feeling that we have simultaneously become capable of forgetting nothing and incapable of remembering anything at all."[31] Thamus's ancient warning materialized. Here, exteriorization comes to redefine and even replace what we consider memory proper. The transition is so profound that Renouard feels driven to speculatively reimagine the creation myth:

> The god Computer, weary of the forgetfulness and debauchery that reigned upon the Earth, swallowed all things and all living beings, and made them into *eternal* images that wandered through his entrails; but the goddess 3D Printer, taking pity upon these ghosts whose lamentations had reached her, lay with the god Computer, after which she gave birth once more to the inhabitants of the Earth, out of a new material in which the *imperfections* of the old bodies had vanished. Thus began the Sixth Sun Age.[32]

Instead of rejecting external memory as in Plato's myth, digital storage is recast as a manna. At first, humans were forgetful, and the machine rose to their aid in this sorry state. Then, a second machine entirely reconfigured their very existence. Setting aside the gendered connotations of machinic logos and technical inception that Renouard invokes, this contemporary revision constructs a near-religious relationship between the human condition and computation. This revision brings to mind Peters's reflection on the theological overtones of Alphabet's self-appointed mission to organize the world's knowledge.[33] Or, borrowing from José Van Dijck, it may be read as an example of how "dataism" is put into practice.[34] In this incipient media-theological turn, humanity is reborn only after being ingested and devoured by the all-knowing machine, transfigured into data, and returned as idealized, unforgetting immortals. Whereas matter is finite, data becomes infinite. In such a schema, totality is within reach insofar as existence is reformatted in binary code. Even absent explicit religious framing, such visions nonetheless rehearse the age-old desire for transcendence via the "entrails" of the machine and being subsumed entirely by its internal processes.

The notion of recorded omniscience, à la Renouard, resonates with themes explored across scholarly writing, science fiction, and artistic experiments. At the close of the twentieth century, available technologies were leveraged in experimental projects that sought to unlock the utopian potential of pervasive, unselective recording. During his much-lauded research project *MyLifeBits* (2001–6), Microsoft's Gordon Bell embarked on a mission to digitally capture every facet of his life, scanning piles of personal records and even wearing a head-mounted camera for several years.[35] The result was a *life log*: "A complete record of your life, a complete e-memory of your time on earth." Bell and Jim Gemmel enthusiastically predict that upgrading from physical memory to e-memory is inevitable, adding that "cloud computers will lead to a single, integrated e-memory experience."[36] Liran Razinsky flags the subtle slippage that occurs when the autobiographical meets digital storage, problematizing the conceit that exhaustive representations could replicate, let alone surpass, knowledge of self.[37] As much as projects like *MyLifeBits* offered early glimpses into a data-driven future, they also normalized self-surveillance by encouraging the voluntary surrender of personal information. The lure of uninterrupted recording, positioned as a bulwark against forgetting, becomes, in the hands of corporations like Microsoft and Amazon, a promise of salvation by storage.

Exhaustiveness feeds into fictions of perfection and vice versa. When Mayer-Schönberger engages with memory, he emphasizes its abundance and ubiquity: "Today, with the help of widespread technology, forgetting has become the exception, and remembering the default [. . .] society's ability to forget has become suspended, replaced by perfect memory."[38] Though he laments the vanishing art of forgetting, how else might we read this statement if not as yet another reiteration of capital's opportunistic refrain—that the ever cheaper and computable stands ready to supersede what is, by contrast, fragile and fragmented recollection? This same disjunction gives rise to Bell's magnum opus, which presumes that technical memory is "objective, dispassionate, prosaic, and unforgivingly accurate." In contrast, "bio-memories fade, vanish, merge, and mutate with time, but your digital memories are unchanging."[39] Perfect memory, it follows, never falters, nor is it capable of, susceptible to, or requiring erasure. This sleight of hand holds only if one accepts that "perfect memory" is synonymous with "perfect storage," the latter presuming the existence of indelible, incorruptible, and boundless repositories of human activity.

In the decades since Nicholas Negroponte triumphantly declared that "the [digital] copy is perfect," such an idealization has unraveled time and again in the face of the realities of online circulation and retention.[40] Both Negroponte and Mayer-Schönberger's perfected forms draw power from the claim that each digital copy is a flawless duplication of the last, untouched by the wear that plagues analog reproduction. At their root, utopian and critical theories accept and promote a sense of abundance that, as both argue, previous media could never support. Analog copies—a photograph, a cassette, a film reel—degrade with every iteration, each one's life shortened by the attempt to live on through reproduction. Digital copies, by contrast, ostensibly promised to liberate humanity from this entanglement with loss, offering a space of unflawed retention. Still, even digital objects buckle under the strain of continuous demand, a reminder that material limits persist even in the boundless domain of cyberspace.[41] That they falter is not an anomaly but a structural consequence of constraints that, although they are never resolved, are systematically disavowed in some theoretical writing, popular discourse, and industry marketing, all of which claim that digital media constitute a "perfect" system of memory.[42] These assumptions hinge on the complete collapse of memory into machinery, wherein the latter presumably exists only to augment the former, and the extent to which these technologies are configured to privilege machinic efficiency over human recollection is disregarded.

THE COMMERCIAL WEB DOES NOT WANT TO FORGET

The web—the freewheeling playground of social media giants, search-engine behemoths, bottomless cloud servers, and the de- and re-territorialized spaces of the state—deletes when required, holding onto the rest. The current digital ecosystem starkly contrasts the utopian visions of early cyberspace pioneers, who once envisioned it as a libertarian, non-hierarchical, and unregulated realm beyond control.[43] Instead, with its supposed inability to "forget," today's internet sustains a heavily stratified, surveilled, and fragmented sphere of interactions.[44] Thus, the core of the academic debate surrounding the end of forgetting lies less in memory studies and more in the concerns raised by privacy scholarship, which links data capture to profitability and control.[45]

The eventual rise of Web 2.0 in the first decade of the 2000s increased users' participation in production and consumption, making once distinct actions fodder for data harvesting.[46] This digital economy, formed around "prosumption" and tracking, as Christian Fuchs observes, flouts privacy concerns in pursuit of financial gain.[47] Targeted advertising plays a large part, feeding off the steady supply of publicly shared information as well as collected behavioral data—every click and action, no matter how minute, becomes consequential in bulk. This default connection between "free" digital products and their users led Shoshana Zuboff to define our era as dominated by "surveillance capitalism."[48] Mining and extraction—literal and metaphorical, material and immaterial—form the backbone of the economic system within which data transforms from mere commodity to capital itself, according to Jathan Sadowski.[49] Sadowski offers a prescient simile: "deleting data because of storage costs would be like burning piles of money or dumping barrels of oil down the drain."[50] The observation is generally correct, except that, as I discuss in the next section, large-scale storage and its upkeep do, indeed, burn through stacks of cash and credit.

This state of affairs is the result of layered historical events and trends. Mid-twentieth-century computing projects, such as the development of the Electronic Discrete Variable Automatic Computer (EDVAC, 1949) and the Universal Automatic Computer (UNIVAC, 1951), were born out of the postwar military-industrial complex. Publicly funded initiatives, including those spearheaded by the Defense Advanced Research Projects Agency (DARPA), fostered academic and commercial innovation.[51] Historian Tung-Hui Hu further ties the rise of computation during the Cold

War to the onset of a "bunker mentality."[52] Safeguarding information from Soviet eyes required securing data in indestructible sites while ensuring its survival through distributed networks. In that geopolitical climate, networks and data storage had to be engineered to withstand risk.[53]

Around the same period, corporate branding likewise began to adopt the language of robustness, portraying technology as the vehicle for perfect storage poised to revolutionize data management. A prime example is IBM's promotional film *The Search at San Jose* (1958), which dramatizes the creation of the Random Access Method of Accounting and Control device (RAMAC, 1956)—the first commercial computer to use external magnetic disk storage. The voice-over sets the scene: "Everywhere, endless rows of filing cabinets presented the same problem, each drawer packed with records that our researchers saw needed constant updating, checking, and cross-filing." If the filing cabinet was once an ingenious fix, as Craig Robertson outlines in his design history of office equipment, by the close of the 1950s it had already begun to seem an insufficient measure against the inundation of information.[54] RAMAC's ability to condense those seemingly infinite rows of smaller storage containers and offer speedy accessibility anticipated vital aspects of networked cloud computing. "[The magnetic disc] file unit may be connected to other computers to provide even larger warehouses of facts." The film—and, by extension, IBM—celebrates the invention as "a new philosophy of record keeping," positioning the computer as central to a "search that has not ended nor will it, so long as man needs more powerful machines than ever before to extend the farthest reaches of the human mind." In this brief promotional film, we witness the paradigm shift that tech companies of the twentieth century catalyzed—from storage as a dull external physical warehouse to digital memory as an inexhaustible extension of human capabilities.

More than half a century later, the language once employed to lure clients into embracing the impenetrable world of data-processing technologies remains alive and well. The naturalization of storage into "memory" has paved the way for today's sociotechnical reimaginings of hardware and software as agile, flexible, and responsive, supposedly like the human mind, and sturdier than a single machine. Data centers are presumed to preserve the entire sum of human activity, which can no longer be sustained without its technical prostheses. It is no coincidence that contemporary culture is steeped in a fascination with, and even fetishization of, data bunkers and cold storage archives. Under the banner of security, stability, and resilience, the legacy of those early technological innovations intersects both commercial and governmental ideologies. As efforts to capture and safeguard information turned steadily outward toward increasingly fortified external repositories, over time, paper yielded to phonograms, photographs, and film, with each medium promising a new threshold of longevity and reach. Magnetic tape arrived soon after, only to be displaced by discs, then by personal hard drives, and eventually by server farms. Storage becomes ever more diffused and invisible—vast, humming, and tucked out of sight. Each such transition marks a swift turn in the ongoing search for sophisticated and compact media, imagined to contain more and therefore forget less, deferring disappearance just a little longer.

In his anthropological study of Cold War–era bunkers repurposed as "data bunker" sites, A. R. E. Taylor introduces "future-proofing" as a business stratagem.[55] This is a tactic of successive steps. It begins by asserting the necessity of data, follows by emphasizing its fragility and casting doubt on the durability of other storage methods and spaces, and concludes by presenting solutions—protocols, procedures, and materials designed to ensure extremely long-term preservation. Taylor traces how pervasive anxieties around loss precipitated an entire industry of such advanced data bunkers, where constant equipment monitoring and maintenance foster a sense of security. In a similar vein, Shane Brennan understands the present as emblematic of the sprawling neoliberal reach of "backup culture."[56] In this paradigm, data security rests entirely on users' willingness not only to relinquish information but also to partake in "risk-mitigation strategies," reproduce countless copies, and invest in myriad storage devices and services. The less the internet forgets, the more robust we believe it to be. The more it remembers, the more consumers are encouraged to place their trust—and faith—in the system.[57] Once users bought into the phantasm of the cloud, the internet assumed another mythic form: a mega-fortress—bulletproof, boundless, and built to remember everything. Safeguarding information for perpetuity is of supreme importance, as other future-oriented projects proclaim; the seeds, sounds, films, and objects stored can be retrieved and consulted after the end of the world.[58]

At its apotheosis, the discourse predicting the end of forgetting sounded an alarm. A decade on, the slogan has morphed into a wish for data resilience in a world increasingly unmoored by conflict, calamity, and ecological collapse as nature begins to repossess what was stripped from it through generations of industrial extraction and purposeful depletion. There may be some consolation in the belief that the internet will remember *for humanity*, assuming the network survives us in the coming decades and centuries. Web 2.0 has evolved into something more, as it has positioned itself as a guardian. As data collection, prediction, and real-time and retroactive big-data analytics reign supreme, Alphabet, Apple, Meta, and Microsoft, among others, have become unlikely defenders of our intimate personal records and of society's most prized collections. As Kara Keeling emphasizes, the logic of Western regimes of capital casts expansion and accumulation as both the guarantor of continual progress and the remedy for its potential failure, a framing that diverges profoundly from other traditions that resist such a linear thrust.[59] At least publicly, the crisis has accordingly shifted from managing excess to immunizing against complete obliteration.

The user is left dreading a world in which the web careens instead into oblivion, a scenario that conjures the possibility of non-storage itself. Renouard contemplates this possibility in his memoir, asking what would happen if the internet stopped remembering for us. "Which is worse? We are caught in a dilemma between the anxiety of losing everything, irretrievable, without any possible remedy, and that of being read, spied upon, now or later, by a distant stranger. Of the two evils, I confess, the first terrifies me more than the second."[60] The binary Renouard draws, exemplary of a particular current of thought in recent years, does little to challenge the underlying political and economic systems at play, as it assumes that data exists only in two forms: utterly unstable or wholly robust. Such a dichotomy leaves the user with but one option: surrender your data to the companies or risk losing everything. Such an all-or-nothing approach suggests that without corporate safeguarding measures, data would be gone. Notably absent from this scenario is any discussion of community-based or radical local alternatives.

Yet even as Big Tech projects itself as a borderless entity—a universal, supranational enterprise that claims to transcend boundaries, taxation demands, and geopolitical conflicts—its reality remains stubbornly particular and situated. Data centers spread, often opportunistically, into places scarred by histories of dispossession and colonial subjugation. Enticed by low costs and toothless local regulation, data complexes expand to the Global South, leaving behind ecological devastation even as they yield few economic benefits.[61] (Cryptocurrency miners likewise migrate around the globe in search of cheap energy, straining fragile power grids until they are unceremoniously expelled.)[62] Predictably, acts of refusal and resistance have emerged. Across South America, local opposition is growing. In Chile and Uruguay, grassroots movements are increasingly contesting their involuntary transformation into major tech hubs.[63] Siting data centers within native territories increasingly complicates existing tensions over land, water, and energy. This encroachment potently illustrates path-dependent convergences between politics and technology. Discussion around "Indigenous data sovereignty" has gained prominence by articulating alternatives for community-controlled data governance and locally owned servers outside corporate domination, while opposition to existing and prospective data infrastructure has grown more pronounced. Communities from the Sámi in northern Europe to Native Hawaiians, as Tonia Sutherland and Gailyn Bopp highlight in the case of the latter, advocate for a relationship between data and environment rooted in sustainability, care, and reciprocity rather than extraction.[64] Like its predecessors, this techno-empire is built on finite reserves, yet comparatively speaking, it moves with far greater mobility, exhausting several sites before seamlessly migrating to the next.

Paradoxically, the move to enshrine the values of security and permanence within the commercial architecture of the internet has unfolded through processes that actively produce environmental degradation and social destabilization, even as these efforts frame themselves in terms of preservation and protection. Too hastily positioning the digital sphere as a space immune to data loss and, by extension, its protector owes much to the memetic legacy of "the internet never forgets." A catchphrase originally coined to critique systems of power and expose asymmetries of control and accountability has been absorbed into fables of total retention—fittingly, given that both are fundamentally immaterial. Beneath the rhetorical polish, the material burdens of digital memory are unequally distributed; while they are claimed to benefit all consumers, they exacerbate the risk to individuals who are most vulnerable to surveillance, commodification, and harm.[65]

THE SPACE OF REMOVE

Academic and popular commentaries that dwell on the internet's prying nature tend to gravitate to anomalous episodes or viral phenomena that underscore the web's aptitude for abruptly reviving and recirculating what was assumed gone, irrelevant, or anodyne. In allowing these rare occurrences to stand in for ubiquitous capture and its potential harms, the image of an unforgetting internet elides the messy, resource-intensive realities of data production and retention, often overlooking the routine deletions that are more than mere byproducts of the internet's material economy. Aggrandizing digital memory as an infinite, collectively shared pool also highlights a deeper issue: the difficulty of separating the idealized vision of digital objects from their practical uses online. As of now, the internet neither guarantees flawless retention nor escapes the limitations of the physical hardware and software on which it depends. Mél Hogan points to a core contradiction at the heart of the system that cannot be easily resolved: "the very coding that allows the easy duplication and quick sprawl of digital content [. . .] is also their *imperfection*."[66]

The externalization of memory rests on a series of contingent concessions relating to users, technical systems, and commercial actors, each calibrating and calibrated to the limits of retention and reproducibility. Digital media inherits a preparatory modus operandi from analog recording and refines it by privileging selective elimination over wholesale clearance in advance. As early as the 1950s, Daniel Rosenberg recounts, an IBM engineer compiled a "negative dictionary," or a "stop list" that instructed the machine to filter determiners and high-frequency function words from being processed and stored on punch cards and tapes.[67] This choice to introduce systematic omission to machine-readable language, seemingly at odds with the structure of human grammar, aimed, quite plainly, "to trade perfection for currency," prioritizing "yielding a maximum of information" and minimizing computational expenditure.[68] Scholars like Jonathan Sterne have noted that shortly thereafter, the process of developing different digital formats revealed a calculated tactical negation, where bandwidth and storage capacities are made to align with the physiological limits of human perception of images and sounds.[69] Information deemed redundant—that is, unnecessary for achieving a reasonable aesthetic experience—was excluded, thereby reducing the size of a single file. Imperfection, therefore, serves as a structuring principle, delineating thresholds, accommodating constraints, and translating scarcity into commodities. Ergo, even in an age of presumed plenty, stored objects must still be reined in, compressed, and their data removed. Adaptiveness is king.

Across the history of computing and regardless of whether it is initiated prior to or post-process, deletion has never meant just one thing, and its execution has morphed and meandered. To put it simply, early machines, reliant on delay lines and cathode ray tubes, had a relatively straightforward relationship with "forgetting." Storage was regenerative, as fleeting as the session itself, existing only in the transient flickers of electric ons and offs (hence, Wiener's doubling down on repetition as a form of prolonging). Delay line memory, which held data as pulses coursing through a medium, could be erased through either natural decay or sequential overwriting.[70] With the Williams Tube, the first device to implement a form of random-access memory (RAM) by storing bits as electrostatic charge, it became possible to erase specific data and bits. From the early 1950s, RAM represented a gradual shift toward memory that was volatile, electrically dependent, and instantly rewritable. Departing from previous systems, it permitted near-instant rewriting, replacing the sluggish, successive erasure of earlier systems. Punch cards, for instance, exemplify an early form of non-volatile memory whose history extends to the eighteenth century and the Jacquard loom of the early 1800s.[71] Once perforated, the punched card functioned as a self-contained object, retaining data irrespective of machine state. Erasure, in this context, normally entailed undoing and disposing of the entire substrate. IBM extensively deployed this form of memory (alongside others) in business computing and data-processing machines well into the 1960s.

In the early 1970s, IBM inaugurated a new generation of hard disk storage that combined magnetic storage with random access.[72] On a hard drive disk, a command to delete, as Matthew Kirschenbaum's forensic inquiry into the depths of the digital illuminates, initiates an asynchronous temporality: what superficially disappears from the screen remains latently inscribed on the drive, a remnant with no direct representation.[73] Rather than expunging its material instantiation, the system consigns data to a state of suspension between unwanted presence and not-quite absence until, after multiple overwrites, every bit is erased beyond the point at which it could be reconstructed. Put another way, the instigation of deletion produces a discordance between the user's volition and the technology's latency, a misalignment of physical reality and intent (presuming the deletion order is not given accidentally). "Data remanence" then is an inversion of the analog's anti-residuality, as traced throughout this book. In the predominant storage media of today, erasure remains less of an immediate effect than a protracted process, including in flash storage and solid-state drives (SSDs).

Flusser's comparative assertion that "electronic memories forget more efficiently than do human memories" is hard to qualify. Although digital deletion may indeed be efficient, it is the presumption of ease that contemporary media scholarship increasingly calls into question.[74] Removing data from physical storage is not a matter of simply pressing a button but a technically laborious process whose complexity often exceeds that of inscription itself. Complete effacement that renders data irretrievable is technically feasible, but only through a sequence of multiple steps that challenge the very notion of immediacy and completeness. It bears repeating that the construct of "total deletion" is a conceptual narrowing that isolates an idealized operation of erasure at the expense of the heterogeneity of actual articulations. To carelessly assert the possibility of absolute erasure is no less naive than to presume that data can be preserved wholly and for perpetuity. It is no coincidence that many essays across two recently published edited volumes, *Your Computer Is on Fire* and *Uncertain Archives: Critical Keywords for Big Data*, collectively foreground the physical, fleshy, and concrete aspects of a "datafied" and computationally governed world, challenging the systematic bracketing of its instability, as if it could be elided without consequence.[75] Accordingly, my concern here is not with "the digital" as an abstract principle, but with the concrete forms it assumes within structures that tether material to various frameworks and forms of organization that mandate routine deletions. I next discuss symptomatic episodes (not mere isolated instances) that reveal the internet's fraught reality; neither perfect nor complete, these are the mirror image of boundless retention without cost.

By the late 1990s, people working regularly with data began to voice concerns distinct from what had become a common fear of ubiquitous data-gathering. Stewart Brand referred to the threat as the pending onset of the "Digital Dark Age."[76] Web archivists understand all too well that describing the internet as an indelible memory machine is more myth than fact. Brand, an early internet visionary, grew increasingly alarmed by the near-certain loss of born-digital materials, given that archiving initiatives are often understaffed and too underfunded to mitigate the situation. A battle is waged against what the theorist Wolfgang Ernst identifies as the very nature of the web: it is a perpetually shifting "dyno-archive."[77] Even as the popular claim that "the internet never forgets" gained traction, a brief survey of events from the past several decades reveals a different story of the internet—one marked by volatility and unpredictability. Built to store, retrieve, and delete, it also easily abandons and misplaces data amid global shutdowns, bugs, and glitches.[78]

Already in 1996, when the web was still in its infancy, Brewster Kahle articulated what might have then seemed like a fever dream: "to archive the entire internet."[79] Now decades in, the founder of the Internet Archive manages to represent both the pragmatics of digital preservation and quixotic idealism, as he seeks (in his words) "to make permanent the digital materials we are all generating," in defiance of the internet's adaptiveness.[80] In addition to constantly crawling publicly available pages of the web, the nonprofit has expanded its holdings across multiple data centers, preserving digitized and born-digital materials alongside facilities housing books and other media. Crucially, it has intervened at key junctures to counter an axiom of the digital economy. The cost-benefit analysis of commercial enterprises is the rule of law on the internet; all the rest, including Kahle's work, is the exception.

Few case studies illustrate the internet's formative years and their afterlife on other servers better than GeoCities. At its peak, the free website-hosting ecosystem was more than just a chaotic patchwork of home pages. It was a thriving and messy hub of digital culture, one of the largest communities of its day. As a social laboratory, users were dubbed "homesteaders" and staked their claim on digital real estate, slowly forming "neighborhoods" based on common interests. GeoCities' aesthetic sported a kind of frenetic customization that has all but disappeared from today's top-down, hyper-designed feeds. Then, in 1999, Yahoo arrived. The purchase of GeoCities itself was not immediately recognized as a death knell, but it retrospectively marked the beginning of its end. With new ownership came new terms of service that exerted a tightening grip over content that had once felt entirely personal. In response, users staged a visual mutiny. In what would be called "The Haunting," they systematically stripped personal sites of their defining features and quirks, draining them of their unique vibrancy and turning once lively pages into husks.[81] If Yahoo intended to assert control, it found itself reigning over a place with no residents. For once, it was not power pulling the plug but the other way around. Although that particular action successfully reversed the company's decision, GeoCities became a ghost town within several years. It did not vanish overnight, but users soon drifted away. Some simply abandoned their pages, some erased them, and others left messages of protest, composing what Katie Mackinnon calls "platform eulogies"—public farewells in which users declare they are further ceasing communication.[82] A decade later, in 2009, Yahoo shuttered the site. Had it not been for the intervention of the Internet Archive and other groups, the remains of GeoCities might have disappeared altogether.[83] A company births a service, another lets it languish, and most eventually die. The Internet Archive and actors such as the Archive Team, for their part, attempt to counter this technosocial entropy by apprehending and sharing fragments of a web on the verge of disappearance.

The proliferation of internet archiving missions racing to capture soon-to-be-defunct platforms and collections reduced to the vestiges of a bygone era accentuates the hollowness of the "internet never forgets" mantra. In a corporate web, no digital space is truly the users' to keep, and not all information can be assumed to persist. When a net archivist suggests that "everything on the internet can be saved," the statement reads not as a claim of capability but as a projection, part conviction, part wish.[84] To envision the Internet Archive or any other nonprofit matching the scale of the web is to imagine a world freed from material finitude, where labor does not exhaust, storage does not fill, and funding never runs dry. Despite considerable means and reserves, even the best endowed institutions and profit-driven businesses have not managed to secure permanence, only to circle the same impasses.

Somewhat naïvely, in 2010, the Library of Congress made a grand announcement. The institution set out to archive a data set donated by Twitter that encompassed tweets published since the platform's 2006 launch, with plans to maintain an ongoing collection. The library's undertaking was grounded in the conviction that social media could serve as a historical resource for the future, representing a snapshot of collective memory: "a record of knowledge and creativity for Congress and the American people."[85] By 2017, the project had come to a halt. The endeavor demanded too much labor, placing significant technical and financial strain on the library, as the overwhelming volume of messages far exceeded the expectations set when the agreement was first made.[86] The ambition of exhaustiveness was abandoned. Moving forward, only select tweets deemed culturally significant would be archived. Even in the digital realm, the finiteness of retentional capacity and workforce labor underscores the material constraints inherent in abundance.[87]

Mayer-Schönberger opens his book by recounting an anecdote meant to illustrate the unforeseen social repercussions of cyberspace's unforgetful nature. A teacher was reportedly denied employment after a long-forgotten photograph, buried in the recesses of the once-dominant social media network MySpace, was unearthed by prospective employers.[88] Yet, closer scrutiny of early internet history reveals that permanence was never assured, and few platforms and objects eluded the combined wear of decay and the unstoppable churn of commercial decisions. Much like GeoCities' decline before it, MySpace now persists as an untended remainder, its user base dispersed into the ever multiplying folds of newer and more exciting corners of the online world. With its decline came, predictably, the perils of maintaining a patchwork of databases. In 2019, 50 million files abruptly disappeared. Officially, the event was attributed to a server "migration accident."[89] Users and journalists were quick to speculate that the disappearance in fact attested to a business no longer able to keep the lights on in the server room (MySpace's documented history of both less intentional data losses and intentional "creative destruction" of existing content only bolstered their case).[90] Whether it was the main cause or one of many, such events undermine the supposed robustness of an infinitely stable and durable virtual space. The web, in its ceaseless self-reconfiguration, is a testament to this interplay between collection and negation—voluntary and involuntary acts alike.

If the relatively short life of the internet has not made it abundantly clear, users relying on platforms as repositories of personal data must remain vigilant and aware of the fickle nature of popular preferences and trends, as the consequences of mass abandonment may all too easily result in the eradication of their content. Should a company choose to shutter its data centers and decommission its cloud backups, the recourses available—limited at best—highlight the asymmetry between platform control and archival dependency. "Platforms are fast, but they're flammable," Paul Edwards proclaims, and with good reason.[91] Once a platform no longer drives the stream of new content and can no longer profit from what it has already stored, removal follows, indifferent to whatever cultural weight the data might carry. More troubling still, vast parts of the internet simply remain unarchived. Negative machines demonstrate no fidelity to memory or meaning. They capture, store, and transmit, but absent utility, they are made to withdraw and foreclose. Perhaps inevitably, then, the last decade has seen a rise in scholarship investigating the frequent corruption, degradation, and disappearance of content in the form of link rot, content drift, updates, and abandoned sites, each marking the end of life of a digital object as the internet expands and ages.[92] Unpaid storage and hosting fees, often dismissed as trivial, are a crucial factor behind this wave of disappearances. Deletion, prompted by an actual or perceived calculus of space and cost, is not confined to dying or sunsetting platforms.

As the internet's most visited online encyclopedia, Wikipedia offers a prime case for unpacking the bureaucratic nature of erasure. Of note is that debates around deletion and other content decisions often borrow from the vocabulary of storage capacity. With its volunteer-driven structure, the knowledge-sharing website relies heavily on peer production to compile and maintain its repository. Wikipedians constantly add, modify, approve, and eliminate various aspects of articles, sometimes removing entire pages. Editors pushing for more aggressive purging of content have earned the moniker "deletionists."[93] They maintain that tighter editorial standards yield a better product by strategically inducing "artificial scarcity." On the other end of the spectrum, "inclusionists" contend that, unbound by the spatial limits of printed matter, Wikipedia should lean into abundance rather than austerity.[94] For them, the supposed freedom from physical constraints invites equally expansive content creation and publication. These opposing curatorial philosophies often culminate in heated disputes over which individuals, entities, events, or objects are deserving of space. Such removals have, in some instances, become flashpoints for fierce editorial debates that reach far beyond factual accuracy, surfacing deeper tensions around exclusionary agendas rooted in nationalism, misogyny, racism, and classism.[95] In the tug-of-war between Wikipedia's available space and its selective deletion practices, the real question is not whether the internet forgets—it does—but rather who and what are erased in the process and under what procedural rationale.

Let me now turn to one of the most prominent players in cloud storage. The plenitude of free digital space users enjoyed until recently is, in fact, a contingent arrangement, where supposedly complimentary storage is subsidized by the commodification of data. Having habituated users to expect limitless retention, the industry now monetizes this very dependency. Storage becomes a premium service, rebranded as indispensable in the guise of safeguarding the records it once freely absorbed. By leaning into growing anxieties about accidental or deliberate deletions of entire caches of data, IT platforms, software providers, and storage corporations increasingly, and not always subtly, push paid subscriptions that are powered and backed up by the cloud. This strategy ensures steady annual profit streams for virtually unchanging products. Users' established trust in these platforms often blinds them to the fact that they are becoming locked into ecosystems that promise reliability and recoverability. The pattern is consistent across the board, from Alphabet, Microsoft, Adobe, Amazon, to the many lesser-known actors operating behind the scenes. Take Google Photos. In 2020, it announced its pivot away from complimentary to premium storage:

> We launched Google Photos more than five years ago with the mission of being the *home for your memories*. What started as an app to manage your photos and videos has evolved into a place to reflect on meaningful moments in your life. Today, more than a trillion photos are stored in Google Photos, and every week 28 billion new photos and videos are uploaded.
>
> Since *so many of you rely on Google Photos to store your memories*, it's important that it's not just a great product, but also continues to meet your needs over the *long haul* [. . .] we are changing our unlimited high quality storage policy.
>
> [. . .] This change also allows us to keep pace with the growing demand for storage. And, as always, we uphold our commitment to not use information in Google Photos for advertising purposes.[96]

The internet may never forget, but now, it remembers at a price. Any data exceeding the newly imposed limit faces deletion, unless users shell out for an upgrade. The move of Google Photos toward a tiered, paid system, along with the company's bulk deletion of inactive free accounts, highlights how the monetary issue has been obscured by the normalization of these platforms as personal archives. Framing it as an act of care, the company passes over the cost of preservation in a bid to "protect your memories for the long haul"—however long or short that might be. A year earlier, Vox had praised Google Photos as "one of the only 'safe,' free places to store lots of photos."[97] The service secured this esteemed title after Flickr, once the dominant platform for photo storage and sharing, announced in 2019 its plan to begin "deleting photos," thereby excising "massive chunks of internet history."[98] This was just one more instance of disposal in what has become a decades-long history of digital discard—and one that the Internet Archive once again sought to mitigate. While digital media accommodate residual structures, it is now the commercial mandate, not a technical constraint, that insists on their removal.

Such actions reveal how the data economy thrives on overwriting and repurposing space whenever revenues fall short and growth stagnates—or simply when they fail to meet the market's sensational projections and valuations. These decisions also illuminate a corporate concentration of power that counterintuitively reinforces the perception of trust and stability. In the end, durability is a product of profitability, nothing more. Once the value of storing materials is depleted, the justification for maintaining and keeping them vanishes, even though the costs associated with storage have significantly decreased over the years. In other words, not even the promise of abundance can guarantee persistence.

For those engaged in the study of cultural memory and the dialectic of collective remembrance and forgetting, the impact of this state of affairs is difficult to disregard. Scholars like Niels Brügger and Anat Ben-David stress the urgency of digital preservation, especially as social platform content, for example, can vanish unopposed.[99] Viewed from a negative vantage point, what emerges in parallel to the question of what societies ought to retain or purge is how endurance as a value in itself becomes an ideological artifact, an effect of systems calibrated toward visibility, optimization, and profit. There may be no concept of the human apart from technics, as Stiegler contended, yet the forces that have compelled tools to become what they now are and to function as they now do harness the technical in service of regimes of desire and calculation. Adaptive retention, insofar as it is a part of what makes "memory" operable, is more than a technical convenience; it is an inscription of a certain logic into a system that aestheticizes retention while instrumentalizing its erasure.

IT'S ALL FOR YOU, IS IT NOT?

This chapter argues that the rhetoric of INF has, over time, transformed from a critique of digital permanence into a tool that ultimately reinforces corporate control over data. It first introduced a familiar metaphor of memory to elucidate technical processes that, too complex for non-experts to comprehend and too abstract to grasp their immediate consequences, were often deferred to a future that appeared distant and of little concern. Attesting to the habitual, default practice of information retention, popular conversation from the early 2000s gravitated to raising awareness of the looming specter of pervasive surveillance. This was meant to be a cautionary tale, in which traces of the past lingered not as fragments of human history but as an effect of data commodification. In this stratified system, the capacity to erase information is now increasingly concentrated in the hands of a few profit-driven corporations. At the same time, social media claims, with a degree of disingenuousness, to empower users—a tenuous assertion crafted by branding department creatives.[100]

As the INF refrain amplified the stark realities of retention, it simultaneously deemphasized the negativity that mass deletion events exposed. In a curious inversion, the call to "forget"—to create ephemeral systems meant to expunge information after a set time—was indeed taken up in various ways, but its revolutionary potential was coopted, metabolized into nothing more than a feature within the commanding machinery of data extraction on Snapchat, WhatsApp, Instagram, and many others.[101] Rather than championing a resistive stance, forgetting became another tool in surveillance capitalism's arsenal. The unintended consequence of this buzz phrase, more than a decade later, is a conceptual distance from the financial powers that commentators originally intended to dismantle—evidenced, almost absurdly, by Amazon's sale of T-shirts bearing the motto, "The Internet Never Forgets."[102] What once seemed, a decade or two ago, to raise the terrifying specter of ubiquitous data collection has now become a widely accepted platitude, repeated ad nauseam.

The takeaway is to challenge the idealization of the stored and to resist treating data as abstract, perfect, and disconnected from its material infrastructure. Alternatives can emerge when our sociotechnical imaginaries confront capacity head on rather than render it invisible or inconsequential. Take, for instance, Ben Grosser's Minus, a finite platform designed to taunt growth-obsessed social media giants. Cleverly limiting users to a predetermined lifetime number of posts, Grosser challenges the endless drive for engagement, asking, "What if a social network wanted less, not more?"[103] Whether this or other radical strategies will offer viable outlets for the internet's many communities, platforms, and apps remains uncertain. Whatever shape online space may yet assume, one thing is clear. The fantasy of complete retention and the latest ideological iteration of the "unforgetting internet" must be refused, not reformed, for it stifles new possibilities of becoming.

Conclusion

YET SOMETHING PERSISTS

• • • The room is dark. I stand in the entryway. The droning of the projector fills the air, a familiar rhythm. Abstract shapes and credits I cannot quite make out flicker on the screen before me, while other slides swirl across the surrounding walls. I wait for the film to start. My attention is drawn to a soft murmur in the background, its sound slightly unnerving. Once it catches your ear, it is hard to ignore it. I take a step forward, hesitant to walk in. As my eyes adjust to the dim light, they settle on the source of the rattling beneath me. Scattered across the floor are countless strips of film stock, daring visitors at the Whitney Museum's exhibition, "Dreamlands: Immersive Cinema and Art, 1905–2016," to tread on them. A beloved medium, reduced to detritus. A group behind me nudges me forward, and I reluctantly move ahead, my gaze darting around to check for any signs forbidding entry. Surely, someone will rush in to enforce the unspoken rule: *do not touch*. But no one comes. With each step, my confidence grows, the crunching sound of film underfoot becoming louder, less foreign. What begins as apprehension quickly morphs into an odd thrill—an illicit sense of having crossed a boundary and gotten away with it. To my surprise, I relish it. And I am not alone. "People made piles and jumped into them, picked up the film and held it up to the light," the artist recalled from a previous installation of the work at the Whitney in 2000.[1] I lingered in this room far longer than in any other in the show, although those rooms were likewise filled with media-driven works. None, however, could quite rival the experience I just had.

In Jud Yalkut's *Destruct Film* (1967), "the viewer," as the curator explains, "stands ankle-deep in celluloid film strewn across the floor and is encouraged to handle, look through, and take away sections of it."[2] Though I left empty-handed, the piece stayed in my thoughts for days. I found myself wondering what Esfir Shub, the editor who salvaged and reused every scrap of footage and whose work I was researching at the time for this book's second chapter, would have made of this. Would she have appreciated this deconstruction of cinematic illusion, this dismantling and exhibition of the normally concealed apparatus behind filmmaking and filmgoing? It was the epitome of experimental art, certainly, but at the same time, an outward display of excess—a material scrap heap, a playground. A scene, I imagine, that some filmmakers, especially those keenly aware of scarcity, might have struggled to comprehend. Perhaps they would have felt envious, maybe also critical of the savoring of extravagant abundance.

The twenty-first-century reconstruction of Yalkut's environment encapsulates negative machines in a nutshell. It brings into sharp relief all the hidden elements that make media function, laying them bare for anyone to examine and walk over. But what could be more invisible than these pieces of film, staged like refuse on the floor? The unseen work that ensures that all the material that could be exhausted before being disposed of would in fact be. For this reason, the process of erasure and its meticulous engineering has been my focus throughout this book. It is the invisible within the already unseen. *Negative Media*, therefore, is a study not of discarded objects but of the ways in which material waste has been minimized, whether more successfully or less so, in the production of various records. Film stock never became reusable in quite the same way as the phonograph cylinder, magnetic tape, or hard drive, although it might have done so under different circumstances. There is no doubt that many technologies and devices do eventually meet their end in the bin, recycling site, or landfill, but this quest for erasure has been far more elusive than tracking objects "thrown down in the streets [revealing] a certain contempt."[3] This discarded material, after all, leaves behind a much more palpable, identifiable trace external to the machine.

If we shift our focus away from rejected fragments and deleted contents, how else might an engagement with the materiality of recording technologies proceed? In the introduction, I proposed that erasure exists in the cracks and shadows of media theory. The challenge is, therefore, to think with what consistently escapes direct scrutiny and which many media theories have left unexamined. What I found was that from the end of the nineteenth century, as today, abundance underpinned many of the claims about what technical objects are and could be (durable, boundless, endlessly expanding, immaterial, immortal, pristine, and perfect). Scarcity was recast as a mere inconvenience, a problem for engineers to resolve.

At an early point in the project, I described a particular erasable feature in a passing conversation with a scholar whose work I admire and have often cited in these pages. After listening to my account, they remarked something to the effect of, "that's interesting, but I'm not sure what there is to say about it." The remark, though offhand, inadvertently captured how inconspicuous erasure and other routine foreclosures can be. This proved to be a crucial moment that made something plain. To me, it made the stakes of this inquiry unmistakably clear long before I had come across a fitting conceptual framework. Theory tends to pass over this kind of negation—neither generic nor universal but situated and functional. If, indeed, recording and erasing are mutually implicated, there should be as much to say about the complicated conditions of production and negation as the plethora of works that scrutinize outputs such as texts, representations, and effects. We might do well as thinkers and users to ask how these become sayable and seeable in the first place.

Erasure is a routine practice that has been refined and revisited over time across the five industries examined in this book—phonography, cinema, magnetic recording for television, office work, and digital media. Be that as it may, in theoretical debates, the action, rather than the concept, barely registers; it remains just a faint blip occasionally picked up on the radar. Each prevailing discourse tends to fixate on one dimension, allowing others to drift into the margins. But to undo is a fundamental, even a constitutive, action for many of the media we rely on today and use to store our data, and it will continue to be so for the foreseeable future. It is a rather thankless task that is too often taken for granted. I therefore opted to explore processes where the same substrate is continually used in production, highlighting dynamic movements and transformations over dejected objects. Such an inquiry cannot occur in isolation; it cannot sever ontological, epistemological, and ideological debates from their specific technical histories and economic contexts.

AND ON IT GOES

Contending with unstable ground is not merely a practical dilemma but a conceptual impasse. The tools we have devised to arrest time, stabilize flux, battle forgetting, conserve energy, and resist entropy seem to function while accommodating the potential negation of said aspirations. Even more so, they do not simply permit disappearance; they require it. Erasure is not incidental but constitutive. It is found in the basic instructions and manuals of our technologies. If this all sounds familiar, it is because this project initially set out to engage with Jacques Derrida's work and examine the concept of *archē* through the history of technical objects. "How do media write under erasure?" was the question, although the technicalities and procedures I encountered in the physical archives have often taken me in other directions. The "archive" as a stand-in term for exteriorized and then internalized regimes of memory, Jeffrey Bowker writes, "operates through being invisibly exclusionary. The invisibility is an important feature here: the archive presents itself as being the set of all possible statements, rather than the law of what can be said."[4] Ergo, under the veil of potentially unconstrained retention are routinized omissions. Indiscriminate inclusion would unmake the archive, stripping it of its authority as an arbiter of the legible and thereby dissolving its authorial power. It cannot, by definition, hold everything. I stay with this statement if only to gather again the theoretical storylines that have unfolded throughout these pages.

Is operative erasure so elusive as to resist analysis altogether? Erasure as a concept might be rather unstable, nomadic even, but negative media theory makes it possible to apprehend certain dimensions of it. At its core, this capability functions as a procedure against and for record-making. Undoing does not simply efface traces but clears the ground so that something else, something newly legible, might take its place. The operation remains incomplete until even the residue of that effacement has vanished, and the act of deletion itself is no longer perceptible. In this way, a medium such as magnetic tape excludes and conceals the mechanisms through which it functions. This implies that multiple facets of media are obscured behind self-presentation. What we are able and are allowed to perceive, and what we infer about its making, often diverges from how media actually work. Recall Boris Groys's formulation of the *structurally invisible.* This, he suggests, is akin to the back of the painting—distinct from the aesthetic object that greets the viewer. Of course, no system of control or containment is without its limits. Occasionally, something slips and fractures its totalizing design. If one looks closely, a glitch or a trace of decay, for instance, can betray the existence of something beyond the visible frame. This may be something unfamiliar, if not outright terrifying, that confronts us with what we have tried so hard to ward off through technics.

One should wonder why erasure has failed to attract sustained interest from those otherwise invested in unpacking the hidden dimension of media. Perhaps it is as simple as that there were always more pressing matters to attend to at every twist and turn. To be sure, operationality lacks the seductive pull of immaterial fantasies, of visions of media transcending physical bounds, of delivering a semblance of an afterlife in the form of traces that can outlast us all. Likewise, broadcast is more readily imagined as a conduit of raw immediacy and liveness than as the source of recordings gathering dust in unattended containers. And certainly, today's grand narrative draws us into another unsettling vision: every thought and action preserved in cold, sterile, humming data centers, with each fragment of data poised to be extracted and scrutinized by an unknown power. What is more, theorists often gravitate to exemplary, memorable, "model" gestures of negation. Robert Rauschenberg's erasure of a De Kooning, for instance, becomes a paradigmatic reference point where the icons and codes of art history are being unmade, painstakingly, by hand. But are we not all Rauschenbergs of a kind, smudging the record not out of malice necessarily but because that is what our tools were built to do? My wager, then, is this: perhaps the inner workings of media could be discerned through the ordinary. The "archive" hides behind mundanity in much the same way that negation, its organizing principle, does.

At the level of nuts and bolts, it becomes evident that no single system or existing network of systems can accommodate "all possible statements," despite promises or warnings to the contrary. Operative erasure is a contemporary iteration and an offshoot of reuse and recycling practices that have long been the domain of storage media. Even inscriptions on stone, after all, can be chiseled away and re-engraved.[5] Over the (very) long twentieth century, the period covered in these pages, erasure was initially mobilized as a strategy to combat material privation and maximize finite resources. As the century unfolded, undoing transformed into a method for grappling with the unrealistic expectation of boundless plenty. In both cases, erasing strategies are tantamount to stretching the boundaries of available storage or getting as close as possible to fully exhausting it.

Few understand this reality better than those who build, preserve, or simply depend on these apparatuses. Through media archaeological excavations of common, abandoned, and never-fully-realized propositions, I set out to expose the considerable distance between engineering realities and technical imaginaries. Erasure, when it appears at all in theoretical or popular accounts, is often pared down to abstraction, divorced from the very mechanisms that tightly bind visibility to it. Sometimes, they simply call it "forgetting." Instead, operative erasure, as I have argued, reflects ingenuity; it is the product of resourceful design, arising from a pragmatic entanglement with material constraints, that turns limited capacity into possibility, friction into form. *Adaptive retention* is, therefore, my way of articulating a nonpassive relation premised on incessant recalibration, wherein the substrate is not merely a surface to be imprinted. By the same token, erasure is no accident but an inevitable response to the physical world.

At their current pace, data centers are poised to consume even more staggering amounts of water and electricity, steadily expanding their carbon footprint and driving a surge in greenhouse gas emissions.[6] For environmentally conscious ventures, now may be the ideal time to urge the R&D department to focus on developing more efficient processes that require less data. For climate-conscious users, this may be a call to examine our own practices. Considering digital minimalism, for example, there are ways to make do with the storage we already have (or can sustain privately) without getting caught up in the commercial race for ever more. Without intentional changes in both industry practices and consumer demands, the environmental burden of the post-digital age will continue to escalate unchecked. In addition to better design practices, advocacy for regulations that cap such construction could also become a crucial step toward a more sustainable existence.

Far from obsolete, operative erasure could be refashioned yet again to tackle some of the most urgent quandaries of the present. The cloud is heavy with dead weight—petabytes of junk data, unused, unusable, and worthless, accumulating unchecked, some estimates warn. As no surprise, junk data is sometimes instrumentalized as a tactic to confound algorithmic legibility, hiding real data between the unwanted and the too much. So much for the myth of immateriality: even the digital has its dump site. Should the historical arc mapped so far hold predictive value, then it is here that operative erasure may yet prove useful. Rather than treat deletion as failure, loss, or accident, it could become a mode of reckoning and curbing the costs of digital storage surplus. It is unlikely that companies would forgo an opportunity to reduce expenditure. The elimination of redundancies could, in fact, be a material intervention in the escalating environmental toll of data accumulation. The risk, inevitably, lies in the entrenchment of data surveillance: further eroding privacy, tightening mechanisms of control, and ceding agency over data to processes that would automate the "law of what can be said." The stakes of such undoing lie in the principles it would be made to affirm, whose wills it would serve, and the values it would inscribe.

This point offers a fitting segue into the economic thread running through the book. We always begin the same way. Each new technology sells the dream of progress by leaps and bounds. Yet the relentless pursuit of retention and celebration of limitless growth has simultaneously created the necessity to come to terms with finiteness. So far, the cases have shown that each new argument for better storage hinged not only on improved retention but also on increasingly sophisticated methods of deletion. Tracing these budding industries allowed for an examination of how erasure refracted market pressures and demands. At first glance, it may seem counterintuitive that profit-driven enterprises, built on the promise of record-keeping, would undermine those very assurances by introducing reusability. Erasure, however, operates with a soft logic; fluid and contingent, it adapts to different contexts. The ability to annul content while preserving the substrate became integral to the scaffolding of various business models. It drives profit and production forward by returning to the same substrate again and again—extracting more from what is already at the system's disposal. More than anything, negation functions as a rationalizing force that privileges efficiency and aims at optimization. Stability and malleability, then, are not opposite poles but coexisting tendencies within these machines.

It would not be an overstatement to note that wealth accumulation as the driving force of capital depends on what can be repeatedly exploited for value. The migration of nearly all aspects of production into the digital sphere fueled the commodification of data as a resource that could be tirelessly circulated and capitalized upon. This has met with some opposition. Take, for instance, the music industry's pivot in response to piracy: it compensated for the decline in record sales by transforming shows into mega-events, sending ticket prices soaring ever higher. To further increase profits, touring was intensified, with the live experience captured and shared on social media, streamed via online platforms, released in special editions, packaged in deluxe box sets, turned into made-to-order merchandise touted by influencers, and more. Everything ends up being fed back into the digital fold somehow. But we must remember that infinite storage is an illusion that ultimately crumbles under its own weight. As shown in the final chapter, even the most powerful corporations, in their bid to minimize cost, end up institutionalizing undoing as a necessary "byproduct." All the while, they tout their services as the gold standard of durability and security. While I share the urgency of critiques centered on extraction and depletion, it remains equally important to also consider how the system recalibrates to work within certain limits. To ignore that is to be surprised by disappearance as if it were not built in. Tracing these loops does not absolve the system; it sharpens our sense of where the pressure points may be.

That negative machines operate by generating through exclusion and excluding through generation is key. Operable erasure and adaptive retention can also attune us to the ways technologies spit out and chew through their "memory" and, in doing so, regulate the contours of social life. Power grips both ends of the rope by way of these mutable relations. At one end is a construct of limitlessness, shaped by modernist and colonialist hopes for epistemic universality. These conjure a comprehensive, knowable vision of a world structured through technics. Today, the promise of plenty serves as a rallying cry for neoliberalism and empire, with storage space weaponized and moralized in the service of those already poised to profit. On the other end, limited capacity becomes a rationale for exclusion, an alibi for what (and who) must be left out. There's simply no room, they say, as if exclusion were a property of logistics alone. Erasability is a reminder that throws a wrench in the circuits of totalization, particularly in its digital guise. However, it is also one of the tools that allows such regimes to persist smoothly. Retention and negation cut both ways. They sanction, but they can also bar ideas, bodies, identities, and beliefs.

In the end, our tools shape us as profoundly as we shape them, a reciprocity that human history has rendered spectacularly clear. Mindful of this, what this book insists on is simple. Records, files, and data are regularly erased. This fact, though itself negated, demands more space in our conversations about topics such as technicity, memory, money, and politics. Perhaps we may also find a measure of consolation in the fact that not everything can be stored. In the oft-cited cautionary tale of Borges's "Funes the Memorious," total recall proves a curse. The world splinters into the unbearable specificity of every registered detail. This raises, of course, the familiar provocation: if the capacity for complete memory were within reach, should we accept? I am not so much interested in answering no or yes to singularity as in the fact that, as it stands, our machines are not yet Borges's protagonist. Server rooms, too, have their thresholds and would eventually give out. And yet, various sociotechnical narratives continue to valorize abundant retention, blind to the bottleneck it would inevitably create and the social and ecological damage it would most certainly exact.

Which brings me to blockchain-based applications, a newly glorified frontier for data. By leaning into limitlessness as a value, some companies go so far as to promote "data permanence" as a digital ideal.[7] Whether blockchain's currently narrow application will evolve into a full-blown ecosystem capable of supplanting the internet as we know it remains an open question. Even less clear is how, in that event, the technology could uphold its promise to document every single transaction and copy. Materially, such an enduring memory seems all but impossible. And politically, we can say that not everyone will pay the same price for it. Until the reveries of Web3 evangelists materialize or crumble, our media nevertheless remain under constraint. For some, it is hardly a loss at all.

In the past few years, internet users have seen a surge in the release and use of large language models (LLMs) and other generative technologies. These AI applications are set to place even greater pressure on data storage systems, due in large part to the immense amount of data required for training. The hunger for information, almost insatiable, thrives undeterred by the steep costs associated with everything storage (including high-performance file storage systems, block storage and object storage). If we are lucky, rising costs may drive the development of strategies to reduce the amount of—and thus the retention of—data required to feed this ravenous golem.[8] When consulted about the size of OpenAI's training set, ChatGPT responded that the company "has not publicly disclosed the exact size of the training set for ChatGPT" but confirmed that it is vast, comprising somewhere between hundreds of billions to trillions of tokens, sourced from various data sets, scraped from the public web—some unlawfully obtained. And the volume of pretraining data sets tends to be even larger. Either way, AI's ascent may spell the end of the business model built on indexing and advertising such as Google's, and, with it, the collapse of the internet in its current form.

While perfectly circular digital economies remain a distant possibility, new start-ups seem to be heading in the opposite direction to sustainability. One strand of techno-solutionism set its sights instead on expanding storage in every conceivable direction on Earth and beyond. Some companies now claim they can ease the strain on the planet's resources by building cloud infrastructure in uncharted territories, including Earth's orbit and even on the moon. This, they argue, is the next frontier of storage: data distributed planetarily and extraplanetarily. For now, we remain confined to this planet, bound by the limitations of our technologies, resources, and physics. There is no escape to the outer reaches of the solar system or the galaxy just yet. If nothing else, humanity remains tethered to Earth and must contend with the repercussions of its storage industries. If media technologies are to continue along the trajectories traced in these chapters, deletion will be ever more necessary, calculated, systematic, and routinized. For this and many other reasons, I hope this effort will initiate a conversation that undoes the undoing of undoing, disrupting the recursive patterns of not attending to the penumbra of production and the possibility of more responsible use of finite resources.

This book is, then, an opening proposition and not, I must confess, a handbook on how to better demagnetize cassette tapes abandoned in a basement or completely scrub a hard drive, nor is it a manual for how to best save and archive 16 mm films or important documents. It is also not an endeavor to track every possible deletion. I have no exhaustive list of all things undone or every technique for undoing to offer. There are, no doubt, many more negations to uncover. And this is why orienting ourselves toward storage or engaging in "storage studies" can prove useful: it offers a framework capable of traversing and integrating multiple strata of production and generation, charting vectors that range from the microscopic of media containers to the macrostructures of technical networks, Earthly and cosmic.

Afterword

AMID ERASURE, WE LIVE

• • • I was working on this book, rewriting what I had already written, when a war began. It kept on. And then another started. This was to be a long meditation on a personal and political erasure, on the machinery of naming and becoming. I meant to write of the time my name was changed according to the standardizing demand of a nation-state and how my own identity as a post-Soviet immigrant has emerged in the negative. Seemingly simple administrative gestures, of course, have their consequences. But both places, Ukraine and Israel/Palestine, are burning. I do not have much of a taste for speaking of the personal anymore.

I find myself, too often now, lost for words. Words that might convince. Words that might console. The count of casualties and bodies steadily climbs. Some people are accounted for, while others are not. Images of carnage blur into one another. In Gaza, hunger is normalized. The longer it continues—and it has already gone on for far too long—the more language escapes me. I search for words that could *do*. What utterance could feasibly interrupt the voracious war machine? This is not posed as a scholarly question. It is not another meditation on whether we can still write during or after.

How about an image?

About a decade ago, the Israeli pavilion at the Venice Architecture Biennale displayed several sandboxes. An unremarkable robotic arm, seemingly innocuous, swept across the surface every few minutes. A needle attached to the mechanism etched future urban plans into the soft substrate. As the arm moved, each previous vision was erased, giving way to another, without memory of what had come before. Caught in perpetual amnesia, the apparatus created its present just as it erased its past. Though the installation was meant to reflect on the modernist building project, it now seems an ever more apt metaphor for this bloody patch of land across time and history. We see no residents. No people. No life. Just nature, technology, and the question of sovereignty. When the value of human life has been so thoroughly eroded, we may call that machine a nation, a god, security, capital. What have you. The motion of the arm does not stop, never ceases. But as we reside amid those scattered particles, we become the invisible medium through which the machine continues negating. And it also effaces us and everything around us. Can sand remember? Can the earth forgive?

The sandboxes evoke a worldview of limited capacity, which we have seen play out in the design of various storage containers, assuming that the old must be cleared to make room for the new. Existence, the lifeworld, and nature are not the same as the boxes we have invented for them—at least, not exactly. Accordingly, any claim within the socio-political that reduces reality to capacities and functional metrics should be regarded with deep suspicion. Under what imagined storage system, under whose command, and in service of whose interests do people become disposable? There are things that must not be considered expendable, must not be rendered as fodder, as surplus. Life, quite simply.

Listening to the sonic backdrop of planes, drones, and helicopters, of sirens slicing through the air and the horns of mass protests, it must be stated with a clear voice. The gambit of scarcity, the claim that there is not enough to go around, is what frames human life as a battle: of resource against resource, of lives weighed and cast in the name of one authority or another. Unless we rewrite the terms, the so-called road to abundance will follow the same worn logic—expansion, consumption, oppression, occupation, extraction. Not sharing. Not working together. Not living together. And the world, unchanged, will go on as it has.

This book is dedicated to my grandparents, some of whom survived the Holodomor and all of whom lived through World War II. If there is an ethical lesson I draw from their stories, it is this: how could one possibly choose anything but to insist—again and again—against violence? We owe a debt to the generations that came before us, those beneath the sand, to ourselves, and certainly to those who will follow. And yet, the twenty-first century, the supposed end of history, has failed miserably in ensuring that atrocities belong only to the history books, as entries on a forgotten crumpled page.

By the time this book appears in print, I hope that there might be space for every single being to live with dignity, though such dreams are too easily deferred, redirected, and denied.

For peace.
October 2024

NOTES

Introduction

1. Ruth Kricheli, "Updating Our Inactive Account Policies," *Google Blog*, May 16, 2023, https://blog.google/technology/safety-security/updating-our-inactive-account-policies/.

2. Jordan Novet, "Google's Plan to Purge Inactive Accounts Isn't Sitting Well with Some Users," *CNBC*, August 19, 2023.

3. Wendy Hui Kyong Chun, *Programmed Visions: Software and Memory* (MIT Press, 2011), 170.

4. For the book that popularized much of this sort of conversation, see Viktor Mayer-Schönberger, *Delete: The Virtue of Forgetting in the Digital Age* (Princeton University Press, 2009).

5. Antony Adshead, "Unexpected Costs Hit Many As They Move to Cloud Storage," *Computer Weekly*, March 5, 2023.

6. See, for instance, Bill Brown, "Thing Theory," *Critical Inquiry* 28, no. 1 (2001): 1–22; Katherine N. Hayles, *Writing Machines* (MIT Press, 2002).

7. Jennifer Gabrys, *Digital Rubbish: A Natural History of Electronics* (University of Michigan Press, 2011); Nicole Starosielski, *The Undersea Network* (Duke University Press, 2015); Kate Crawford, *The Atlas of AI: Power, Politics, and the Planetary Costs of Artificial Intelligence* (Yale University Press, 2021); Jussi Parikka, *A Geology of Media* (University of Minnesota Press, 2015).

8. Sean Cubitt, *Finite Media: Environmental Implications of Digital Technologies* (Duke University Press, 2017), 7.

9. See, for instance, Mark J. P. Wolf, ed., *The Routledge Companion to Media Technology and Obsolescence* (Routledge, 2019); Jens Schröter, "Erasure As Planned Obso-

lescence," in *Obsolescence programmée. Perspectives culturelles*, ed. Ella Mingazova, Bruno Dupont, and Carole Guesse (Presses Universitaire de Liège, 2022), 83–99.

10. Thomas Robert Malthus, *An Essay on the Principle of Population* (Cambridge University Press, 1992); Michael Perelman, "Marx and Resource Scarcity," *Capitalism Nature Socialism* 4, no. 2 (1993): 65–84.

11. Fredrik Albritton Jonsson and Carl Wennerlind, *Scarcity: A History from the Origins of Capitalism to the Climate Crisis* (Harvard University Press, 2023).

12. Harold A. Innis, *Empire and Communications* (Dundurn Press, 2007); James W. Carey, "Technology and Ideology: The Case of the Telegraph," *Prospects* 8 (1983): 303–25; Marshall McLuhan, *The Gutenberg Galaxy: The Making of Typographic Man* (University of Toronto Press, 2011).

13. John Muir, *Life and Letters in the Ancient Greek World* (Routledge, 2009); Jonathan Goldberg, *Writing Matter: From the Hands of the English Renaissance* (Stanford University Press, 1990); Peter Stallybrass, Roger Chartier, J. Franklin Mowery, and Heather Wolfe, "Hamlet's Tables and the Technologies of Writing in Renaissance England," *Shakespeare Quarterly* 55, no. 4 (2004): 379–419.

14. Catherine Girard, "Painture: The Temporal and Emotional Labor of Stale Bread in the French Studio," *West 86th: A Journal of Decorative Arts, Design History, and Material Culture* 31, no. 1 (Spring–Summer 2024).

15. See, for example, Ann Blair, "Reading Strategies for Coping with Information Overload, ca. 1550–1700," *Journal of the History of Ideas* 64, no. 1 (2023): 11–28.

16. John Perry Barlow, "Selling Wine without Bottles: The Economy of Mind on the Global Net," *Duke Law and Technology Review* 18, no.1 (2019): 10 (my emphasis).

17. See, for instance, Thomas Richards, *The Imperial Archive: Knowledge and the Fantasy of Empire* (Verso, 1993).

18. Brian Michael Murphy, "Data Storage Is Reaching the Limits of Physics," *Wall Street Journal*, August 25, 2022.

19. Friedrich A. Kittler, *Discourse Networks, 1800/1900* (Stanford University Press, 1990).

20. Jonathan Sterne, *MP3: The Meaning of a Format* (Duke University Press, 2012); Mayer-Schönberger, *Delete*; Cory Arcangel, "On Compression," in *This Is a Couple Thousand Short Films about Glenn Gould: A Book in Relation to a Project of the Same Name*, ed. Cory Arcangel, Paul Morley, and Steven Bode (Film and Video Umbrella, 2008), 220–32; Daniel Palmer, "The Rhetoric of the JPEG," in *The Photographic Image in Digital Culture* (Routledge, 2013), 149–64.

21. Shannon Mattern, "Bureaucracy's Playthings," in *Computer Architectures: Constructing the Common Ground*, ed. Theodora Vardouli and Olga Touloumi (Routledge, 2019), 160–70; Craig Robertson, *The Filing Cabinet: A Vertical History of Information* (University of Minnesota Press, 2021).

22. "Media studies, however, only make sense when media make senses." Friedrich Kittler, "Number and Numeral," *Theory, Culture & Society* 23, no. 7–8 (2006): 55.

23. Dieter Mersch, "Tertium Datur. Introduction to a Negative Media Theory," *Matrizes* 7, no. 1 (2013): 207–22.

24. Jacques Derrida, *Of Grammatology* (Johns Hopkins University Press, 1997).

25. Martin Heidegger, *Being and Time* (Harper San Francisco, 1962).

26. For instance, Stephen Graham and Nigel Thrift, "Out of Order: Understanding Repair and Maintenance," *Theory, Culture & Society* 24, no. 3 (2007): 1–25.

27. Marshall McLuhan and Quentin Fiore, *The Medium Is the Massage* (Random House, 1967).

28. Joseph Vogl, "Becoming-media: Galileo's Telescope," *Grey Room* 29 (2007): 16.

29. Sybille Krämer, *Medium, Messenger, Transmission: An Approach to Media Philosophy* (Amsterdam University Press, 2015), 31.

30. Boris Groys, *Under Suspicion: A Phenomenology of Media* (Columbia University Press, 2012).

31. Groys, *Under Suspicion*, 35.

32. Jay David Bolter and Richard Grusin, *Remediation: Understanding New Media* (Cambridge, MA: MIT Press, 2000), 5.

33. Victor I. Stoichita, *Short History of the Shadow* (Reaktion Books, 1997), 7.

34. Akira Mizuta Lippit, *Atomic Light (Shadow Optics)* (University of Minnesota Press, 2005).

35. John Durham Peters, *Speaking into the Air: A History of the Idea of Communication* (University of Chicago Press, 1999); Amanda Lagerkvist, *Existential Media: A Media Theory of the Limit Situation* (Oxford University Press, 2022); Amit Pinchevski, *By Way of Interruption: Levinas and the Ethics of Communication* (Duquesne University Press, 2005); Michel Serres, *The Parasite* (University of Minnesota Press, 2013).

36. Alexander R. Galloway, Eugene Thacker, and McKenzie Wark, *Excommunication: Three Inquiries in Media and Mediation* (University of Chicago Press, 2013).

37. Mersch, "Tertium Datur," 216.; Schröter, "Erasure As Planned Obsolescence."

38. Bruno Latour, "Where Are the Missing Masses? The Sociology of a Few Mundane Artifacts," in *Shaping Technology/Building Society: Studies in Sociotechnical Change*, ed. John Law and Wiebe E. Bijker (MIT Press, 1992): 225–58; Gilbert Simondon, *On the Mode of Existence of Technical Objects* (University of Minnesota Press), 18.

39. See, for instance, Peter Krapp, *Noise Channels: Glitch and Error in Digital Culture* (University of Minnesota Press, 2011); Carolyn L. Kane, *High-Tech Trash: Glitch, Noise, and Aesthetic Failure* (University of California Press, 2019).

40. Jonathan Goldstein, "#45 Sgt. John Kapphahn," *Heavyweight*, September 29, 2022.

41. Norbert Wiener, *Cybernetics: Or Control and Communication in the Animal and the Machine* (MIT Press, 2019), 8.

42. Eira Tansey, "Archives without Archivists," *Reconstruction: Studies in Contemporary Culture* 16, no. 1 (2016), 2.

43. Lise Jaillant, "More Data, Less Process: A User-centered Approach to Email and Born-digital Archives," *The American Archivist* 85, no. 2 (2022): 533–55.

44. Johan Fredrikzon and Chris Haffenden, "Towards Erasure Studies: Excavating the Material Conditions of Memory and Forgetting," *Memory, Mind & Media* 2 (2023): 2.

45. Paul Ricœur, *Memory, History, Forgetting* (University of Chicago Press, 2004);

Jacques Derrida, *Archive Fever: A Freudian Impression* (University of Chicago, 1996); Avishai Margalit, *The Ethics of Memory* (Harvard University Press, 2002).

46. Sigmund Freud, "A Note upon the 'Mystic Writing-Pad,'" in *The Standard Edition of the Complete Psychological Works, Volume XIX*, ed. and trans. James Strachey (Hogarth Press, 1961), 227. (Original German edition published 1925.)

47. Freud, "A Note upon the 'Mystic Writing-Pad,'" 229.

48. Thomas Elsaesser, "Freud as Media Theorist: Mystic Writing-Pads and the Matter of Memory," *Screen* 50, no. 1 (2009): 100–113.

49. Sigmund Freud, "Civilization and Its Discontents," in *The Standard Edition of the Complete Psychological Works, Volume XIX*, ed. and trans. Strachey, 72.

50. R. John Williams, "Surface Writing," *Representations* 165, no. 1 (2024): 24.

51. Friedrich A. Kittler, "Forgetting," *Discourse* 3 (1981): 99.

52. For some by-now-classic readings of what it means to give and/or reconstruct voice, see Saidiya Hartman, "Venus in Two Acts," *Small Axe: A Journal of Criticism* 12, no. 2 (2008): 1–14; Gayatri Chakravorty Spivak, "~~Megacity~~," *Grey Room* 1 (2000): 9–25; Michel-Rolph Trouillot, *Silencing the Past: Power and the Production of History* (Beacon Press, 2015); Ann Laura Stoler, *Along the Archival Grain: Epistemic Anxieties and Colonial Common Sense* (Princeton University Press, 2008).

53. Michel Foucault, *Discipline and Punish: The Birth of the Prison* (Vintage Books, 1977); Jacques Rancière, *The Politics of Aesthetics: The Distribution of the Sensible*, trans. Gabriel Rockhill (Continuum, 2004); Gayatri Chakravorty Spivak, "Can the Subaltern Speak?" in *Imperialism*, ed. Peter H. Cain and Mark Harrison (Routledge, 2023), 171–219.

54. Allen Feldman, *Archives of the Insensible: Of War, Photopolitics, and Dead Memory* (University of Chicago Press, 2015).

55. Harriet I. Flower, *The Art of Forgetting: Disgrace and Oblivion in Roman Political Culture* (University of North Carolina Press, 2006); Michael Camille, "Obscenity under Erasure," in *Obscenity: Social Control and Artistic Creation in the European Middle Ages*, ed. Jan M. Ziolkowski (Brill, 1998); Juliet Fleming, *Graffiti and the Writing Arts of Early Modern England* (Reaktion, 2001); Peter Galison, "Blacked-out Spaces: Freud, Censorship and the Re-territorialization of Mind," *The British Journal for the History of Science* 45, no. 2 (2012): 235–66; Joshua Craze, "Excerpts from a Grammar of Redaction," in *Dissonant Archives: Contemporary Visual Culture and Contested Narratives in the Middle East*, ed. Anthony Downey (Bloomsbury Publishing, 2015), 385–400.

56. Peter Galison, "Removing Knowledge," *Critical Inquiry* 31, no. 1 (2004): 229–43. In legal contexts, the textual operation of erasure had to be regulated and authorized. Doherty and colleagues speculate that the substrate of sheepskin parchment was used for legal deeds as early as the thirteenth century because it left visible marks of erasure and thus prevented writers from making untraceable amendments to the text. Histories of Prussian bureaucracy also note different protocols and procedures for document authorization and cancellation. See Sean Paul Doherty, Stuart Henderson, Sarah Fiddyment, Jonathan Finch, and Matthew J. Collins, "Scratching the

Surface: The Use of Sheepskin Parchment to Deter Textual Erasure in Early Modern Legal Deeds," *Heritage Science* 9 (2021): 1–6; Cornelia Vismann, *Files: Law and Media Technology* (Stanford University Press, 2008).

57. Gina Giotta, "Disappeared: Erasure in the Age of Mechanical Writing," PhD diss., (University of Iowa, 2011).

58. Erkki Huhtamo and Jussi Parikka, *Media Archaeology: Approaches, Applications, and Implications* (University of California Press, 2011).

59. Jonathan Sterne, *The Audible Past: Cultural Origins of Sound Reproduction* (Duke University Press, 2003); Kittler, *Discourse Networks*; Douglas Kahn, *Noise, Water, Meat: A History of Sound in the Arts* (MIT Press, 1999).

60. Jean-Louis Comolli, *Cinema against Spectacle: Technique and Ideology Revisited* (Amsterdam University Press, 2015), 99.

61. For a study of the importance of the landing, see Lorenz Engell, "Apollo TV: The Copernican Turn of the Gaze," *World Picture* 7 (2012): 4.

62. Susan Murray, "Reviving the Technical in Television History," in *A Companion to the History of American Broadcasting*, ed. Aniko Bodroghkozy (Wiley, 2018), 193.

63. Robertson, *The Filing Cabinet*.

64. Julian Stallabrass, "Trash," in *The Object Reader*, ed. Fiona Candlin and Raiford Guins (Routledge, 2009), 418.

65. Mayer-Schönberger, *Delete*.

Chapter 1

1. Charles Grivel, "The Phonograph's Horned Mount," in *Wireless Imagination: Sound, Radio, and the Avant-garde*, ed. Douglas Kahn and Gregory Whitehead (MIT Press, 1992), 36.

2. In his first patent application, Edison stated his intent "to record in *permanent characters* the human voice and other sounds, from which characters such sounds may be reproduced and rendered audible again at a future time." Thomas A. Edison, "Improvement in Phonograph or Speaking Machines," Patent US200521A, issued February 19, 1878 (my emphasis).

3. Edward H. Johnson, "A Wonderful Invention: Speech Capable of Indefinite Repetition from Automatic Records," *Scientific American*, November 17, 1877, 304.

4. Jeffrey Sconce, *Haunted Media: Electronic Presence from Telegraphy to Television* (Duke University Press, 2000); Carolyn Marvin, *When Old Technologies Were New: Thinking about Electric Communication in the Late Nineteenth Century* (Oxford University Press, 1988); John Durham Peters, *Speaking into the Air: A History of the Idea of Communication* (University of Chicago Press, 1999).

5. Amanda Lagerkvist, *Existential Media: A Media Theory of the Limit Situation* (Oxford University Press, 2022), 172.

6. Johnson, "A Wonderful Invention," 304.

7. Roland Gelatt, *The Fabulous Phonograph, 1877–1977* (Collier Books, 1977).

8. Thomas A. Edison, "The Phonograph and Its Future," *North American Review* 126 (May–June 1878): 527–36. Although discussions of recording recur frequently

across writings on sound in various disciplines, I wish to set aside the debate on aesthetic quality (whether real or presumed).

9. Emily Thompson, "Machines, Music, and the Quest for Fidelity: Marketing the Edison Phonograph in America, 1877–1925," *The Musical Quarterly* 79, no. 1 (1995): 137.

10. Wolfgang Ernst, *Digital Memory and the Archive*, ed. Jussi Parikka (University of Minnesota Press, 2012), 60.

11. Jonathan Sterne, *Audible Past: Cultural Origins of Sound Reproduction* (Duke University Press, 2003), 183.

12. Johnson, "A Wonderful Invention," 304.

13. Johnson, "A Wonderful Invention."

14. Kittler wrote extensively on the relationship between the literary representation of the phonograph and the figure of Dracula, both portrayed as entities with life unnaturally extended, hovering closer to death than to life. Friedrich A. Kittler, "Dracula's Legacy," in *Literature, Media, Information Systems*, ed. John Johnston (Routledge, 2013), 50–84.

15. "The Talking Phonograph," *Scientific American*, December 22, 1877, 384–85.

16. Friedrich A. Kittler, *Gramophone, Film, Typewriter*, trans. Geoffrey Winthrop-Young and Michael Wutz (Stanford University Press, 1999).

17. Barbara Engh, "After 'His Master's Voice,'" *New Formation* 38 (1999): 54.

18. Peters, *Speaking into the Air*, 144,

19. Mark Katz, *Capturing Sound: How Technology has Changed Music* (University of California Press, 2010).

20. Jane Eade, "The Theatre of Death," *Oxford Art Journal* 36, no. 1 (2013): 109–25.

21. Sterne, *Audible Past*.

22. However, this commercial competition did not amount to much in the end; Edison would dominate the cylinder market until it gave way to the vogue for (non-reusable) flat discs. Kurt Nauck, *Indestructible and U-S Everlasting Cylinders: An Illustrated History and Cylinderography* (Mainspring Press, 1907).

23. Quoted in Peters, *Speaking into the Air*, 142.

24. Grivel, "The Phonograph's Horned Mount"; Douglas Kahn, "Death in Light of the Phonograph: Raymond Roussel's *Locus Solus*," in *Wireless Imagination: Sound, Radio, and the Avant-garde*, ed. Douglas Kahn and Gregory Whitehead (MIT Press, 1992), 69–104. See also Sebastian D. G. Knowles, "Death by Gramophone," *Journal of Modern Literature* 27, no. 1 (2003): 1–13; Allen S. Weiss, *Breathless: Sound Recording, Disembodiment, and the Transformation of Lyrical Nostalgia* (Wesleyan University Press, 2002).

25. Quoted in Grivel, "The Phonograph's Horned Mount," 39.

26. Edison, "The Phonograph and Its Future."

27. Certainly, other technologies have been examined through the prism of death, which has indeed become a dominant mode of theorization of photography and the moving image. In focusing on the phonograph, I intend to suggest not that its story is unique, but rather that it is representative of a trend within media studies. See Roland Barthes, *Camera Lucida: Reflections on Photography* (Macmillan, 1981); Siegfried Kracauer, *Theory of Film: The Redemption of Physical Reality* (Oxford University

Press, 1965); André Bazin, "The Ontology of the Photographic Image," *Film Quarterly* 13, no. 4 (1960): 4–9.

28. Philip Rosen, *Change Mummified: Cinema, Historicity, Theory* (University of Minnesota Press, 2001), 22.

29. Sterne, *Audible Past,* 286.

30. For discussion of memory and tools, see Jacques Derrida, *Archive Fever: A Freudian Impression* (University of Chicago Press, 1998); Mary J. Carruthers, *The Book of Memory: A Study of Memory in Medieval Culture* (Cambridge University Press, 1992).

31. Andrea F. Bohlman and Peter McMurray, "Tape: Or, Rewinding the Phonographic Regime," *Twentieth-Century Music* 14, no. 1 (2017): 3–24.

32. Bohlman and McMurray, "Tape: Or, Rewinding the Phonographic Regime."

33. See, for example, Walter J. Fewkes, "On the Use of the Phonograph in the Study of the Languages of the American Indian," *Science* 378 (1890): 267–69; Irene Hilden, *Absent Presences in the Colonial Archive: Dealing with the Berlin Sound Archive's Acoustic Legacies* (Leuven University Press, 2022); Brian Hochman, *Savage Preservation: The Ethnographic Origins of Modern Media Technology* (University of Minnesota Press, 2014).

34. Sterne, *Audible Past,* 191–92.

35. Gelatt, *The Fabulous Phonograph,* 19.

36. Kittler, *Gramophone, Film, Typewriter,* 27.

37. Casey Cep, "The Real Nature of Thomas Edison's Genius," *New Yorker,* October 21, 2019.

38. Darren Wershler, Lori Emerson, and Jussi Parikka, *The Lab Book: Situated Practices in Media Studies* (University of Minnesota Press, 2022), 53; Edmund Morris, *Edison* (Random House, 2019).

39. Wershler, Emerson, and Parikka, *The Lab Book.*

40. For a discussion of technological precursors, see Sterne, *Audible Past;* Lisa Gitelman, *Scripts, Grooves and Writing Machines: Representing Technology in the Edison Era* (Stanford University Press, 1999).

41. Lisa Gitelman, "Souvenir Foils: On the Status of the Print at the Origin of Recorded Sound," in *New Media 1740–1915,* ed. Lisa Gitelman and Geoffrey B. Pingree (MIT Press, 2003), 157–74.

42. Edison, "The Phonograph and Its Future."

43. Annegret Fauser, "The Marvels of Technology," *Musical Encounters at the 1889 Paris World's Fair* (Boydell & Brewer, 2005), 297–312.

44. In fact, some evidence suggests that the ability to reuse the same cylinder was crucial to the exchange of cylinders across vast distances. For example, consider this description of an epistolary exchange of sound recordings:

> [I] found him listening with an air of great satisfaction to a record which he had on his machine. I thought that he probably had been dictating a letter to his stenographer, and was not a little surprised when he told me that he had just received a letter from his brother in Panama. "My brother has a phonograph,

too," he said, "and it was his idea that we might use it as a substitute for letters [. . .] It doesn't cost us much, either. The record goes as third-class mail and we use the same one for a long while. After I have listened to this as often as I wish I will shave it off and make it serve for carrying the answer." ("Send Greetings through Record," *Talking Machine World* 7, no. 5 [March 15, 1911]: 34)

45. Raymond R. Wile, "Cylinder Record Materials," *ARSC Journal* 22, no. 2 (1996): 163.

46. "If the messages which it contains are not worth keeping," Edison wrote, then using a knife and "shaving off the surface of the phonogram seven thousandths of an inch thick [. . .] gives a fresh surface." Thomas A. Edison, "The Phonograph at Work," *New York Evening Post*, November 18, 1887.

47. The "Perfected" Wax Cylinder Phonograph, Doc. 3209, in Daniel J. Weeks, Alexandra R. Rimer, Theresa M. Collins, Louis Carlat, Paul B. Israel, and Thomas A. Edison, *The Papers of Thomas A. Edison: Competing Interests, January 1888–December 1889* (Johns Hopkins University Press, 2021).

48. Various patents submitted by Edison refer specifically to shaver-related inventions: Thomas A. Edison, "Burnishing Attachment for Phonographs," Patent 382,414, issued May 8. 1888; "Method of Preparing Phonograph Recording Surfaces," Patent 393,465, issued November 27, 1888; "Phonograph," Patent 430,276, issued June 17, 1890; "Phonograph," Patent 430,278, issued June 17, 1890; "Device for Turning Off Phonogram Blanks," Patent 448,780, issued March 24, 1891; "Turning-off Device for Phonographs," Patent 448,781, issued March 24, 1891; "Smoothing Tool for Phonogram Blanks," Patent 457,344, issued August 11, 1891; "Phonograph," Patent 465,972, issued December 29, 1891; "Phonograph Cutting Tool," Patent 484,583, issued October 18, 1892; "Phonograph," Patent 488,189, issued December 20, 1892; and "Phonograph," Patent 609,268, issued August 16, 1898.

Edison was not the only enthusiast of sound recording who devoted his time to thinking about the operation of recording and erasing; other inventors also filed patents, from 1890 to 1912: Oscar Phelps Austin, "Process of Resurfacing Phonogram-Blanks," Patent 429,079, issued May 27, 1890; Thomas H. Macdonald, "Graphophone," Patent 654,317, issued July 24, 1900; P. T. Dodge, "Erasing Attachment for Phonographs," Patent 449,349, issued March 31, 1891; E. H. Amet, "Erasing Attachment for Phonographs," Patent 521,456, issued June 19, 1894; E. E. Bardsley, "Attachment for Graphophones," Patent 592,758, issued November 2, 1897; R. Nelles, "Phonograph Erasing Device," Patent 656,366, issued August 21, 1900; John W. Steele, "Graphophone Shaving Device," Patent 668,230, issued February 19, 1901; Charles A. G. Pritchard, "Graphophone-Record Shaver," Patent 669,207, issued March 5, 1901; E. R. Johnson, "Cutting Tool for Sound-Recording Machines," Patent 778,975, issued January 3, 1905; J. F. Ott, "Machine for Shaving Sound Records," Patent 796,857, issued August 8, 1905; J. D. Rockhill, "Trimmer for Phonograph Records," Patent 974,435, issued November 1, 1910; and G. C. La Mountain, "Trimmer for Phonograph Records," Patent 1032338, issued July 9, 1912.

49. A trade publication estimated the cost to be "$5,000 each per year." More pertinent to the current discussion, the article also takes note of "an interesting feature of the array of 'tools of the trade' to be found at the headquarters of the congressional reporters is *the shaving machine. The function of this apparatus is to rejuvenate the*

records so that they can be used again and again. After a record has served its purpose [. . .] the cylinder is placed in the shaving machine." "Talking Machines in National Legislature," *Talking Machine World* 4, no. 4 (April 15, 1908): 6 (my emphasis).

50. *Phonogram* 1, no. 2 (1891): 33.

51. Simon Werrett, *Thrifty Science: Making the Most of Materials in the History of Experiment* (University of Chicago Press, 2019).

52. Kyle S. Barnett, "Furniture Music: The Phonograph As Furniture, 1900–1930," *Journal of Popular Music Studies* 18, no. 3 (2006): 301–24; JoAnne Yates, *Control through Communication: The Rise of System in American Management* (Johns Hopkins University Press, 1989); Craig Robertson, *The Filing Cabinet: A Vertical History of Information* (University of Minnesota Press, 2021).

53. National Phonograph Company, *The Phonograph and How to Use It* (National Phonograph Co., 1900), 16.

54. Benjamin Welton, "The Man Arthur Conan Doyle Called 'America's Sherlock Holmes,'" *The Atlantic*, November 20, 2013.

55. "Indianapolis Gleanings," *The Talking Machine World* 7, no. 9 (September 15, 1911).

56. "The Four-minute Recorder and New Shaving Machine," *The Phonograph Monthly* 10, no. 8 (August 1912): 3–5.

57. National Phonograph Company, *The Phonograph and How to Use It*, 123.

58. For more on the boxy nature of media, see Christopher Cook, "Entertainment in a Box: Domestic Design and the Radiogram and Television," *Music in Art* 35, no. 1–2 (2010): 266; Paul Frosh, "The Face of Television," *Annals of the American Academy of Political and Social Science* 625 (2009): 87–102.

59. Thompson, "Machines, Music, and the Quest for Fidelity," 144.

60. I use the term "sound reproduction" while fully acknowledging the complexities and challenges that come with its inherent ambiguity. See Patrick Feaster, "Phonography," in *Keywords in Sound*, ed. David Novak and Matt Sakakeeny (Duke University Press, 2015), 139–50.

61. Thomas A. Edison, "Device for Turning off Phonogram-blanks," US Patent 448,780, issued July 7, 1888.

62. See, for example, Leonard DeGraaf, "Confronting the Mass Market: Thomas Edison and the Entertainment Phonograph," *Business and Economic History* 24, no. 1 (1995): 88–96.

63. Gelatt, *The Fabulous Phonograph*, 168; Peter Shambarger, "Cylinder Records: An Overview," *ARSC Journal* 26, no. 2 (1995): 138.

64. Patrick Feaster, "'A Compass of Extraordinary Range': The Forgotten Origins of Phonomanipulation," *ARSC Journal* 42, no. 2 (2011): 163–203.

65. Thomas Y. Levin, "Tones from Out of Nowhere: Rudolph Pfenninger and the Archaeology of Synthetic Sound," *Grey Room* 12 (2003): 32–37, at 41.

66. Grivel, "The Phonograph's Horned Mount," 32.

67. Simon Nelson Patten, *The New Basis of Civilization*, vol. 1 (Harvard University Press, 1968).

68. Bernard Stiegler, *Technics and Time, 2: Disorientation* (Stanford University Press, 1998), 11.

Chapter 2

1. Alain Badiou, *Cinema*, trans. Susan Spitzer (Polity, 2010), 88.

2. Béla Balázs, "Bela Balazs: The Future of Film," in *The Film Factory: Russian and Soviet Cinema in Documents 1896–1939*, ed. Ian Christie and Richard Taylor (Routledge, 2012), 144.

3. Sergei Eisenstein, "Sergei Eisenstein: Bela Forgets the Scissors," in *The Film Factory: Russian and Soviet Cinema in Documents 1896–1939*, ed. Christie and Taylor, 145.

4. Béla Balázs, *Theory of the Film: Growth of a New Art* (Dennis Dobson, Ltd., 1952).

5. Admittedly, given my interest in undoing, several issues are bound to remain outside the scope of the discussion, including the editor's tacit feel for creating rhythm and flow, and broader issues like acting, staging, and camerawork.

6. Terms used to describe filmmaking and its relevant processes are not simply descriptive. The interplay between words like "cutting," "editing," and "montage" lays bare a bias toward synthesis and assemblage in the theories discussed in this chapter. In the English-language release of Pudovkin's *Film Technique*, the translator invoked the difficulty of communicating film theory across linguistic and cultural borders. The note flags that the "only possible English equivalent" to Pudovkin's chosen term "montage" is "editing." However, the translator explains that in England—at the time of writing—an "editor" is too often perceived as someone who performs relatively menial tasks, that is, akin to a "cutter." The translator thus opts to keep "montage" when describing "the mounting or amassing of all the affective impulses." Pudovkin, *Film Technique and Film Acting*, trans. and ed. Ivor Montagu (Grove Press, 1958), 207. This distinction, drawn not on sand but on celluloid, further distances the creative from the technical. For the translator, the perceived impoverishment of artistic force in the English word "editing" echoes the diminishment of the importance of severance and discard in "editing," or whatever name we choose to give the process. I deliberately retain a degree of freedom in discussing the messy intermingling of these categories to trace what slips through the conceptual cracks.

7. Richard Taylor, *The Politics of the Soviet Cinema 1917–1929* (Cambridge University Press, 1979); Vance Kepley Jr., "'Cinefication': Soviet Film Exhibition in the 1920s," *Film History* 6, no. 2 (1994): 262–77; Kristin Thompson, "Government Policies and Practical Necessities in the Soviet Cinema of the 1920s," in *The Red Screen: Politics, Society, Art in Soviet Cinema*, ed. Anna Lawton (Routledge, 1992).

8. David Bordwell, "The Idea of Montage in Soviet Art and Film," *Cinema Journal* 11, no. 2 (1972): 9.

9. Alla Gadassik, "Ėsfir Shub on Women in the Editing Room: 'The Work of Montazhnitsy' (1927)," *Apparatus: Film, Media and Digital Cultures of Central and Eastern Europe* 6 (2018). Italics in original.

10. Vsevolod Pudovkin, Esfir Shub, et al., "To All Creative Workers in Soviet Cinema," in *The Film Factory: Russian and Soviet Cinema in Documents 1896–1939*, ed. Christie and Taylor, 322.

11. Vladimir Lenin, quoted in Anatoli Lunacharsky, "Cinema—The Greatest of the Arts," in *The Film Factory: Russian and Soviet Cinema in Documents 1896–1939*, ed. Christie and Taylor, 154.

12. Kepley, "'Cinefication,'" 268.

13. Taylor offers a lengthy discussion of the nuances between "propaganda" and "agitation," the latter spreading a single rallying cry over a blanket promotion of values, although both can coexist in one object. Taylor, *Politics of the Soviet Cinema*, 27; Robert Bird, "The Film Train Stops at Mosfilm: Aleksandr Medvedkin and the Operative Film Factory," in *In the Studio: Visual Creation and Its Material Environments*, ed. Brian R. Jacobson (University of California Press, 2020), 145–65.

14. Jamie Miller, "Soviet Cinema, 1929–41: The Development of Industry and Infrastructure," *Europe-Asia Studies* 58, no. 1 (2006): 103.

15. Anna Kolesnikov, "The Geocultural Provenance of Narratives: The Case of the Kuleshov Effect," *Film History: An International Journal* 32, no. 2 (2020): 62.

16. Lev Kuleshov, *Selected Works: Fifty Years in Film*, trans. Nina Shcherbakova (Raduga Publishers, 1987), 206.

17. Yuri Tsivian, "The Wise and Wicked Game: Re-Editing and Soviet Film Culture of the 1920s," *Film History* 8, no. 3 (1996): 327–43.

18. See Balázs, *Theory of the Film*, 119.

19. Kuleshov, *Selected Works*.

20. Kuleshov, *Selected Works*, 208.

21. For a reading of the legacy and concretization of multiple experiments into the one described above, see Kolesnikov, "The Geocultural Provenance of Narratives."

22. Dziga Vertov, *Kino-Eye: The Writings of Dziga Vertov*, trans. Kevin O'Brien, ed. Annette Michelson (University of California Press, 1984), 71.

23. Dziga Vertov, "We, a Version of a Manifesto," in *The Film Factory: Russian and Soviet Cinema in Documents 1896–1939*, ed. Christie and Taylor, 70.

24. Vertov, *Kino-Eye*.

25. Devin Fore, *Soviet Factography: Reality without Realism* (University of Chicago Press, 2024), 141.

26. Dziga Vertov, "The Factory of Facts," in *The Film Factory: Russian and Soviet Cinema in Documents 1896–1939*, ed. Christie and Taylor, 151.

27. Richard Taylor, "Eisenstein: A Soviet Artist," in *The Eisenstein Reader*, trans. Richard Taylor and William Powell, ed. Richard Taylor (BFI Publishing, 1998), 1.

28. Sergei Eisenstein, *The Film Sense*, trans. Jay Leyda (Meridian Books, 1957), 9.

29. Sergei Eisenstein, *The Eisenstein Reader*, trans. Richard Taylor and William Powell, ed. Richard Taylor (BFI Publishing, 1998), 59.

30. Esfir Shub, *Zhizn' moia–kinematograf* (Iskusstvo, 1972), 66.

31. Shub, *Zhizn' moia*; Esfir Shub, "Esfir Shub: Selected Writings," trans. Anastasia Kostina, ed. Liubov Dyshlyuk, *Feminist Media Histories* 2, no. 1 (2016): 11.

32. Shub, quoted in Jay Leyda, *Films Beget Films* (George Allen & Unwin, 1964), 27.

33. Shub, *Zhizn' moia*; Shub, "Esfir Shub: Selected Writings."

34. Shub, quoted in Leyda, *Films Beget Films*, 27.

35. Shub, "Esfir Shub: Selected Writings," 19. See also Alla Gadassik, "A Skillful Isis: Esfir Shub and the Documentarian as Caretaker," in *A Companion to Documentary Film History*, ed. Joshua Malitsky (John Wiley & Sons, 2021), 174.

36. Shub, "Esfir Shub: Selected Writings," 22.

37. Mikhail Yampolsky and Derek Spring, "Reality at Second Hand," *Historical Journal of Film, Radio and Television* 11, no. 2 (1991): 161–62.

38. Dragan Batančev, "Economics of Shortage and the Archival Impulse in Revolutionary Socialist Cinema," *The Projector* 23, no. 2 (2023): 1–11.

39. Kepley, "Cinefication," 266.

40. Taylor, *The Politics of the Soviet Cinema*, 75

41. Taylor, *The Politics of the Soviet Cinema*, 72.

42. Vance Kepley Jr., "The Origins of Soviet Cinema: A Study in Industry Development," *Quarterly Review of Film & Video* 10, no. 1 (1985): 22–38.

43. Miller, "Soviet Cinema," 110–11.

44. Thompson, "Government Policies and Practical Necessities."

45. Kepley, "Cinefication," 264.

46. Kepley, "The Origins of Soviet Cinema."

47. These were arrangements fraught with suspicion that eventually culminated in the dissolution of relations. L. Akselrod, "Dokumenty po istorii nacionalizacii russkoj kinematografii," in *Iz istorii kino: Materialy i dokumenty* (Akademii nauk USSR, 1953), 32–33.

48. Kepley, "The Origins of Soviet Cinema," 27.

49. Bohdan Y. Nebesio, "Competition from Ukraine: VUFKU and the Soviet Film Industry in the 1920s," *Historical Journal of Film, Radio and Television* 29, no. 2 (2009): 161.

50. Valery Ivanovich Fomin, "Rozhdenie sovetskogo kino 1917–1930," in *Otchet o nauchno-issledovatel'skoj rabote: Istorija kinootrasli v Rossii: Upravlenie, kinoproizvodstvo, prokat*, June 1, 2020, 274, https://culture.gov.ru/upload/mkrf/mkdocs2013/21_01_2013_2.pdf#page=23.07. My translation.

51. N. F. Preobrazhenskii, "Vospominanija o rabote VFKO," in *Iz istorii kino: Materialy i dokumenty* (Akademii nauk USSR, 1953), 90. My translation.

52. Some of his surviving films have recently resurfaced in a private collection. Following his death, his son reportedly destroyed much of the estate after failing to secure buyers. Akhmet Gazdiev, "Kavkaz na kinoplenke Nikolaja Minervina," *Bezformata*, November 30, 2016, https://magas.bezformata.com/listnews/kavkaz-na-kinoplenke-nikolaya-minervina/52785599/.

53. Akselrod, "Dokumenty po istorii nacionalizacii russkoj kinematografii," 34.

54. Kuleshov, *Selected Works*, 215. Jay Leyda mentions in passing that other *agitki* films were also shot on Minervin's positive stock, identifying this technical choice as the primary reason such films have not endured. See Jay Leyda, *Kino: A History of The Russian and Soviet Film* (George Allen & Unwin, 1960), 151.

55. Gazdiev, "Kavkaz na kinoplenke Nikolaja Minervina."

56. Advertisement for Minervin's studio in the early 1920s. *Kino-fot* 6 (January 8, 1923).

57. Kepley, "The Origins of Soviet Cinema," 33–34.

58. Batančev, "Economics of Shortage."

59. Ian Christie and Richard Taylor, "Party Cinema Conference Resolution: The Results of Cinema Construction in the USSR and the Tasks of Soviet Cinema," "RAPP

Resolution on Cinema 1929," and "RAPP Resolution on Cinema 1930," all in *The Film Factory: Russian and Soviet Cinema in Documents 1896–1939*, ed. Chistie and Taylor.

60. Miller, "Soviet Cinema," 115–19.

61. Taylor, *The Politics of the Soviet Cinema, 1917–1929*, 48.

62. Michelle Aubert, "Materials Issues in Film Archiving: A French Experience," *MRS Bulletin* 28, no. 7 (2003): 506.

63. Siobhan Angus, *Camera Geologica: An Elemental History of Photography* (Duke University, 2024), 92–93.

64. Fore, *Soviet Factography*, 27–78.

65. Catherine Walworth, *Soviet Salvage: Imperial Debris, Revolutionary Reuse, and Russian Constructivism* (Pennsylvania State University Press, 2017), 135.

66. Tsivian, "The Wise and Wicked Game," 336.

67. Esfir Shub, "The Manufacture of Facts," in *The Film Factory: Russian and Soviet Cinema in Documents 1896–1939*, ed. Christie and Taylor, 152–53.

68. Joshua Malitsky, "Esfir Shub and the Film Factory-Archive: Soviet Documentary from 1925–1928," *Screening the Past* 17 (2004).

69. Leyda, *Film Begets Film*, 28.

70. For a reading of gender representations in Soviet cinema, see Judith Mayne, *Kino and the Woman Question: Feminism and Soviet Silent Film* (Ohio State University Press, 1989).

71. Vladimir Korolevich, "On the First Words," in *Lines of Resistance: Dziga Vertov and the Twenties*, ed. Yuri Tsivian (Le Giornate del cinema muto, 2004), 202.

72. For more on women in the Soviet Union and the film industry, see Lilya Kaganovsky, "Film Editing As Women's Work: Ėsfir' Shub, Elizaveta Svilova, and the Culture of Soviet Montage," *Apparatus: Film, Media and Digital Cultures of Central and Eastern Europe* 6 (2018).

73. For instance, David Meuel, *Women Film Editors: Unseen Artists of American Cinema* (McFarland, 2016).

74. Bill Nichols, "Remaking History: Jay Leyda and the Compilation Film," *Film History* 26, no. 4 (2014): 146.

75. Nichols, "Remaking History," 146.

76. Yampolsky, "Reality at Second Hand," 162–64.

77. For a deeper engagement with the concepts of the raw and the cooked as they intersect with media technologies, see Lisa Gitelman, ed., *Raw Data Is an Oxymoron* (MIT Press, 2013).

78. Pudovkin, *Film Technique and Film Acting*, 26.

79. This took place after he had made *Red Front* with Minervin's stock. Kuleshov, *Selected Works*, 216–19.

80. Quoted in Leyda, *Kino*, 164.

81. Lev Kuleshov, "Montage as the Foundation of Cinematography," in *Kuleshov on Film: Film Writings by Lev Kuleshov*, trans. and ed. Ronald Levaco (University of California Press, 1974), 43.

82. Kuleshov, "Montage as the Foundation of Cinematography," 43, 45.

83. Vertov, *Kino-Eye*, 95.

84. Bordwell, "The Idea of Montage in Soviet Art and Film," 10.

85. Without question, archivists, conservators, and restorers habitually think of cinema as a storage medium. However, professional conversation most often revolves around long-term preservation and warding off decay. See, for example, Paolo Cherchi Usai, *The Death of Cinema: History, Cultural Memory and the Digital Dark Age* (Bloomsbury, 2019). My interest in film lies not in safeguarding but in reusing, repurposing, and continuously transforming it.

86. Murch, Walter. *In the Blink of an Eye.* (Silman-James Press, 2001): 8.

87. For a critical undertaking of this oft-told account of cinematic genealogies, see Georges Sadoul and Yvonne Templin, "English Influences on the Work of Edwin S. Porter," *Hollywood Quarterly* 3, no. 1 (1947): 41–50. The authors credit British directors James Williamson and G. A. Smith with the invention of editing, drawing on news photography for stereoscopes and magic lanterns.

88. Leyda, *Film Begets Film*, 37.

89. Alice Lovejoy, "Celluloid Geopolitics: Film Stock and the War Economy, 1939–47," *Screen* 60, no. 2 (2019): 224–41.

90. See, for example, William Stevenson, "Cutting Remarks," *Film Comment* 26, no. 4 (1990): 70–74.

91. Viktor Shklovsky, "The Work of Re-editing," in *The Film Factory: Russian and Soviet Cinema in Documents 1896–1939*, ed. Christie and Taylor, 168.

92. "The Volunteer Cutter," *Camera: The Digest of the Media Picture Industry* 11, no. 4 (1919): 4.

93. Edgar Burcksen, quoted in Lori Landay, "The Moviola and Other Analog Film Editing Machines," in *The Routledge Companion to Media Technology and Obsolescence* (Routledge, 2018), 136–47.

94. Gadassik, "A Skillful Isis," 175.

95. See, for instance, Laura Mulvey, "Visual Pleasure and Narrative Cinema," in *Feminism and Film Theory* (Routledge, 2013), 57–68; Christian Metz, *The Imaginary Signifier: Psychoanalysis and the Cinema* (Indiana University Press, 1981); Jean-Louis Baudry, "Ideological Effects of the Basic Cinematographic Apparatus," *Film Quarterly* 28, no. 2 (1974): 39–47.

96. Jean-Pierre Oudart, "Dossier Suture: Cinema and Suture," *Screen* 18, no. 4 (1977): 36–43. Daniel Dayan adds an ideological aspect that he finds lacking in such discussions. See Daniel Dayan, "The Tutor-code of Classical Cinema," *Film Quarterly* 28, no. 1 (1974): 22–31.

Chapter 3

1. Paul Valéry, quoted in Paul Virilio, *The Original Accident* (Polity, 2007), 5.

2. Vilém Flusser, *Gestures*, trans. Nancy Ann Roth (University of Minnesota Press, 2014), 145.

3. For work on video, see David Antin, "Video: The Distinctive Features of the Medium," in *Video Art* (Institute of Contemporary Art, University of Pennsylvania, 1975), 57–74; Roy Ames, *On Video* (Routledge, 1999); Michael Z. Newman, *Video Revolutions: On the History of a Medium* (Columbia University Press, 2014); Mark

McKenna, *Nasty Business: The Marketing and Distribution of the Video Nasties* (Edinburgh University Press, 2020).

4. See Jane Feuer, "The Concept of Live Television: Ontology As Ideology," in *Regarding Television: Critical Approaches—An Anthology*, ed. Ann E. Kaplan (University Publications of America, 1983), 12–23; Mimi White, "The Attractions of Television: Reconsidering Liveness," in *MediaSpace: Place, Scale and Culture in a Media Age*, ed. Nick Couldry and Anna McCarthy (Routledge, 2004), 75–91; William Lafferty, "'A New Era in TV Programming' Becomes 'Business as Usual': Videotape Technology, Local Stations, and Network Power, 1957–1961," *Quarterly Review of Film & Video* 16, no. 3–4 (1997): 405–19; Elana Levine, "Distinguishing Television: The Changing Meanings of Television Liveness," *Media, Culture & Society* 30, no. 3 (2008): 393–409; Jonathan Sterne, "Television under Construction: American Television and the Problem of Distribution, 1926–62," *Media, Culture & Society* 21, no. 4 (1999): 503–30.

5. For film archiving, see Penelope Houston, *Keepers of the Frame: The Film Archives* (British Film Institute, 1994); Grazia Ingravalle, *Archival Film Curatorship: Early and Silent Cinema from Analog to Digital* (Amsterdam University Press, 2014); Haidee Wasson, *Museum Movies: The Museum of Modern Art and the Birth of Art Cinema* (University of California Press, 2005).

6. NASA, "Update: Apollo 11 Tapes," August 16, 2006, https://www.nasa.gov/mission_pages/apollo/apollo_tapes.html.

7. NASA TV, "Briefing on Apollo 11 Moonwalk Video," July 16, 2009, video, 54:24, https://www.youtube.com/watch?v=xAPRS8DM6Mk.

8. Let me address the inevitable questions regarding moon conspiracies. Paradoxically, for those who maintain that the moon landing is a bogus nonevent straight from a Hollywood set, the loss of the tapes did little to support their epistemological inquiries, which, for decades, had relied on scrutinizing details in the footage to deny the veracity of the event.

9. This was not without critique. The most notable of philosophical oppositions to the space program was articulated by Hannah Arendt. See Hannah Arendt, "The Conquest of Space and the Stature of Man," *The New Atlantis* 18 (2007): 43–55.

10. Lorenz Engell, "Apollo TV: The Copernican Turn of the Gaze," *World Picture* 7 (2012): 4, 1.

11. For a discussion of the outline of the media events paradigm, see Daniel Dayan and Elihu Katz, *Media Events: The Live Broadcasting of History* (Harvard University Press, 1994).

12. Lynn Spigel, *Make Room for TV: Television and the Family Ideal in Postwar America TV* (University of Chicago Press, 1992), 1.

13. Dayan and Katz, *Media Events.*

14. Marshall McLuhan, *The Global Village: Transformations in World Life and Media in the 21st Century* (Oxford University Press, 1992), 4.

15. Paul Virilio, *Open Sky*, trans. Julie Rose (Verso, 2008), 131 (emphasis in original).

16. Rudolf Arnheim, "A Forecast of Television," in *Understanding Television: Essays on Television as a Social and Cultural Force*, ed. Richard Adler (Praeger, 1981), 191, 194.

17. Siegfried Zielinski, *Audiovisions: Cinema and Television as Entr'actes in History* (Amsterdam University Press, 1999), 143.

18. For a comprehensive list of early patents and initiatives, see Albert Abramson, *The History of Television, 1880 to 1941* (McFarland & Co., 1987).

19. Derek Kompare, "Transcribed Adventures: Radio and the Recording," in *Rerun Nation: How Repeats Invented American Television*, ed. Derek Kompare (Routledge, 2005).

20. Robert Vianello, "The Power Politics of 'Live' Television," *Journal of Film and Video* 37, no. 3 (Summer 1985): 26–29.

21. See Zielinski, *Audiovisions*; William Boddy, *Fifties Television: The Industry and Its Critics* (University of Illinois Press, 1990).

22. Jeff Martin, "The Dawn of Tape: Transmission Device As Preservation Medium," *The Moving Image* 5, no. 1 (2005): 45–66. That is, the capacity for retention does not automatically lead to archiving and preservation.

23. Boddy, *Fifties Television*, 8.

24. Vianello, "The Power Politics of 'Live' Television," 29.

25. Andrew Crisell, *Liveness and Recording in the Media* (Palgrave Macmillan, 2012).

26. Herbert Zettl, "The Rare Case of Television Aesthetics," *Journal of the University Film Association* 30, no. 2 (1978): 3.

27. Samuel Weber, "Television: Set and Screen," in *Mass Mediauras: Form, Technics, Media* (Stanford University Press, 1996), 117.

28. Pierre Nora, "Monster Events," *Discourse* 5 (1983): 10.

29. Pierre Nora, "The Return of the Event," in *Histories: French Constructions of the Past*, ed. Jacques Revel and Lynn Avery Hunt (New Press, 1995), 175.

30. Nora, "The Return of the Event," 443.

31. Jacques Derrida, "Above All, No Journalists," in *Religion and Media*, ed. Hent de Vries and Samuel Weber (Stanford University Press, 2001), 62.

32. Collins in *Chasing the Moon*, dir. Robert Stone (PBS, 2019).

33. Richard L. Nafzger, interview by Sandra Johnson, NASA Headquarters Oral History Project: Edited Oral History Transcript, Greenbelt, MD, June 12, 2013.

34. For further historical discussion of the various aspects of the space program, see Roger D. Launius, *Reaching for the Moon: A Short History of the Space Race* (Yale University Press, 2019).

35. Nafzger interview (my emphasis). For more context, see also David Meerman Scott and Richard Jurek, *Marketing the Moon: The Selling of the Apollo Lunar Program* (MIT Press, 2014); Roger D. Launius, "Opposing Apollo: Political Resistance to the Moon Landings," *New Space* 2, no. 2 (2014): 74–80.

36. On learning that, although a working Westinghouse color camera was aboard the command and service module (and had already been tested on the Apollo 10), it would ultimately not be used to capture the moon landing, the engineer Max Faget protested that the landing "is to be recorded in such a stingy manner." Quoted in Bill Wood, "Apollo TV Essay," *Apollo Lunar Surface Journal* (2005): 17.

37. Scott and Jurek, *Marketing the Moon*.

38. Cronkite, in Stone, *Chasing the Moon.*

39. Stone, *Chasing the Moon.*

40. CBS News, *The Historic Conquest of the Moon as Reported to the American People*, aired 10:56:20 PM EDT, July 20, 1969 (Columbia Broadcasting System, 1970), 6.

41. NASA TV, "Briefing on Apollo 11 Moonwalk Video."

42. Lynn Spigel, "From Domestic Space to Outer Space: The 1960s Fantastic Family Sit-Com," in *Close Encounters: Film, Feminism, and Science Fiction*, ed. Constance Penley, Elisabeth Lyon, Lynn Spigel, and Janet Bergstrom (University of Minnesota Press, 1991), 205.

43. Admittedly, though, NASA had already contracted Westinghouse for an exploration-adequate camera design in 1964 and the astronauts were trained to use the camera despite its contentious status among those involved in planning the missions.

44. Nafzger interview.

45. For more detail and for images that exemplify the visible difference between the slow scan and its conversion, see Colin Mackellar, "Comparison Photographs of the Apollo 11 Lunar Television As Seen at Goldstone, Honeysuckle Creek, Parkes and Houston," NASA, December 2005, https://history.nasa.gov/alsj/a11/a11TVcomparisons.pdf.

46. Nafzger interview (my emphasis).

47. Nafzger interview.

48. NASA, n.d. (c. 2009), "The Apollo 11 Telemetry Data Recording: A Final Report," https://www.hq.nasa.gov/alsj/a11/Apollo_11_TV_Tapes_Report.pdf.

49. Although Oberlin Smith published a letter in *The Electric World* suggesting that an iron ribbon or a cotton thread covered with steel dust instead of Edison's tinfoil could be a cheaper and more durable carrier for sound recording, he never produced a working model. Smith's intervention therefore went unnoticed for roughly fifty years. Oberlin Smith, "Some Possible Form of the Phonograph," *The Electric World*, September 8, 1888, 116.

50. Peter McMurray, "Once upon Time: A Superficial History of Early Tape," *Twentieth-Century Music* 14, no. 1 (2017): 27.

51. Mark H. Clark and Henry Nielsen, "The Telegraphone," in *Magnetic Recording: The First 100 Years*, ed. Eric D. Daniel, C. Denis Mee, and Mark H. Clark (IEEE Press, 1999).

52. Ampex, V-1000 Videotape Recorder: Industrial Manual, Ampex Corporation Records, Stanford University, M1230, box 15, p. DRP-1.

53. Jeff Martin's "The Dawn of Tape" is one exception.

54. McMurray, "Once upon Time."

55. Clark and Nielsen, "The Telegraphone," 19.

56. Quoted in Abramson, *The History of Television*, 2.

57. William Lafferty, "The Blattnerphone: An Early Attempt to Introduce Magnetic Recording into the Film Industry," *Cinema Journal* 22, no. 4 (1983): 18–37.

58. Semi Joseph Begun, "Device to Prevent Accidental Erasure of Magnetic Re-

cording," US Patent 2,508,485, issued May 23, 1950; "Demagnetizing Apparatus for Magnetic Recorders," US Patent 2,535,481A, issued December 26, 1950; "Apparatus for Demagnetizing a Magnetic Recording-Reproducer," US Patent 2,538,893, issued January 23, 1951; "Automatic Erase for Magnetic Recorders," US Patent, 2,589,035, issued March 11, 1952; "Magnetic Reproducing Device with Means to Prevent Accidental Erasure of Record Medium," US Patent 2,594,848A, issued April 29, 1952; "Apparatus for Demagnetizing Magnetic Recording-Reproducing Heads," US Patent 2,604,548, issued July 22, 1952; "Erase Head for Use with Commercial Alternating Current or Equivalent," US Patent 2,604, issued January 23, 1952.

59. Basil Lane, "75 Years of Magnetic Recording: From Steel to Plastic," *Wireless World* (May 1975): 225.

60. Begun, "Device to Prevent Accidental Erasure of Magnetic Recording."

61. NASA TV, "Briefing on Apollo 11 Moonwalk Video."

62. NASA, "The Apollo 11 Telemetry Data Recording," 16.

63. NASA, "The Apollo 11 Telemetry Data Recording," 10.

64. David Leonard, "Search for Apollo 11 TV Tapes Moves into High Gear," August 24, 2006, https://www.space.com/2793-search-apollo-11-tv-tapes-moves-high-gear.html.

65. Leonard, "Search for Apollo 11 TV Tapes," 12–13.

66. NASA, "The Apollo 11 Telemetry Data Recording," 12.

67. Heather Pringle, "NASA Dives into Its Past to Retrieve Vintage Satellite Data," *Science* 327, no. 5971 (2010): 1322–23; John Sarkissian, "The Search for Lost Apollo 11 Tapes," *CSIROscope*, March 20, 2013, https://blog.csiro.au/the-search-for-lost-apollo-11-tapes/.

68. Richard L. Hess, "Tape Degradation Factors and Challenges in Predicting Tape Life," *ARSC Journal* 39, no. 2 (2008): 258.

69. Stephen A. Schwartz, Ronald W. Beers, Miroslav Dolák, David T. Schwartz, and Darlene D. Rush, "Space Operations: NASA Is Not Properly Safeguarding Valuable Data from Past Missions," Report to the Chairmen, Committee on Science, Space, and Technology, House of Representatives (1990), 3.

70. Quoted in Marc Kaufman, "NASA Stumped in Search for Moon Tapes," *NBC News*, January 31, 2007.

71. Nora, "Monster Events," 14.

72. For instance, although the BBC today boasts an impressive collection of British television and radio recordings, Jason Jacobs describes the BBC's procedures and attitudes toward its magnetic tape collection as follows: "Even when the recording of programmes was seen as a positive necessity, this did not invalidate the conceptual and aesthetic horizons within which television was perceived: as strictly ephemeral. The dominance of such a standpoint can be seen (or, rather, it cannot) in the way videotaped material from the 1960s was routinely wiped by the BBC and ITV television companies, partly in order to reuse tapes and to save space, but crucially because tapes and space were more valuable than the preservation of television programmes." Jason Jacobs, *The Intimate Screen: Early British Television Drama* (Clarendon Press, 2000), 11.

73. “Douglas Edwards and the News,” promotional material by Merlin Engineering Works, Ampex Corporation Records, Stanford University, M1230, box 39.

74. Meanwhile, the institutional archiving of programs took a different path that only emerged several years later with TV archives and museums. See Lynn Spigel, “Our TV Heritage: Television, the Archive, and the Reasons for Preservation,” in *A Companion to Television*, ed. Janet Wasko (Blackwell Publishing, 2005).

75. Lucas Hilderbrand, *Inherent Vice: Bootleg Histories of Videotape and Copyright* (Duke University Press, 2009).

76. “[Apollo 11]. Original, First-Generation NASA Videotape Recordings of the Apollo 11 Lunar EVA,” Sotheby’s, https://www.sothebys.com/en/buy/auction/2019/space-exploration/apollo-11-original-first-generation-nasa-videotape.

77. Mark A. Greene, “I’ve Deaccessioned and Lived to Tell About It: Confessions of an Unrepentant Reappraiser,” *Archival Issues* 30, no.1 (2006): 7.

78. Martin Gammon, *Deaccessioning and Its Discontents: A Critical History* (MIT Press, 2018).

79. Greene, “I’ve Deaccessioned and Lived to Tell About It.”

80. Gammon, *Deaccessioning and Its Discontents.*

81. Nafzger interview (my emphasis).

Chapter 4

1. From *Species of Spaces and Other Pieces* by Georges Perec, published by Penguin Classics. Copyright © Translation and Notes copyright © John Sturrock, 1997, 1999. *Especes d’Espaces* copyright © Editions Galilee, 1994. Reprinted by permission of Penguin Books Limited.

2. Marshall McLuhan, “The Typewriter: Into the Age of the Iron Whim,” in *Understanding Media: The Extensions of Man* (MIT Press, 1994), 262.

3. McLuhan, “The Typewriter,” 262.

4. Abigail J. Sellen and Richard H. R. Harper, *The Myth of the Paperless Office* (MIT Press, 2003).

5. See Lisa Gitelman, *Paper Knowledge: Toward a Media History of Documents* (Duke University Press, 2014); Ben Kafka, “A Riot on Every Page: Archive, Bureaucracy, Paranoia,” in *Peter Piller Archive, Materials (G) Albedo* (Walther, 2014).

6. Sybille Krämer, “Writing, Notational Iconicity, Calculus: On Writing as a Cultural Technique,” *MLN* 118, no. 3 (2003): 522.

7. John Durham Peters, *The Marvelous Clouds: Toward a Philosophy of Elemental Media* (University of Chicago Press, 2015), 291.

8. Jacques Derrida, “Paper or Me, You Know . . . ,” in *Paper Machine* (Stanford University Press, 2005), 52.

9. Cornelia Vismann, “Out of File, Out of Mind,” in *New Media, Old Media: A History and Theory Reader*, ed. Wendy Hui Kyong Chun, Anna Watkins Fisher, and Thomas Keenan (Routledge, 2005), 99.

10. Vismann, “Out of File, Out of Mind,” 100. See also Cornelia Vismann, *Files: Law and Media Technology*, trans. Geoffrey Winthrop-Young (Stanford University Press, 2008), 125–29.

11. Darren Sean Wershler-Henry, *The Iron Whim: A Fragmented History of Typewriting* (Cornell University Press, 2007), 35.

12. Lisa Gitelman, *Scripts, Grooves, and Writing Machines* (Stanford University Press, 2000).

13. Scholars have traced the different needs and uses that converged with this invention, including as an aid for people with disabilities and as a tool for the blind; see discussions in Wershler-Henry, *The Iron Whim*; Friedrich Kittler, *Gramophone, Film, Typewriter*, trans. Geoffrey Winthrop-Young and Michael Wutz (Stanford University Press, 1999).

14. Harold A. Innis, *Empire and Communications* (Dundurn Press, 2007); Max Weber, "Chapter XI Bureaucracy," in *Economy and Society* (University of California Press, 1987), 957.

15. Vismann, *Files: Law and Media Technology*, 129.

16. James R. Beniger, *The Control Revolution: Technological and Economic Origins of the Information Society* (Harvard University Press, 1986).

17. JoAnne Yates, *Control through Communication: The Rise of System in American Management* (Johns Hopkins University Press, 1989).

18. Yates, *Control through Communication*, 1–20. See also Craig Robertson, *The Filing Cabinet: A Vertical History of Information* (University of Minnesota Press, 2021).

19. Yates, *Control through Communication*, 43; see also Kim England and Kate Boyer, "Women's Work: The Feminization and Shifting Meanings of Clerical Work," *Journal of Social History* 42, no. 2 (2009): 311.

20. Kittler, *Gramophone, Film, Typewriter*, 183.

21. Kittler, *Gramophone, Film, Typewriter*, 221.

22. Gitelman, *Paper Knowledge*, 1.

23. Elizabeth L. Eisenstein, *The Printing Revolution in Early Modern Europe* (Cambridge University Press, 2012), 56.

24. Lothar Müller, *White Magic: The Age of Paper* (Polity Press, 2014), 83; Wershler-Henry, *The Iron Whim*.

25. Anthony Grafton, "Correctors Corruptors? Notes on the Social History of Editing," in *Editing Texts = Texte Edieren*, ed. Glenn W. Most (Vandenhoeck & Ruprecht, 1998), 54–76.

26. Ann Blair, "Errata Lists and the Reader as Corrector," in *Agents of Change: Print Culture Studies after Elizabeth L. Eisenstein*, ed. Sabrina Alcorn Baron, Eric N. Lindquist, and Eleanor F. Shevlin (University of Massachusetts Press, 2007), 21–41.

27. Adam Smyth, "Errors and Corrections: 'My Galley Charged with Forgetfulness,'" in *Material Texts in Early Modern England* (Cambridge University Press, 2018), 77.

28. Multigraph Collective, *Interacting with Print: Elements of Reading in the Era of Print Saturation* (University of Chicago Press, 2018).

29. Matthew G. Kirschenbaum, *Track Changes: A Literary History of Word Processing* (Belknap Press of Harvard University Press, 2016), 34.

30. Earl G. Blackstone and Sofrona L. Smith, *Improvement of Instruction in Typewriting* (Prentice-Hall, 1936), vi.

31. Blackstone and Smith, *Improvement of Instruction in Typewriting*, vi.

32. Blackstone and Smith, *Improvement of Instruction in Typewriting*, 452.

33. Paul Benzon, *Archival Fictions: Materiality, Form, and Media History in Contemporary Literature* (MIT Press, 2021), 29.

34. Blackstone and Smith, *Improvement of Instruction in Typewriting*, 412.

35. Wershler-Henry, *The Iron Whim*, 147.

36. Isaac Pitman, *A Manual of the Typewriter: A Practical Guide to Commercial, Literary, Legal, Dramatic and All Classes of Typewriting Work* (Isaac Pitman & Sons, 1893), 25.

37. Eberhard Faber, "The Sudden Disappearance of Miss Take: A Short Story," promotional materials for typewriter erasers. Available at the *Contrapuntalism* blog, https://contrapuntalism.blog/2016/01/20/the-sudden-disappearance-of-miss-take/

38. Including, but not limited to, Hélène Cixous, "The Laugh of the Medusa," *Signs: Journal of Women in Culture and Society* 1, no. 4 (1976): 875–93; Donna Haraway, "Situated Knowledges: The Science Question in Feminism and the Privilege of Partial Perspective," *Feminist Studies* 14, no. 3 (1988): 575–99; Judith Butler, *Gender Trouble* (Routledge, 2002); Sara Ahmed, *Queer Phenomenology: Orientations, Objects, Others* (Duke University Press, 2020).

39. Rachel Plotnick, "Tethered Women, Mobile Men: Gendered Mobilities of Typewriting," *Mobile Media & Communication* 8, no. 2 (2020): 188–208.

40. Kirschenbaum, *Track Changes.*

41. Hannah Sullivan, *The Work of Revision* (Harvard University Press, 2013).

42. Perec, *Species of Spaces and Other Pieces*, 12.

43. Craig Douglas Dworkin, *No Medium* (MIT Press, 2013); Benzon, *Archival Fictions.*

44. Benzon, *Archival Fictions*, 25.

45. Wershler-Henry, *The Iron Whim*, 43.

46. Wershler-Henry, *The Iron Whim.*

47. Letter, John G. Callan to Mr. Henry J. Guild, March 31, 1932, John G. Callan Papers, HBS Archives, Baker Library, Harvard Business School.

48. John G. Callan, "Typewriter Paper of Deferred Indelibility and Method of Preparing the Same," US Patent 1994, 750, issued March 19, 1935. The best known of the mills to produce the paper was Eaton's Paper Company, which sublicensed from Brightwater Paper Company to produce this special bond.

49. Letter, Brightwater Paper Company, mailing materials for Cosmic Bond, John G. Callan Collection, HBS Archives, Baker Library, Harvard Business School.

50. Memorandum, "Statement of Method of Making 'Delible' and Similar Typewriter Bond Paper," sent to A. B. Marsh, November 24, 1934, John G. Callan Papers, HBS Archives, Baker Library, Harvard Business School.

51. Letter, Henry J. Guild to John G. Callan, August 9, 1934, John G. Callan Papers, HBS Archives, Baker Library, Harvard Business School.

52. Quoted from promotional material, no further information available. John G. Callan Collection, HBS Archives, Baker Library, Harvard Business School.

53. Quoted from promotional material, no further information available. John G. Callan Collection, HBS Archives, Baker Library, Harvard Business School.

54. Memorandum, "Statement of Method of Making 'Delible.'"

55. For a history of rubber erasers, see Henry Petroski, *The Pencil: A History of Design and Circumstance* (Random House, 1992).

56. Petroski, *Pencil History*, 511, 514. See also Carlin Wing, "Episodes in the Life of Bounce," *Cabinet* 56 (Winter 2014–2015).

57. Eberhard Faber Catalog, n.d., 81. https://ia902609.us.archive.org/1/items/466SheafferCatalogOfDeskSets1970s39Pages_201410/25 3-eberhard-faber-catalog-of-wood-pencils-erasers-1923-part-2–50-pages.pdf.

58. This idea has had a rather recent renaissance. In 2009, Xerox was granted a patent for erasable paper or "reimageable transient documents." Grace T. Brewington, Anthony S. Condello, Daniel M. Bray, "Erase and Writing Continuous for Erasable Media," Patent EP2287005B1, priority August 17, 2009.

59. Although it should be noted that Graham initially attempted to produce something similar to Corrasable Bond. As she recalled in a radio interview in 1969, the Liquid Paper company also produced a paper that was based on "the idea of correction [. . .] same correction method except it is the paper coated with white carbon system." See Bette Nesmith Graham, Interview by Walt Nielson, Radio Station KXXK, May 10, 1969, 3, North Texas State University, Business Oral History Collection.

60. The concept of "palimpsest" differs in the fields of art history and literary studies; for the latter, the term "palimpsest" is used to describe multiplicity, a text within a text within a text (à la Roland Barthes and Gérard Genette). For the former, it denotes a text beneath a text beneath a text. See Richard Galpin, "Erasure in Art: Destruction, Deconstruction, and Palimpsest," February 1998, https://www.richardgalpin.co.uk/erasureinart.

61. Promotional materials of the Liquid Paper company from the 1980s point to a different location as "found in mom's basement."

62. Bette Nesmith Graham, Speech at the New Enterprise Club Harvard Business School, March 9, 1977, 2, North Texas State University, Business Oral History Collection.

63. Quoted in R. J. Powell, "Memory of 'White-Out' Shan't Be Erased," *Wall Street Journal*, October 16, 1986, 1.

64. Nesmith Graham, Interview by Walt Nielson, Radio Station KXXK, May 10, 1969, 7.

65. Bette Nesmith Graham, Speech to Rotary Club, n.d., 5, North Texas State University, Business Oral History Collection.

66. Nesmith Graham, Interview by Ruth Anderson, 16, North Texas State University, Business Oral History Collection.

67. Nesmith Graham, Interview by Ruth Anderson, 19, North Texas State University, Business Oral History Collection.

68. Ethlie Ann Vare and Greg Ptacek, "Mothers of Invention: For Women, History Is Patently Wrong," *Chicago Tribune*, January 31, 1988.

69. Vare and Ptacek, "Mothers of Invention: For Women, History Is Patently Wrong."

70. Bette Nesmith Graham, Interview by Ruth Anderson, 15, North Texas State University, Business Oral History Collection.

71. Bruno Latour and Steve Woolgar, *Laboratory Life: The Construction of Scientific Facts* (Princeton University Press, 1986). See also Timothy Lenoir, ed., "Inscription Practices and Materialities of Communication," in *Inscribing Science: Scientific Texts and the Materiality of Communication* (Stanford University Press, 1998); Hans-Jörg Rheinberger, "Economy of Scribble," in *An Epistemology of the Concrete: Twentieth-century Histories of Life* (Duke University Press, 2010).

72. Arthur Schawlow, B. P. Stoicheff, and Suzanne Riess, *Optics and Laser Spectroscopy: Bell Telephone Laboratories, 1951–1961, and Stanford University since 1961: Oral history transcript* (1988), 100. https://archive.org/details/opticslaserspectooscharich.

73. Letter, A. M. Johnson to Arthur L. Schawlow, April 7, 1972, box 81, Arthur Schawlow Papers, Special Collection, Stanford University.

74. Patricia Daukantas, "Credible (and Edible) Lasers: The Life of Arthur L. Schawlow," *Optics and Photonics News* 22, no. 5 (2011): 22–28.

75. He refiled the application after some modifications. Arthur Schawlow, "Method of and Apparatus for Erasing," US Patent 3,553,421A, filed November 7, 1968, and issued January 5, 1971.

76. Schawlow, "Method of and Apparatus for Erasing"; Theodor W. Hänsch, "Edible Lasers and Other Delights of the 1970s," *Optics & Photonics News* (2005). Hänsch recounts his time working as a postdoctoral fellow at Schawlow's lab, where they tested, among other things, laser dyes using edible gelatin.

77. Schawlow, "Method of and Apparatus for Erasing."

78. Schawlow, "Method of and Apparatus for Erasing."

79. Schawlow, "Method of and Apparatus for Erasing."

80. Schawlow, Stoicheff, and Riess, *Optics and Laser Spectroscopy*, 213.

81. Arthur L. Schawlow, Letter to Jean-Pierre Dreyfus, December 5, 1975, Arthur Schawlow Papers, box 81, Special Collection, Stanford University.

82. Arthur L. Schawlow, Letter to Eric H. Pinnington, March 28, 1969, Arthur Schawlow Papers, box 82, Special Collection, Stanford University.

83. Niels J. Reimers, Letter to C. Frederick Ekman, August 18, 1971, Arthur Schawlow Papers, box 81, Special Collection, Stanford University.

84. Ronald R. Larsen, Letter to Niels Reimers with NSF draft, January 23, 1973, Arthur Schawlow Papers, box 82, Special Collection, Stanford University; and G. Marks, Letter to Arthur L. Schawlow, October 25, 1967, Arthur Schawlow Papers, box 82, Special Collection, Stanford University.

85. Arthur Schawlow, Interview with Walter Cronkite, in *The Laser: A Light Fantastic*, dir. Peter Poor, CBS News, 1967. https://archive.org/details/gov.archives.arc.53891.

86. Schawlow, Interview with Cronkite, in *The Laser: A Light Fantastic.*

87. Katherine D. Wheeler, Letter to Arthur L. Schawlow, February 1, 1965, Arthur Schawlow Papers, box 82, Special Collection, Stanford University.

88. In several letters, he indicated that the initial cost would amount to a $2,000 retail price per unit when produced "by hand, one at a time." A "moderate production" would bring down the cost to $200. If this launch were to succeed, further reduction of production costs would be possible in the event the process was automated. See, for instance, Arthur L. Schawlow, Letter to Robert H. Alpen, March 16, 1971, Arthur Schawlow Papers, box 81, Special Collection, Stanford University.

89. Arthur L. Schawlow, Letter, to A. M. Johnson, May 22, 1972, Arthur Schawlow Papers, box 81, Special Collection, Stanford University.

90. Jens Schröter, "The Laser: On the Quantum Materiality of Media in the Twentieth Century," *NECSUS: European Journal of Media Studies* 11, no. 2 (2022): 46–68.

91. Schawlow, Stoicheff, and Riess, *Optics and Laser Spectroscopy,* 14.

92. One typing ball could be replaced by another depending on typeface preferences.

93. John Harwood, *The Interface: IBM and the Transformation of Corporate Design, 1945–1976* (University of Minnesota Press, 2011), 187.

94. Emerson W. Pugh, Lyle R. Johnson, and John H. Palmer, *IBM's 360 and Early 370 Systems* (MIT Press, 1991), 612.

95. "Typewriter of the Electronic Era," *Business Day, New York Times,* November 23, 1984.

96. F. J. Steinberg, "IBM Introduces a Typewriter That Erases," *Computers and Automation* (May 1973): 43.

97. D. Elbert and G. Waldrip, "Adhesively Eradicable Transfer Medium," US Patent 3,825,470, issued July 23, 1974.

98. IBM Correcting Selectric II promotional brochure, n.d., courtesy of the IBM archives.

99. For a discussion of this device, see Kirschenbaum, *Track Changes,* 2016.

100. Tom Eblen, "IBM Retiree Tells How He Helped Invent Word Processing in Lexington," *Lexington Herald Leader,* April 21, 2014.

101. Raymond F. Pieslak and Charles M. Jochem, *Magnetic Tape Selectric Typewriter* (Vocational-Technical Curriculum Laboratory, Rutgers University, 1974), 138.

102. IBM Corp., "IBM Magnetic Tape Selectric Composer: Record Unit Training Guide MT/ST Models II and IV (for Graphics)," 1968, https://ia800805.us.archive.org/26/items/IBM-MTSC-TrainingGuide/IBM%20Magnetic%20Tape%20Selectric%20Composer%20training%20guide.pdf.

103. Steven J. DeRose and Andries Van Dam, "Document Structure and Markup in the FRESS Hypertext System," *Markup Languages* 1, no. 1 (1999): 7–32.

104. Belinda Barnet, "Crafting the User-centered Document Interface: The Hypertext Editing System (HES) and the File Retrieval and Editing System (FRESS)," *Digital Humanities Quarterly* 4, no. 1 (2010).

105. Perec, *Species of Spaces and Other Pieces,* 210.

106. Bruno Latour, "Visualisation and Cognition: Drawing Things Together," *Knowledge and Society: Studies in the Sociology of Culture and Present* 6 (1986): 2.

107. Wershler-Henry, *The Iron Whim*.

108. Rachel Plotnick, "The Unclean Human-machine Interface," in *Computer Architectures* (Routledge, 2019), 114.

Chapter 5

1. Vilém Flusser, "On Memory (Electronic or Otherwise)," *Leonardo* 23, no. 4 (1990): 397–99.

2. Angela Moscaritolo, "Google's Schmidt Concerned by Lack of Internet 'Delete Button,'" *PC Mag*, May 6, 2013.

3. Richard Esguerra, "Google CEO Eric Schmidt Dismisses the Importance of Privacy," *Electronic Frontier Foundation,* December 10, 2009, https://www.eff.org/deeplinks/2009/12/google-ceo-eric-schmidt-dismisses-privacy.

4. Viktor Mayer-Schönberger, *Delete: The Virtue of Forgetting in the Digital Age* (Princeton University Press, 2009). In a similar vein, see Kate Eichhorn, *The End of Forgetting: Growing up with Social Media* (Harvard University Press, 2019).

5. Mayer-Schönberger, *Delete,* ix.

6. Mayer-Schönberger, *Delete,* ix. Consequently, numerous activists and scholars have proposed various transient models for reimagining the internet, beginning with Martin Dodge and Rob R. Kitchin, "'Outlines of a World Coming into Existence': Pervasive Computing and the Ethics of Forgetting," *Environment and Planning B: Planning and Design* 34, no. 3 (2007): 431–45; Liam J. Bannon, "Forgetting As a Feature, Not a Bug: The Duality of Memory and Implications for Ubiquitous Computing," *CoDesign* 2, no. 01 (2006): 3–15. A recent manifestation of this logic can be identified in the revival of "selective forgetting" within AI development, where the concept reemerges, albeit in a different guise. Although it is less concerned with data storage, the emphasis on forgetting in AI training and learning echoes familiar biotechnical discourses: "enabling AI with more humanlike processes, like adaptive forgetting, is one way to foster more flexible performance." Quoted in Amos Zeeberg, "How Selective Forgetting Can Help AI Learn Better," *Quanta Magazine*, February 28, 2024, https://www.quantamagazine.org/how-selective-forgetting-can-help-ai-learn-better-20240228/.

7. Chris Conley, "The Right to Delete," *AAAI Spring Symposium Series* (2011).

8. And so did regulatory bodies. Although not erased, access to information can be severed. The 2014 ruling by the EU's Court of Justice, often dubbed the "right to be forgotten" (legally, the "right to erasure"), compelled Google to allow users to request the removal of harmful search results. Although a significant legal development, it offers limited control over published content. Users do not hold full authority; companies, guided by their own policies, ultimately decide. As May Crockett asserts, these regulatory attempts fall short of granting true control, leaving erasure often incomplete. May Crockett, "The Internet (Never) Forgets," *SMU Science & Technology Law Review* 19, no. 2 (2017): 151–81.

9. Julian Stallabrass, *Gargantua: Manufactured Mass Culture* (Verso, 1996), 418.

10. Anita L. Allen, "Dredging Up the Past: Lifelogging, Memory, and Surveillance," *The University of Chicago Law Review* 75, no. 1 (2008): 63.

11. Luciano Floridi, *The Fourth Revolution: How the Infosphere Is Reshaping Human Reality* (Oxford University Press, 2014).

12. To clarify before I proceed, some common deletions that are undeniably intriguing—for example, those performed by content moderators, whose labor of negation shapes social media, or streaming services, which regularly deplatform films and TV shows from their catalog due to fees and licensing agreements—are outside this chapter's immediate scope and engagement with storage. As platforms such as YouTube, Meta, X, and Snap transitioned from "sharing enterprises" and "social facilitators" to media corporations, they prompted cries for regulation. Until recently, most of the tech giants complied and promised to exercise greater control over what content could circulate and remain on their platforms. These decisions entail determining what is appropriate, viewable, and sensible. As Tarleton Gillespie explains, the paid profession of content moderation emerged from the chaotic confrontation between advocates for free speech within semi-public spaces and the rising demand for censorship of harmful content, including misinformation, defamation, harassment, and racism. Consequently, this gave rise to professional content moderators who perform the "front-line screening" work, deciding which materials to remove or keep, as Sarah Roberts highlights. Unlike the volunteer moderation seen in early internet spaces like bulletin board systems (BBS), current social media moderation is a multifaceted process involving numerous actors, including algorithmic tools and human decision-makers. Although terms of service and community guidelines offer some general parameters about prohibited content, Roberts emphasizes how these anonymous workers must make nuanced decisions regarding what constitutes a violation worthy of removal, often working within unclear and shifting guidelines. Tarleton Gillespie, *Custodians of the Internet: Platforms, Content Moderation, and the Hidden Decisions That Shape Social Media* (Yale University Press, 2018); Sarah T. Roberts, *Behind the Screen: Content Moderation in the Shadows of Social Media* (Yale University Press, 2019), 3; Sarah T. Roberts, "Digital Detritus: 'Error' and the Logic of Opacity in Social Media Content Moderation," *First Monday* 23, no. 3–5 (2018).

13. Sam Biddle, "Facebook Engineers: We Have No Idea Where We Keep All Your Personal Data," *The Intercept*, September 7, 2022, https://theintercept.com/2022/09/07/facebook-personal-data-no-accountability/; Catherine Thorbecke, "Why Deleting Something from the Internet Is 'Almost Impossible,'" *CNN*, September 18, 2022.

14. John Durham Peters, *The Marvelous Clouds: Toward a Philosophy of Elemental Media* (University of Chicago Press, 2015), 315.

15. Plato, *Plato: Collected Dialogues*, trans. R. Hackforth, ed. Edith Hamilton and Huntington Cairns (Princeton University Press, 1955).

16. Jacques Derrida, *Post Card: From Socrates to Freud and Beyond* (University of Chicago Press, 1987); Bernard Stiegler, *Technics and Time 1: The Fault of Epimetheus* (Stanford University Press, 1998); Paul Ricœur, *Memory, History, Forgetting* (University of Chicago Press, 2004).

17. Jacques Derrida, *Mémoires for Paul de Man* (Columbia University Press, 1986), 107.

18. Flusser, "On Memory (Electronic or Otherwise)," 397.

19. Elena Esposito, "Tools to Remember an Ever-Changing Past," in *Forgetting Machines: Knowledge Management Evolution in Early Modern Europe*, ed. Alberto Cevolini (Brill, 2016), 335–44.

20. Esposito, "Tools to Remember an Ever-Changing Past," 339.

21. Esposito, "Tools to Remember an Ever-Changing Past," 339.

22. Bernard Stiegler, *Technics and Time 2: Disorientation* (Stanford University Press, 1998).

23. Wendy Hui Kyong Chun, *Programmed Visions: Software and Memory* (MIT Press, 2011), 98.

24. Chun, *Programmed Vision*, 160.

25. Herbert G. Wells, "World Brain: The Idea of a Permanent World Encyclopedia," *Encyclopédie française* 18 (1937): 24–11; John Presper Eckert, "A Survey of Digital Computer Memory Systems," *Proceedings of the IRE* 41, no. 10 (1953): 1393–1406; John Von Neumann, "First Draft of a Report on the EDVAC," *IEEE Annals of the History of Computing* 15, no. 4 (1993): 27–75.

26. Alan Turing, "Intelligent Machinery (1948)," in *The Essential Turing: Seminal Writings in Computing, Logic, Philosophy, Artificial Intelligence, and Artificial Life: Plus The Secrets of Enigma*, ed. B. Jack Copeland (Oxford University Press, 2004), 431.

27. Norbert Wiener, *Cybernetics: Or Control and Communication in the Animal and the Machine* (MIT Press, 2019), 167.

28. Vannevar Bush, "As We May Think," *The Atlantic Monthly*, July 1945.

29. Vannevar Bush, "Memex Revisited," in *New Media, Old Media*, ed. Wendy Hui Kyong Chun and Thomas Keenan (Routledge, 2006), 90.

30. Maël Renouard, *Fragments of an Infinite Memory* (New York Review Books, 2021).

31. Renouard, *Fragments of an Infinite Memory*, 174.

32. Renouard, *Fragments of an Infinite Memory*, 34 (my emphasis).

33. Peters, *The Marvelous Clouds*, 315–76.

34. José Van Dijck, "Datafication, Dataism and Dataveillance: Big Data between Scientific Paradigm and Ideology," *Surveillance & Society* 12, no. 2 (2014): 197–208.

35. Gordon Bell and Jim Gemmel, *Total Recall: How the E-Memory Revolution Will Change Everything* (Dutton, 2009).

36. Bell and Gemmel, *Total Recall*, 28.

37. Liran Razinsky, "The Dream of Absolute Memory: On Digital Self-Representation," *Lit: Literature Interpretation Theory* 31, no. 2 (2020): 182–201.

38. Mayer-Schönberger, *Delete*, 2, 4.

39. Bell and Gemmel, *Total Recall*, 57.

40. Nicholas Negroponte, *Being Digital* (Vintage, 1996), 58.

41. Examining data corruption, as Hito Steyerl does in her analysis of the "poor image," reveals that the quality of digital materials can degrade as easily as it can be enhanced. When textual and audiovisual objects are copied and transferred be-

tween users and across platforms, they encounter varying demands, such as format, size, and quality. As these digital objects circulate far and wide, multiple versions emerge—some of superior quality, others muddled or overlaid with additional elements, and still others fragmented by partial cuts and pastes. See Hito Steyerl, "In Defense of the Poor Image," *e-flux* 10, no. 11 (2009).

42. Jean-François Blanchette, "A Material History of Bits," *Journal of the American Society for Information Science and Technology* 62, no. 6 (2011): 1042–57.

43. Fred Turner, *From Counterculture to Cyberculture: Stewart Brand, the Whole Earth Network, and the Rise of Digital Utopianism* (University of Chicago Press, 2006).

44. Alexander R. Galloway and Eugene Thacker, *The Exploit: A Theory of Networks* (University of Minnesota Press, 2013).

45. José Van Dijck, "From Shoebox to Performative Agent: The Computer As Personal Memory Machine," *New Media & Society* 7, no. 3 (2005): 311–32; Joanne Garde-Hansen, Andrew Hoskins, and Anna Reading, eds., *Save As . . . Digital Memories* (Springer, 2009); David Lyon, *Surveillance Studies: An Overview* (Polity Press, 2007).

46. Tim O'Reilly, "What Is Web 2.0: Design Patterns and Business Models for the Next Generation of Software," September 30, 2005, https://papers.ssrn.com/sol3/papers.cfm?abstract_id=1008839.

47. Christian Fuchs, "A Contribution to the Critique of the Political Economy of Google," *Fast Capitalism* 8, no. 1 (2011): 31–50.

48. Shoshana Zuboff, *The Age of Surveillance Capitalism: The Fight for a Human Future at the New Frontier of Power* (Public Affairs, 2019). See also Nick Srnicek, *Platform Capitalism* (Polity Press, 2017).

49. Jathan Sadowski, "When Data Is Capital: Datafication, Accumulation, and Extraction," *Big Data & Society* 6, no. 1 (2019): 1–12.

50. Sadowski, "When Data Is Capital," 1.

51. Paul N. Edwards, *The Closed World: Computers and the Politics of Discourse in Cold War America* (MIT Press, 1996).

52. Tung-Hui Hu, *A Prehistory of the Cloud* (MIT Press, 2015).

53. Alexander R. Galloway, *Protocol: How Control Exists after Decentralization* (MIT Press, 2004).

54. Craig Robertson, *The Filing Cabinet: A Vertical History of Information* (University of Minnesota Press, 2021).

55. A. R. E. Taylor, "Future-proof: Bunkered Data Centers and the Selling of Ultra-secure Cloud Storage," *Journal of the Royal Anthropological Institute* 27, no. 1 (2021): 76–94.

56. Shane Brennan, "Making Data Sustainable: Backup Culture and Risk Perception," in *Sustainable Media*, ed. Nicole Starosielski and Janet Walker (Routledge, 2016), 56–76.

57. Sarah Pink, Debora Lanzeni, and Heather Horst conducted an ethnographic study on the anxiety surrounding the potential loss of digital information. Cognizant of the risk of involuntary deletions, participants in the study developed practical

routines and psychological strategies to mitigate their anxieties regarding data security. These included measures such as backing up files both locally and in the cloud to ensure the relative safety of their digital information. Sarah Pink, Debora Lanzeni, and Heather Horst, "Data Anxieties: Finding Trust in Everyday Digital Mess," *Big Data & Society* 5, no. 1 (2018): 1–14. See also Natasha Dow Schüll, "Digital Containment and Its Discontents," *History and Anthropology* 29, no. 1 (2018): 42–48.

58. Mél Hogan and Sarah T. Roberts, "Archiving for Extinction," *Media-N* 19, no. 1 (2023): 7–26.

59. Kara Keeling, *Queer Times, Black Futures* (New York University Press, 2019).

60. Renouard, *Fragments of an Infinite Memory*, 157.

61. See, for example, Aniruddha Ghosal and Vincent Thian, "Malaysia Is Betting on Data Centers to Boost its Economy. But Experts Warn They Come at a Price," *AP*, February 19, 2025; Patrick Brodie, "Data Infrastructure Studies on an Unequal Planet," *Big Data & Society* 10, no. 1 (2023): 1–14.

62. Peter Guest, "Bitcoin Mining Was Booming in Kazakhstan. Then It Was Gone," *MIT Technology Review*, January 12, 2023.

63. Gerry McGovern and Sue Branford, "The Cloud vs. Drought: Water Hog Data Centers Threaten Latin America, Critics Say," *Mongabay*, November 2, 2023, https://news.mongabay.com/2023/11/the-cloud-vs-drought-water-hog-data-centers-threaten-latin-america-critics-say/.

64. Sati Sargsyan, "Data Centers and Indigenous Sovereignty," in *Centering the Margins of Digital Culture*, ed. A. Kaun and P. Åker (Södertörn University Press, 2023), 9–38; Tonia Sutherland and Gailyn Bopp, "The Pacific Futures of Subsea Data Centers," *New Media & Society* 25, no. 2 (2023): 345–60.

65. Nanna Bonde Thylstrup, Daniela Agostinho, Annie Ring, Catherine D'Ignazio, and Kristin Veel, "Big Data As Uncertain Archives," in *Uncertain Archives: Critical Keywords for Big Data*, ed. Thylstrup et al. (MIT Press, 2021), 1–28.

66. Mél Hogan, "The Archive As Dumpster," *Pivot: A Journal of Interdisciplinary Studies and Thought* 4, no. 1 (2015): 20 (my emphasis).

67. Daniel Rosenberg, "Word," in *Uncertain Archives*, ed. Thylstrup et al., 579–83.

68. Hans Peter Luhn, "Key Word-in-context Index for Technical Literature (kwic index)," *American Documentation* 11, no. 4 (1960): 288.

69. Jonathan Sterne, *MP3: The Meaning of a Format* (Duke University Press, 2012); Mayer-Schönberger, *Delete*; Cory Arcangel, "On Compression," in *This Is a Couple Thousand Short Films about Glenn Gould: A Book in Relation to a Project of the Same Name*, ed. Cory Arcangel, Paul Morley, and Steven Bode (Film and Video Umbrella, 2008), 220–32; Daniel Palmer, "The Rhetoric of the JPEG," in *The Photographic Image in Digital Culture* (Routledge, 2013), 149–64.

70. Eckert, "A Survey of Digital Computer Memory Systems," 1394.

71. Robert S. Wahl, "The History of Punched Cards: Using Paper to Store Information," in *The Routledge Companion to Media Technology and Obsolescence*, ed. Mark J. P. Wolf (Routledge, 2019), 27–45.

72. James Allen-Robertson, "The Materiality of Digital Media: The Hard Disk

Drive, Phonograph, Magnetic Tape and Optical Media in Technical Close-up," *New Media & Society* 19, no. 3 (2017): 455–70.

73. Matthew G. Kirschenbaum, *Mechanisms: New Media and the Forensic Imagination* (MIT Press, 2008).

74. Flusser, "On Memory (Electronic or Otherwise)," 397. For a view of the material burden, see, for example, Mimi Onuoha, "What It Takes to Truly Delete Data," *FiveThirtyEight*, January 30, 2017, https://fivethirtyeight.com/features/what-it-takes-to-truly-delete-data/.

75. Thomas S. Mullaney, Benjamin Peters, Mar Hicks, and Kavita Philip, *Your Computer Is on Fire* (MIT Press, 2021); Thylstrup et al., *Uncertain Archives*.

76. Stewart Brand, "Escaping the Digital Dark Age," *Library Journal* 124, no. 2 (1999): 46–48.

77. Wolfgang Ernst, *Digital Memory and the Archive*, trans. Jussi Parikka (University of Minnesota Press, 2012).

78. Chun, *Programmed Visions*, 95.

79. Brewster Kahle, "Archiving the Internet," *Scientific American* 3 (1997), 1.

80. Brewster Kahle and Ana Parejo Vadillo, "The Internet Archive: An Interview with Brewster Kahle," *19: Interdisciplinary Studies in the Long Nineteenth Century* 2015, no. 21 (2015).

81. See C. J. Reynolds and Blake Hallinan, "The Haunting of GeoCities and the Politics of Access Control on the Early Web," *New Media & Society* 23, no. 11 (2021): 3268–89. For additional discussions of by-now-dead platforms, see *Internet Histories* 6, no. 1–2 (2022).

82. Katie Mackinnon, "The Death of GeoCities: Seeking Destruction and Platform Eulogies in Web Archives," *Internet Histories* 6, no. 1–2 (2022): 237–52.

83. Similarly, after its acquisition, the photo-sharing platform Webshots purged more than a decade's worth of user-generated content spanning the period from 1999 to 2012. In response, the Internet Archive intervened—yet again—to salvage what was almost lost.

84. Quoted in Jessica Ogden, "'Everything on the Internet Can Be Saved': Archive Team, Tumblr and the Cultural Significance of Web Archiving," *Internet Histories* 6, no. 1–2 (2022): 113–32.

85. Gayle Osterberg, "Update on the Twitter Archive at the Library of Congress," Library of Congress (blog), December 26, 2017, https://blogs.loc.gov/loc/2017/12/update-on-the-twitter-archive-at-the-library-of-congress-2/?loclr=twloc.

86. Library of Congress, "Update on the Twitter Archive at the Library of Congress," December 2017, https://blogs.loc.gov/loc/files/2017/12/2017dec_twitter_white-paper.pdf.

87. Kahle, "Archiving the Internet," 1.

88. Mayer-Schönberger, *Delete*, 1–10.

89. Alex Hern, "Myspace Loses All Content Uploaded before 2016," *The Guardian*, March 18, 2019.

90. Frances Corry, "The Production of Destruction: How Employee Values Shape Platform Afterlives," *New Media & Society* (2024): 1–18.

91. Paul N. Edwards, "Platforms Are Infrastructures on Fire," in *Your Computer Is on Fire*, ed. Mullaney et al., 313–36.

92. Francine Barone, David Zeitlyn, and Viktor Mayer-Schönberger, "Learning from Failure: The Case of the Disappearing Web Site," *First Monday* 20, no. 4–5 (2015); Jonathan Zittrain, John Bowers, and Clare Stanton, "The Paper of Record Meets an Ephemeral Web: An Examination of Linkrot and Content Drift within *The New York Times*," Berkman Klein Center for Internet & Society at Harvard University, April 26, 2021, https://ssrn.com/abstract=3833133; Shawn Walker and Sheetal Agarwal, "The Missing Link: A Preliminary Typology for Understanding Link Decay in Social Media," *IConference Proceedings*, 2016, http://hdl.handle.net/2142/89413; Hany SalahEldeen and Michael Nelson, "Losing My Revolution: How Many Resources Shared on Social Media Have Been Lost?" presented at "Theory and Practice of Digital Libraries," Second International Conference, Paphos, Cyprus, September 23–27, 2012; Nanna Bonde Thylstrup, "The World's Digital Memory Is at Risk," *New York Times*, June 21, 2023; Sharon Ringel, "Studying Absence: The Ephemerality of Digital News Contexts," *Digital Journalism* (2023): 1–15; H. C. Huurdeman, J. Kamps, T. Samar et al., "Lost But Not Forgotten: Finding Pages on the Unarchived Web," *International Journal of Digital Libraries* 16 (2015): 247–65.

93. Vasilis Kostakis, "Identifying and Understanding the Problems of Wikipedia's Peer Governance: The Case of Inclusionists Versus Deletionists," *First Monday* 15, no. 31 (2010).

94. Kostakis, "Identifying and Understanding the Problems of Wikipedia's Peer Governance."

95. Anat Leshnick, "Deletion Discussions on Hebrew Wikipedia: Negotiating Global and Local Ideologies," *New Media & Society* (2022): 1–17; Heather Ford and Judy Wajcman, "'Anyone Can Edit,' Not Everyone Does: Wikipedia's Infrastructure and the Gender Gap," *Social Studies of Science* 47, no. 4 (2017): 511–27 ; Ed Erhart, "Why Didn't Wikipedia Have an Article on Donna Strickland, Winner of a Nobel Prize?" *WikiMedia*, October 4, 2018, https://wikimediafoundation.org/news/2018/10/04/donna-strickland-wikipedia/.

96. Shimrit Ben-Yair, "Updating Google Photos' Storage Policy to Build for the Future," *The Keyword* (Google blog), November 11, 2020, https://blog.google/products/photos/storage-changes/ (my emphasis).

97. Kaitlyn Tiffany, "Flickr Will Soon Start Deleting Photos—and Massive Chunks of Internet History," *Vox*, February 6, 2019, https://www.vox.com/the-goods/2019/2/6/18214046/flickr-free-storage-ends-digital-photo-archive-history.

98. Tiffany, "Flickr Will Soon Start Deleting Photos."

99. Among their many relevant writings on this topic, see Niels Brügger, *The Archived Web: Doing History in the Digital Age* (MIT Press, 2018); Anat Ben-David, "Counter-archiving Facebook," *European Journal of Communication* 35, no. 3 (2020): 249–64; Anat Ben-David, "What Does the Web Remember of Its Deleted Past? An Archival Reconstruction of the Former Yugoslav Top-level Domain," *New Media & Society* 18, no. 7 (2016): 1103–19.

100. Arguably, even the act of deleting one's account presents inherent limitations.

While many critics and activists advocate for social media account deletion as a form of resistance, the ability to withdraw and disconnect from the internet and its associated social spaces is not equally accessible to all. As Benjamin Peters points out, "a generation ago the hip rushed online; today the self-proclaimed cool minorities are logging off because, unlike most, they can." Benjamim Peters, "How Do We Live Now? In the Aftermath of Ourselves," in *Your Computer Is on Fire*, ed. Mullaney et al., 277.

101. Ella Klik, "Ephemeral Design: Platform Capitalism and the Making of a Feature," *New Media & Society* (2023): 1–17.

102. For a history of the development of this storage business, see Nathan Ensmenger, "The Cloud Is a Factory," in *Your Computer Is on Fire*, ed. Mullaney et al., 29–50.

103. For more information, see Ben Grosser, "Minus," blog post, https://bengrosser.com/projects/minus/.

Conclusion

1. Sabrina Gschwandtner, "Interview with Jud Yalkut," *Millennium Film Journal* 42 (2004).

2. Chrissie Iles, "Dream Reels: Video Films and Environments by Jud Yalkut," catalog, Whitney Museum of American Art, 2000.

3. Julian Stallabrass, "Trash," in *The Object Reader*, ed. Fiona Candlin and Raiford Guins (Routledge, 2009), 408. See also Max Liboiron and Josh Lepawsky, *Discard Studies: Wasting, Systems, and Power* (MIT Press, 2022); Greg Kennedy, *An Ontology of Trash: The Disposable and Its Problematic Nature* (SUNY Press, 2012).

4. Geoffrey C. Bowker, *Memory Practices in the Sciences* (MIT Press, 2008), 14.

5. See, for instance, Kay Boers, Becca Grose, Rebecca U. Sherwood, and Guy Walker, eds., *Erasure in Late Antiquity* (Trivent Publishing, 2024).

6. See, for instance, Isabel O'Brien, "Data Center Emissions Probably 662% Higher Than Big Tech Claims. Can It Keep Up the Ruse?" *The Guardian*, September 15, 2024.

7. Wayne Jones, "Can Data Really Be Stored Forever?" *ardrive*, https://ardrive.io/can-data-really-be-storedforever/.

8. See, for instance, Samyam Rajbhandari, Jeff Rasley, Olatunji Ruwase, and Yuxiong He, "Zero: Memory Optimizations toward Training Trillion Parameter Models," *SC20: International Conference for High Performance Computing, Networking, Storage and Analysis, IEEE* (2020): 1–16.

BIBLIOGRAPHY

Abramson, Albert. *The History of Television, 1880 to 1941*. McFarland & Co., 1987.

Adshead, Antony. "Unexpected Costs Hit Many as They Move to Cloud Storage." *Computer Weekly*, March 5, 2023.

Advertisement for Minervan's studio. *Kino-fot* 6, January 8, 1923.

Ahmed, Sara. *Queer Phenomenology: Orientations, Objects, Others*. Duke University Press, 2020.

Akselrod, L. "Dokumenty po istorii nacionalizacii russkoj kinematografii." In *Iz istorii kino: Materialy i dokumenty*. Akademii nauk USSR, 1953.

Allen, Anita L. "Dredging Up the Past: Lifelogging, Memory, and Surveillance." *The University of Chicago Law Review* 75, no. 1 (2008): 47–74.

Allen-Robertson, James. "The Materiality of Digital Media: The Hard Disk Drive, Phonograph, Magnetic Tape and Optical Media in Technical Close-up." *New Media & Society* 19, no. 3 (2017): 455–70.

Ames, Roy. *On Video*. Routledge, 1999.

Angus, Siobhan. *Camera Geologica: An Elemental History of Photography*. Duke University Press, 2024.

Antin, David. "Video: The Distinctive Features of the Medium." In *Video Art*. Institute of Contemporary Art, University of Pennsylvania, 1975.

"[Apollo 11]. Original, First-Generation NASA Videotape Recordings of the Apollo 11 Lunar EVA." Sotheby's. https://www.sothebys.com/en/buy/auction/2019/space-exploration/apollo-11-original-first-generation-nasa-videotape.

Arcangel, Cory. "On Compression." In *This Is a Couple Thousand Short Films about Glenn Gould: A Book in Relation to a Project of the Same Name*, edited by Cory Arcangel, Paul Morley, and Steven Bode. Film & Video Umbrella, 2008.

Arendt, Hannah. "The Conquest of Space and the Stature of Man." *The New Atlantis* 18 (2007): 43–55.

Arnheim, Rudolf. "A Forecast of Television." In *Understanding Television: Essays on Television as a Social and Cultural Force*, edited by Richard Adler. Praeger, 1981.

Aubert, Michelle. "Materials Issues in Film Archiving: A French Experience." *MRS Bulletin* 28, no. 7 (2003): 506–10.

Badiou, Alain. *Cinema*. Translated by Susan Spitzer. Polity, 2010.

Balázs, Béla. "Bela Balazs: The Future of Film." In *The Film Factory: Russian and Soviet Cinema in Documents 1896–1939*, edited by Ian Christie and Richard Taylor. Routledge, 2012.

Balázs, Béla. *Theory of the Film: Growth of a New Art*. Dennis Dobson, Ltd., 1952.

Bannon, Liam J. "Forgetting As a Feature, Not a Bug: The Duality of Memory and Implications for Ubiquitous Computing." *CoDesign* 2, no. 1 (2006): 3–15.

Barlow, John Perry. "Selling Wine without Bottles: The Economy of Mind on the Global Net." *Duke Law and Technology Review* 18, no. 1 (2019): 8–31.

Barnet, Belinda. "Crafting the User-centered Document Interface: The Hypertext Editing System (HES) and the File Retrieval and Editing System (FRESS)." *Digital Humanities Quarterly* 4, no. 1 (2010).

Barnett, Kyle S. "Furniture Music: The Phonograph As Furniture, 1900–1930." *Journal of Popular Music Studies* 18, no. 3 (2006): 301–24.

Barone, Francine, David Zeitlyn, and Viktor Mayer-Schönberger. "Learning from Failure: The Case of the Disappearing Web Site." *First Monday* 20, no. 4–5 (2015).

Batančev, Dragan. "Economics of Shortage and the Archival Impulse in Revolutionary Socialist Cinema." *The Projector* 23, no. 2 (2023): 1–11.

Barthes, Roland. *Camera Lucida: Reflections on Photography*. Macmillan, 1981.

Baudry, Jean-Louis. "Ideological Effects of the Basic Cinematographic Apparatus." *Film Quarterly* 28, no. 2 (1974): 39–47.

Bazin, André. "The Ontology of the Photographic Image." *Film Quarterly* 13, no. 4 (1960): 4–9.

Bell, Gordon, and Jim Gemmell. *Total Recall: How the E-Memory Revolution will Change Everything*. Dutton, 2009.

Ben-David, Anat. "Counter-archiving Facebook." *European Journal of Communication* 35, no. 3 (2020): 249–64.

Ben-David, Anat. "What Does the Web Remember of Its Deleted Past? An Archival Reconstruction of the Former Yugoslav Top-level Domain." *New Media & Society* 18, no. 7 (2016): 1103–19.

Beniger, James R. *The Control Revolution: Technological and Economic Origins of the Information Society*. Harvard University Press, 1986.

Ben-Yair, Shimrit. "Updating Google Photos' Storage Policy to Build for the Future." *The Keyword* (Google blog), November 11, 2020. https://blog.google/products/photos/storage-changes/.

Benzon, Paul. *Archival Fictions: Materiality, Form, and Media History in Contemporary Literature*. MIT Press, 2021.

Biddle, Sam. "Facebook Engineers: We Have No Idea Where We Keep All Your Personal Data." *The Intercept*, September 7, 2022. https://theintercept.com/2022/09/07/facebook-personal-data-no-accountability/.

Bird, Robert. "The Film Train Stops at Mosfilm: Aleksandr Medvedkin and the Operative Film Factory." In *In the Studio: Visual Creation and Its Material Environments*, edited by Brian R. Jacobson. University of California Press, 2020.

Blackstone, Earl G. and Sofrona L. Smith. *Improvement of Instruction in Typewriting.* Prentice-Hall, 1936.

Blair, Ann. "Errata Lists and the Reader As Corrector." In *Agents of Change: Print Culture Studies after Elizabeth L. Eisenstein*, edited by Sabrina Alcorn Baron, Eric N. Lindquist, and Eleanor F. Shevlin. University of Massachusetts Press, 2007.

Blair, Ann. "Reading Strategies for Coping with Information Overload, ca. 1550–1700." *Journal of the History of Ideas* 64, no. 1 (2023): 11–28.

Blanchette, Jean-François. "A Material History of Bits." *Journal of the American Society for Information Science and Technology* 62, no. 6 (2011): 1042–57.

Boddy, William. *Fifties Television: The Industry and Its Critics.* University of Illinois Press, 1990.

Boers, Kay, Becca Grose, Rebecca U. Sherwood, and Guy Walker, eds. *Erasure in Late Antiquity.* Trivent Publishing, 2024.

Bohlman, Andrea F., and Peter McMurray. "Tape: Or, Rewinding the Phonographic Regime." *Twentieth-Century Music* 14, no. 1 (2017): 3–24.

Bordwell, David. "The Idea of Montage in Soviet Art and Film." *Cinema Journal* 11, no. 2 (1972): 9–17.

Bowker, Geoffrey C. *Memory Practices in the Sciences.* MIT Press, 2008.

Brand, Stewart. "Escaping the Digital Dark Age." *Library Journal* 124, no. 2 (1999): 46–48.

Brennan, Shane. "Making Data Sustainable: Backup Culture and Risk Perception." In *Sustainable Media*, edited by Nicole Starosielski and Janet Walker. Routledge, 2016.

Brodie, Patrick. "Data Infrastructure Studies on an Unequal Planet." *Big Data & Society* 10, no. 1 (2023): 1–14.

Brown, Bill. "Thing Theory." *Critical Inquiry* 28, no. 1 (2001): 1–22.

Brügger, Niels. *The Archived Web: Doing History in the Digital Age.* MIT Press, 2018.

Bush, Vannevar. "As We May Think." *The Atlantic Monthly*, July 1945.

Bush, Vannevar. "Memex Revisited." In *New Media, Old Media*, edited by Wendy Hui Kyong Chun and Thomas Keenan. Routledge, 2006.

Butler, Judith. *Gender Trouble.* Routledge, 2002.

Camille, Michael. "Obscenity under Erasure." In *Obscenity: Social Control and Artistic Creation in the European Middle Ages*, edited by Jan M. Ziolkowski. Brill, 1998.

Carey, James W. "Technology and Ideology: The Case of the Telegraph." *Prospects* 8 (1983): 303–25.

Carruthers, Mary J. *The Book of Memory: A Study of Memory in Medieval Culture.* Cambridge University Press, 1992.

CBS News. *The Historic Conquest of the Moon As Reported to the American People.* Aired July 20, 1969, 10:56:20 PM EDT. Columbia Broadcasting System, 1970.

Cep, Casey. "The Real Nature of Thomas Edison's Genius." *New Yorker*, October 21, 2019.

Chun, Wendy Hui Kyong. *Programmed Visions: Software and Memory.* MIT Press, 2011.

Cixous, Hélène. "The Laugh of the Medusa." *Signs: Journal of Women in Culture and Society* 1, no. 4 (1976): 875–93.

Clark, Mark H., and Henry Nielsen. "The Telegraphone." In *Magnetic Recording: The First 100 Years*, edited by Eric D. Daniel, C. Denis Mee, and Mark H. Clark. IEEE Press, 1999.

Comolli, Jean-Louis. *Cinema against Spectacle: Technique and Ideology Revisited.* Amsterdam University Press, 2015.

Conley, Chris. "The Right to Delete." *AAAI Spring Symposium Series*, 2011.

Cook, Christopher. "Entertainment in a Box: Domestic Design and the Radiogram and Television." *Music in Art* 35, no. 1–2 (2010): 261–70.

Corry, Frances. "The Production of Destruction: How Employee Values Shape Platform Afterlives." *New Media & Society* (2024): 1–18.

Crawford, Kate. *The Atlas of AI: Power, Politics, and the Planetary Costs of Artificial Intelligence.* Yale University Press, 2021.

Craze, Joshua. "Excerpts from a Grammar of Redaction." In *Dissonant Archives: Contemporary Visual Culture and Contested Narratives in the Middle East*, edited by Anthony Downey. Bloomsbury Publishing, 2015.

Crisell, Andrew. *Liveness and Recording in the Media.* Palgrave Macmillan, 2012.

Crockett, May. "The Internet (Never) Forgets." *SMU Science & Technology Law Review* 19, no. 2 (2017): 151–81.

Cubitt, Sean. *Finite Media: Environmental Implications of Digital Technologies.* Duke University Press, 2017.

Daukantas, Patricia. "Credible (and Edible) Lasers: The Life of Arthur L. Schawlow." *Optics and Photonics News* 22, no. 5 (2011): 22–28.

Dayan, Daniel. "The Tutor-code of Classical Cinema." *Film Quarterly* 28, no. 1 (1974): 22–31.

Dayan, Daniel, and Elihu Katz. *Media Events: The Live Broadcasting of History.* Harvard University Press, 1994.

DeGraaf, Leonard. "Confronting the Mass Market: Thomas Edison and the Entertainment Phonograph." *Business and Economic History* 24, no. 1 (1995): 88–96.

DeRose, Steven J., and Andries Van Dam. "Document Structure and Markup in the FRESS Hypertext System." *Markup Languages* 1, no. 1 (1999): 7–32.

Derrida, Jacques. "Above All, No Journalists." In *Religion and Media*, edited by Hent de Vries and Samuel Weber. Stanford University Press, 2001.

Derrida, Jacques. *Archive Fever: A Freudian Impression.* University of Chicago, 1996.

Derrida, Jacques. *Mémoires for Paul de Man.* Columbia University Press, 1986.

Derrida, Jacques. *Of Grammatology.* Johns Hopkins University Press, 1997.

Derrida, Jacques. "Paper or Me, You Know . . ." In *Paper Machine.* Stanford University Press, 2005.

Derrida, Jacques. *Post Card: From Socrates to Freud and Beyond.* University of Chicago Press, 1987.

Dodge, Martin, and Rob R. Kitchin. "'Outlines of a World Coming into Existence': Pervasive Computing and the Ethics of Forgetting." *Environment and Planning B: Planning and Design* 34, no. 3 (2007): 431–45.

Doherty, Sean Paul, Stuart Henderson, Sarah Fiddyment, Jonathan Finch, and Matthew J. Collins. "Scratching the Surface: The Use of Sheepskin Parchment to Deter Textual Erasure in Early Modern Legal Deeds." *Heritage Science* 9 (2021): 1–6.

Dworkin, Craig Douglas. *No Medium*. MIT Press, 2013.

Eade, Jane. "The Theatre of Death." *Oxford Art Journal* 36, no. 1 (2013): 111.

Eberhard Faber. Catalog of Wood Pencils and Erasers, n.d. https://ia902609.us.archive.org/1/items/466SheafferCatalogOfDeskSets1970s39Pages_201410/253-eberhard-faber-catalog-of-wood-pencils-erasers-1923-part-2-50-pages.pdf.

Eberhard Faber. "The Sudden Disappearance of Miss Take: A Short Story." Promotional materials for typewriter eraser. *Contrapuntalism* (blog), January 20, 2016.

Eblen, Tom. "IBM Retiree Tells How He Helped Invent Word Processing in Lexington." *Lexington Herald Leader*, April 21, 2014.

Eckert, John Presper. "A Survey of Digital Computer Memory Systems." *Proceedings of the IRE* 41, no. 10 (1953): 1393–1406.

Edison, Thomas A. "The 'Perfected' Wax-Cylinder Phonograph Doc. 3209." In *The Papers of Thomas A. Edison: Electrifying New York and Abroad, April 1881–March 1883*, edited by Daniel J. Weeks, Alexandra R. Rimer, Theresa M. Collins, Louis Carlat, and Paul B. Israel. Johns Hopkins University Press, 1989.

Edison, Thomas A. "The Phonograph and Its Future." *North American Review*, no. 126 (May–June 1878): 527–36.

Edison, Thomas A. "The Phonograph at Work." *New York Evening Post*, November 18, 1887.

Edwards, Paul N. *The Closed World: Computers and the Politics of Discourse in Cold War America*. MIT Press, 1996.

Edwards, Paul N. "Platforms Are Infrastructures on Fire." In *Your Computer Is on Fire*, edited by Thomas S. Mullaney, Benjamin Peters, Mar Hicks, and Kavita Philip. MIT Press, 2021.

Eisenstein, Elizabeth L. *The Printing Revolution in Early Modern Europe*. Cambridge University Press, 2012.

Eisenstein, Sergei. "Bela Forgets the Scissors." In *The Film Factory: Russian and Soviet Cinema in Documents 1896–1939*, edited by Ian Christie and Richard Taylor. Routledge, 2012.

Eisenstein, Sergei. *The Eisenstein Reader*. Translated by Richard Taylor and William Powell; edited by Richard Taylor. BFI Publishing, 1998.

Eisenstein, Sergei. *The Film Sense*. Translated by Jay Leyda. Meridian Books, 1957.

Elsaesser, Thomas. "Freud As Media Theorist: Mystic Writing-Pads and the Matter of Memory." *Screen* 50, no. 1 (2009): 100–113.

Engell, Lorenz. "Apollo TV: The Copernican Turn of the Gaze." *World Picture* 7 (2012): 1–10.

Engh, Barbara. "After 'His Master's Voice.'" *New Formation* 38 (1999): 54–63.

England, Kim, and Kate Boyer. "Women's Work: The Feminization and Shifting Meanings of Clerical Work." *Journal of Social History* 42, no. 2 (2009): 307–40.

Ensmenger, Nathan. "The Cloud Is a Factory." In *Your Computer Is on Fire*, edited by Thomas S. Mullaney, Benjamin Peters, Mar Hicks, and Kavita Philip. MIT Press, 2021.

Erhart, Ed. "Why Didn't Wikipedia Have an Article on Donna Strickland, Winner of a Nobel Prize?" *WikiMedia*, October 4, 2018. https://wikimediafoundation.org/news/2018/10/04/donna-strickland-wikipedia/.

Ernst, Wolfgang. *Digital Memory and the Archive*. Translated by Jussi Parikka. University of Minnesota Press, 2012.

Esguerra, Richard. "Google CEO Eric Schmidt Dismisses the Importance of Privacy." *Electronic Frontier Foundation*, December 10, 2009. https://www.eff.org/deeplinks/2009/12/google-ceo-eric-schmidt-dismisses-privacy.

Esposito, Elena. "Tools to Remember an Ever-Changing Past." In *Forgetting Machines: Knowledge Management Evolution in Early Modern Europe*, edited by Alberto Cevolini. Brill, 2016.

Fauser, Annegret. "The Marvels of Technology." In *Musical Encounters at the 1889 Paris World's Fair*. Boydell & Brewer, 2005.

Feaster, Patrick. "'A Compass of Extraordinary Range': The Forgotten Origins of Phonomanipulation." *ARSC Journal* 42, no. 2 (2011): 163–203.

Feaster, Patrick. "Phonography." In *Keywords in Sound*, edited by David Novak and Matt Sakakeeny. Duke University Press, 2015.

Feldman, Allen. *Archives of the Insensible: Of War, Photopolitics, and Dead Memory*. University of Chicago Press, 2015.

Feuer, Jane. "The Concept of Live Television: Ontology As Ideology." In *Regarding Television: Critical Approaches: An Anthology*, edited by Ann E. Kaplan. University Publications of America, 1983.

Fewkes, Walter J. "On the Use of the Phonograph in the Study of the Languages of the American Indian." *Science* 378 (1890): 267–69.

Fleming, Juliet. *Graffiti and the Writing Arts of Early Modern England*. Reaktion Books, 2001.

Floridi, Luciano. *The Fourth Revolution: How the Infosphere Is Reshaping Human Reality*. Oxford University Press, 2014.

Flower, Harriet I. *The Art of Forgetting: Disgrace and Oblivion in Roman Political Culture*. University of North Carolina Press, 2006.

Flusser, Vilém. *Gestures*. Translated by Nancy Ann Roth. University of Minnesota Press, 2014.

Flusser, Vilém. "On Memory (Electronic or Otherwise)." *Leonardo* 23, no. 4 (1990): 397–99.

Fomin, Valery Ivanovich. "Rozhdenie sovetskogo kino 1917–1930." In *Otchet o nauchno-issledovatel'skoj rabote: Istorija kinootrasli v Rossii: Upravlenie, kinoproizvodstvo, prokat*, June 1, 2020. https://culture.gov.ru/upload/mkrf/mkdocs2013/21_01_2013_2.pdf#page=23.07.

Ford, Heather, and Judy Wajcman. "'Anyone Can Edit,' Not Everyone Does: Wikipedia's Infrastructure and the Gender Gap." *Social Studies of Science* 47, no. 4 (2017): 511–27.

Fore, Devin. *Soviet Factography: Reality without Realism*. University of Chicago Press, 2024.

Foucault, Michel. *Discipline and Punish: The Birth of the Prison*. Vintage Books, 1977.

"The Four-minute Recorder and New Shaving Machine." *The Phonograph Monthly* 10, no. 8 (August 1912): 3–5.

Fredrikzon, Johan, and Chris Haffenden. "Towards Erasure Studies: Excavating the Material Conditions of Memory and Forgetting." *Memory, Mind & Media* 2 (2023).

Freud, Sigmund. *The Standard Edition of the Complete Psychological Works, Volume XIX*. Edited and translated by James Strachey. London: The Hogarth Press, 1961 [1930].

Frosh, Paul. "The Face of Television." *Annals of the American Academy of Political and Social Science* 625 (2009): 87–102.

Fuchs, Christian. "A Contribution to the Critique of the Political Economy of Google." *Fast Capitalism* 8, no. 1 (2011): 31–50.

Gabrys, Jennifer. *Digital Rubbish: A Natural History of Electronics*. University of Michigan Press, 2011.

Gadassik, Alla. "Ėsfir Shub on Women in the Editing Room: 'The Work of Montazhnitsy' (1927)." *Apparatus: Film, Media and Digital Cultures of Central and Eastern Europe* 6 (2018).

Gadassik, Alla. "A Skillful Isis: Esfir Shub and the Documentarian As Caretaker." In *A Companion to Documentary Film History*, edited by Joshua Malitsky. John Wiley & Sons, 2021.

Galison, Peter. "Blacked-out Spaces: Freud, Censorship and the Re-territorialization of Mind." *The British Journal for the History of Science* 45, no. 2 (2012): 235–66.

Galison, Peter. "Removing Knowledge." *Critical Inquiry* 31, no. 1 (2004): 229–43.

Galloway, Alexander R. *Protocol: How Control Exists after Decentralization*. MIT Press, 2004.

Galloway, Alexander R., and Eugene Thacker. *The Exploit: A Theory of Networks*. University of Minnesota Press, 2013.

Galpin, Richard. "Erasure in Art: Destruction, Deconstruction, and Palimpsest." February 1998. https://www.richardgalpin.co.uk/erasureinart.

Gammon, Martin. *Deaccessioning and Its Discontents: A Critical History*. MIT Press, 2018.

Garde-Hansen, Joanne, Andrew Hoskins, and Anna Reading, eds. *Save As . . . Digital Memories*. Springer, 2009.

Gazdiev, Akhmet. "Kavkaz na kinoplenke Nikolaja Minervina." *Bezformata*, November 30, 2016. https://magas.bezformata.com/listnews/kavkaz-na-kinoplenke-nikolaya-minervina/52785599/.

Gelatt, Roland. *The Fabulous Phonograph, 1877–1977*. Collier Books, 1977.

Ghosal, Aniruddha, and Vincent Thian. "Malaysia Is Betting on Data Centers to Boost Its Economy. But Experts Warn They Come at a Price." *AP*, February 19, 2025.

Gillespie, Tarleton. *Custodians of the Internet: Platforms, Content Moderation, and the Hidden Decisions That Shape Social Media*. Yale University Press, 2018.

Giotta, Gina. "Disappeared: Erasure in the Age of Mechanical Writing." PhD diss., University of Iowa, 2011.

Girard, Catherine. "Painture: The Temporal and Emotional Labor of Stale Bread in the French Studio." *West 86th: A Journal of Decorative Arts, Design History, and Material Culture* 31, no. 1 (Spring–Summer 2024).

Gitelman, Lisa. *Paper Knowledge: Toward a Media History of Documents*. Duke University Press, 2014.

Gitelman, Lisa, ed. *Raw Data Is an Oxymoron*. MIT Press, 2013.

Gitelman, Lisa. *Scripts, Grooves, and Writing Machines*. Stanford University Press, 2000.

Gitelman, Lisa. "Souvenir Foils: On the Status of the Print at the Origin of Recorded Sound." In *New Media 1740–1915*, edited by Lisa Gitelman and Geoffrey B. Pingree. MIT Press, 2003.

Goldberg, Jonathan. *Writing Matter: From the Hands of the English Renaissance*. Stanford University Press, 1990.

Goldstein, Jonathan. "#45 Sgt. John Kapphahn." *Heavyweight* (podcast), September 29, 2022. https://podtail.com/en/podcast/heavyweight/-45-sgt-john-kapphahn/.

Grafton, Anthony. "Correctors Corruptors? Notes on the Social History of Editing." In *Editing Texts = Texte Edieren*, edited by Glenn W. Most. Vandenhoeck & Ruprecht, 1998.

Graham, Stephen, and Nigel Thrift, "Out of Order: Understanding Repair and Maintenance." *Theory, Culture & Society* 24, no. 3 (2007): 1–25.

Greene, Mark A. "I've Deaccessioned and Lived to Tell About It: Confessions of an Unrepentant Reappraiser." *Archival Issues* 30, no.1 (2006): 7–22.

Grivel, Charles. "The Phonograph's Horned Mount." In *Wireless Imagination: Sound, Radio, and the Avant-garde*, edited by Douglas Kahn and Gregory Whitehead. MIT Press, 1992.

Grosser, Ben. "Minus." Blog post. https://bengrosser.com/projects/minus/.

Groys, Boris. *Under Suspicion: A Phenomenology of Media*. Columbia University Press, 2012.

Guest, Peter. "Bitcoin Mining Was Booming in Kazakhstan. Then It Was Gone." *MIT Technology Review* (January 12, 2023).

Hänsch, Theodor W. "Edible Lasers and Other Delights of the 1970s." *Optics & Photonics News* (2005).

Haraway, Donna. "Situated Knowledges: The Science Question in Feminism and the Privilege of Partial Perspective." *Feminist Studies* 14, no. 3 (1988): 575–99.

Hartman, Saidiya. "Venus in Two Acts." *Small Axe: A Journal of Criticism* 12, no. 2 (2008): 1–14.

Harwood, John. *The Interface: IBM and the Transformation of Corporate Design, 1945–1976*. University of Minnesota Press, 2011.

Hayles, Katherine N. *Writing Machines*. MIT Press, 2002.

Heidegger, Martin. *Being and Time*. Harper San Francisco, 1962.

Hern, Alex. "Myspace Loses All Content Uploaded before 2016." *The Guardian*, March 18, 2019.

Hess, Richard L. "Tape Degradation Factors and Challenges in Predicting Tape Life." *ARSC Journal* 39, no. 2 (2008): 240–74.

Hilden, Irene. *Absent Presences in the Colonial Archive: Dealing with the Berlin Sound Archive's Acoustic Legacies*. Leuven University Press, 2022.

Hilderbrand, Lucas. *Inherent Vice: Bootleg Histories of Videotape and Copyright*. Duke University Press, 2009.

Hochman, Brian. *Savage Preservation: The Ethnographic Origins of Modern Media Technology*. University of Minnesota Press, 2014.

Hogan, Mél. "The Archive As Dumpster." *Pivot: A Journal of Interdisciplinary Studies and Thought* 4, no. 1 (2015).

Hogan, Mél, and Sarah T. Roberts. "Archiving for Extinction." *Media-N* 19, no. 1 (2023): 7–26.

Houston, Penelope. *Keepers of the Frame: The Film Archives*. British Film Institute, 1994.

Hu, Tung-Hui. *A Prehistory of the Cloud*. MIT Press, 2015.

Huhtamo, Erkki, and Jussi Parikka. *Media Archaeology: Approaches, Applications, and Implications*. University of California Press, 2011.

Huurdeman, H. C., J. Kamps, T. Samar, et al. "Lost But Not Forgotten: Finding Pages on the Unarchived Web." *International Journal of Digital Libraries* 16 (2015): 247–65.

IBM Corp. "IBM Magnetic Tape Selectric Composer: Record Unit Training Guide MT/ST Models II and IV (for Graphics)," 1968. https://ia800805.us.archive.org/26/items/IBM-MTSC-TrainingGuide/IBM%20Magnetic%20Tape%20Selectric%20Composer%20training%20guide.pdf.

Iles, Chrissie. *Dream Reels: Video Films and Environments by Jud Yalkut*. Catalog. Whitney Museum of American Art, 2000.

"Indianapolis Gleanings." *The Talking Machine World* 7, no. 9 (September 15, 1911).

Ingravalle, Grazia. *Archival Film Curatorship: Early and Silent Cinema from Analog to Digital*. Amsterdam University Press, 2014.

Innis, Harold A. *Empire and Communications*. Dundurn Press, 2007.

Internet Histories 6, no. 1–2 (2022).

Jacobs, Jason. *The Intimate Screen: Early British Television Drama*. Clarendon Press, 2000.

Jaillant, Lise. "More Data, Less Process: A User-centered Approach to Email and Born-digital Archives." *The American Archivist* 85, no. 2 (2022): 533–55.

Johnson, Edward H. "A Wonderful Invention: Speech Capable of Indefinite Repetition from Automatic Records." *Scientific American*, November 17, 1877, 304.

Jonsson, Fredrik Albritton, and Carl Wennerlind. *Scarcity: A History from the Origins of Capitalism to the Climate Crisis*. Harvard University Press, 2023.

Kafka, Ben. "A Riot on Every Page: Archive, Bureaucracy, Paranoia." In *Peter Piller Archive, Materials (G) Albedo*. Walther, 2014.

Kahle, Brewster. "Archiving the Internet." *Scientific American* 3 (1997): 1.

Kahle, Brewster, and Ana Parejo Vadillo. "The Internet Archive: An Interview with

Brewster Kahle." *19: Interdisciplinary Studies in the Long Nineteenth Century*, no. 21 (2015).

Kahn, Douglas. "Death in Light of the Phonograph: Raymond Roussel's Locus Solus." In *Wireless Imagination: Sound, Radio, and the Avant-garde*, edited by Douglas Kahn and Gregory Whitehead. MIT Press, 1992.

Kahn, Douglas. *Noise, Water, Meat: A History of Sound in the Arts*. MIT Press, 1999.

Kane, Carolyn L. *High-Tech Trash: Glitch, Noise, and Aesthetic Failure*. University of California Press, 2019.

Katz, Mark. *Capturing Sound: How Technology Has Changed Music*. University of California Press, 2010.

Kaufman, Marc. "NASA Stumped in Search for Moon Tapes." *NBC News*, January 31, 2007.

Keeling, Kara. *Queer Times, Black Futures*. New York University Press, 2019.

Kennedy, G. *An Ontology of Trash: The Disposable and Its Problematic Nature*. SUNY Press, 2012.

Kepley, Vance, Jr. "'Cinefication': Soviet Film Exhibition in the 1920s." *Film History* 6, no. 2 (1994): 262–77.

Kepley, Vance, Jr. "The Origins of Soviet Cinema: A Study in Industry Development." *Quarterly Review of Film & Video* 10, no. 1 (1985): 22–38.

Kirschenbaum, Matthew G. *Mechanisms: New Media and the Forensic Imagination*. MIT Press, 2008.

Kirschenbaum, Matthew G. *Track Changes: A Literary History of Word Processing*. Belknap Press of Harvard University Press, 2016.

Kittler, Friedrich A. *Discourse Networks, 1800/1900*. Stanford University Press, 1990.

Kittler, Friedrich A. "Dracula's Legacy." In *Literature, Media, Information Systems*, edited by John Johnston. Routledge, 2013.

Kittler, Friedrich A. "Forgetting." *Discourse* 3 (1981): 88–121.

Kittler, Friedrich A. *Gramophone, Film, Typewriter*. Translated by Geoffrey Winthrop-Young and Michael Wutz. Stanford University Press, 1999.

Kittler, Friedrich A. "Number and Numeral." *Theory, Culture & Society* 23, no. 7–8 (2006): 51–61.

Klik, Ella. "Ephemeral Design: Platform Capitalism and the Making of a Feature." *New Media & Society* (2023): 1–17.

Knowles, Sebastian D. G. "Death by Gramophone." *Journal of Modern Literature* 27, no. 1 (2003): 1–13.

Kolesnikov, Anna. "The Geocultural Provenance of Narratives: The Case of the Kuleshov Effect." *Film History: An International Journal* 32, no. 2 (2020): 55–79.

Kompare, Derek. "Transcribed Adventures: Radio and the Recording." In *Rerun Nation: How Repeats Invented American Television*. Routledge, 2005.

Korolevich, Vladimir. "On the First Words." In *Lines of Resistance: Dziga Vertov and the Twenties*, edited by Yuri Tsivian. Le Giornate del cinema muto, 2004.

Kostakis, Vasilis. "Identifying and Understanding the Problems of Wikipedia's Peer Governance: The Case of Inclusionists versus Deletionists." *First Monday* 15, no. 31 (2010).

Kracauer, Siegfried. *Theory of Film: The Redemption of Physical Reality.* Oxford University Press, 1965.

Krämer, Sybille. *Medium, Messenger, Transmission: An Approach to Media Philosophy.* Amsterdam University Press, 2015.

Krämer, Sybille. "Writing, Notational Iconicity, Calculus: On Writing as a Cultural Technique." *MLN* 118, no. 3 (2003): 518–37.

Krapp, Peter. *Noise Channels: Glitch and Error in Digital Culture.* University of Minnesota Press, 2011.

Kricheli, Ruth. "Updating Our Inactive Account Policies." *Google Blog,* May 16, 2023. https://blog.google/technology/safety-security/updating-our-inactive-account-policies/.

Kuleshov, Lev. "Montage as the Foundation of Cinematography." In *Kuleshov on Film: Film Writings by Lev Kuleshov,* translated and edited by Ronald Levaco. University of California Press, 1974.

Kuleshov, Lev. *Selected Works: Fifty Years in Film.* Translated by Nina Shcherbakova. Raduga Publishers, 1987.

Lafferty, William. "The Blattnerphone: An Early Attempt to Introduce Magnetic Recording into the Film Industry." *Cinema Journal* 22, no. 4 (1983): 18–37.

Lafferty, William. "'A New Era in TV Programming' Becomes 'Business as Usual': Videotape Technology, Local Stations, and Network Power, 1957–1961." *Quarterly Review of Film & Video* 16, no. 3–4 (1997): 405–19.

Lagerkvist, Amanda. *Existential Media: A Media Theory of the Limit Situation.* Oxford University Press, 2022.

Landay, Lori. "The Moviola and Other Analog Film Editing Machines." In *The Routledge Companion to Media Technology and Obsolescence,* edited by Mark Wolf. Routledge, 2018.

Lane, Basil. "75 Years of Magnetic Recording: From Steel to Plastic." *Wireless World* (May 1975).

Latour, Bruno. "Visualisation and Cognition: Drawing Things Together." *Knowledge and Society: Studies in the Sociology of Culture and Present* 6 (1986): 1–40.

Latour, Bruno. "Where Are the Missing Masses? The Sociology of a Few Mundane Artifacts." In *Shaping Technology/Building Society: Studies in Sociotechnical Change,* edited by John Law and Wiebe E. Bijker. MIT Press, 1992.

Latour, Bruno, and Steve Woolgar. *Laboratory Life: The Construction of Scientific Facts.* Princeton University Press, 1986.

Launius, Roger D. "Opposing Apollo: Political Resistance to the Moon Landings." *New Space* 2, no. 2 (2014): 74–80.

Launius, Roger D. *Reaching for the Moon: A Short History of the Space Race.* Yale University Press, 2019.

Lenoir, Timothy, ed. "Inscription Practices and Materialities of Communication." In *Inscribing Science: Scientific Texts and the Materiality of Communication.* Stanford University Press, 1998.

Leonard, David. "Search for Apollo 11 TV Tapes Moves into High Gear." August 24, 2006. https://www.space.com/2793-search-apollo-11-tv-tapes-moves-high-gear.html.

Leshnick, Anat. "Deletion Discussions on Hebrew Wikipedia: Negotiating Global and Local Ideologies." *New Media & Society* (2022): 1–17.

Levin, Thomas Y. "Tones from out of Nowhere: Rudolph Pfenninger and the Archaeology of Synthetic Sound." *Grey Room* 12 (2003): 32–37.

Levine, Elana. "Distinguishing Television: The Changing Meanings of Television Liveness." *Media, Culture & Society* 30, no. 3 (2008): 393–409.

Leyda, Jay. *Films Beget Films*. George Allen & Unwin, 1964.

Leyda, Jay. *Kino: A History of the Russian and Soviet Film*. George Allen & Unwin, 1960.

Liboiron, Max, and Josh Lepawsky. *Discard Studies: Wasting, Systems, and Power*. MIT Press, 2022.

Library of Congress. "Update on the Twitter Archive at the Library of Congress." December 2017. https://blogs.loc.gov/loc/files/2017/12/2017dec_twitter_white-paper.pdf.

Lippit, Akira Mizuta. *Atomic Light (Shadow Optics)*. University of Minnesota Press, 2005.

Lovejoy, Alice. "Celluloid Geopolitics: Film Stock and the War Economy, 1939–47." *Screen* 60, no. 2 (2019): 224–41.

Luhn, Hans Peter. "Key Word-in-context Index for Technical Literature (kwic index)." *American Documentation* 11, no. 4 (1960): 288–95.

Lunacharsky, Anatoli. "Cinema—The Greatest of the Arts." In *The Film Factory: Russian and Soviet Cinema in Documents 1896–1939*, edited by Ian Christie and Richard Taylor. Routledge, 2012.

Lyon, David. *Surveillance Studies: An Overview*. Polity Press, 2007.

Mackellar, Colin. "Comparison Photographs of the Apollo 11 Lunar Television As Seen at Goldstone, Honeysuckle Creek, Parkes and Houston." NASA, December 2005. https://history.nasa.gov/alsj/a11/a11TVcomparisons.pdf.

Mackinnon, Katie. "The Death of GeoCities: Seeking Destruction and Platform Eulogies in Web Archives." *Internet Histories* 6, no. 1–2 (2022): 237–52.

Malitsky, Joshua. "Esfir Shub and the Film Factory-Archive: Soviet Documentary from 1925–1928." *Screening the Past* 17 (2004).

Malthus, Thomas Robert. *An Essay on the Principle of Population*. Cambridge University Press, 1992.

Margalit, Avishai. *The Ethics of Memory*. Harvard University Press, 2002.

Martin, Jeff. "The Dawn of Tape: Transmission Device As Preservation Medium." *The Moving Image* 5, no. 1 (2005): 45–66.

Marvin, Carolyn. *When Old Technologies Were New: Thinking about Electric Communication in the Late Nineteenth Century*. Oxford University Press, 1988.

Mattern, Shannon. "Bureaucracy's Playthings." In *Computer Architectures: Constructing the Common Ground*, edited by Theodora Vardouli and Olga Touloumi. Routledge, 2019.

Mayer-Schönberger, Viktor. *Delete: The Virtue of Forgetting in the Digital Age*. Princeton University Press, 2009.

Mayne, Judith. *Kino and the Woman Question: Feminism and Soviet Silent Film*. Ohio State University Press, 1989.

McGovern, Gerry, and Sue Branford. "The Cloud vs. Drought: Water Hog Data Centers Threaten Latin America, Critics Say." *Mongabay*, November 2, 2023. https://news.mongabay.com/2023/11/the-cloud-vs-drought-water-hog-data-centers-threaten-latin-america-critics-say/.

McKenna, Mark. *Nasty Business: The Marketing and Distribution of the Video Nasties*. Edinburgh University Press, 2020.

McLuhan, Marshall. *The Global Village: Transformations in World Life and Media in the 21st Century*. Oxford University Press, 1992.

McLuhan, Marshall. *The Gutenberg Galaxy: The Making of Typographic Man*. University of Toronto Press, 2011.

McLuhan, Marshall. "The Typewriter: Into the Age of the Iron Whim." In *Understanding Media: The Extensions of Man*. MIT Press, 1994.

McLuhan, Marshall, and Quentin Fiore. *The Medium Is the Massage*. Random House, 1967.

McMurray, Peter. "Once upon Time: A Superficial History of Early Tape." *Twentieth-Century Music* 14, no. 1 (2017): 25–28.

Mersch, Dieter. "Tertium Datur. Introduction to a Negative Media Theory." *Matrizes* 7, no. 1 (2013): 207–22.

Metz, Christian. *The Imaginary Signifier: Psychoanalysis and the Cinema*. Indiana University Press, 1981.

Meuel, David. *Women Film Editors: Unseen Artists of American Cinema*. McFarland, 2016.

Miller, Jamie. "Soviet Cinema, 1929–41: The Development of Industry and Infrastructure." *Europe-Asia Studies* 58, no. 1 (2006): 103–24.

Morris, Edmund. *Edison*. Random House, 2019.

Moscaritolo, Angela. "Google's Schmidt Concerned by Lack of Internet 'Delete Button.'" *PC Mag*, May 6, 2013.

Muir, John. *Life and Letters in the Ancient Greek World*. Routledge, 2009.

Mullaney, Thomas S., Benjamin Peters, Mar Hicks, and Kavita Philip. *Your Computer Is on Fire*. MIT Press, 2021.

Müller, Lothar. *White Magic: The Age of Paper*. Polity Press, 2014.

The Multigraph Collective. *Interacting with Print: Elements of Reading in the Era of Print Saturation*. University of Chicago Press, 2018.

Mulvey, Laura. "Visual Pleasure and Narrative Cinema." In *Feminism and Film Theory*. Routledge, 2013.

Murphy, Brian Michael. "Data Storage Is Reaching the Limits of Physics." *Wall Street Journal*, August 25, 2022.

Murray, Susan. "Reviving the Technical in Television History." In *A Companion to the History of American Broadcasting*, edited by Aniko Bodroghkozy. Wiley, 2018.

Nafzger, Richard L. Interview by Sandra Johnson. NASA Headquarters Oral History Project: Edited Oral History Transcript. Greenbelt, MD, June 12, 2013.

NASA. "The Apollo 11 Telemetry Data Recording: A Final Report." c. 2009. https://www.hq.nasa.gov/alsj/a11/Apollo_11_TV_Tapes_Report.pdf.

NASA TV. "Briefing on Apollo 11 Moonwalk Video." Video, 54:24. July 16, 2009. https://www.youtube.com/watch?v=xAPRS8DM6Mk.

NASA. "Update: Apollo 11 Tapes." August 16, 2006. https://www.nasa.gov/mission_pages/apollo/apollo_tapes.html.

National Phonograph Company. *The Phonograph and How to Use It.* National Phonograph Company, 1900.

Nauck, Kurt. *Indestructible and U-S Everlasting Cylinders: An Illustrated History and Cylinderography.* Mainspring Press, 1907.

Nebesio, Bohdan Y. "Competition from Ukraine: VUFKU and the Soviet Film Industry in the 1920s." *Historical Journal of Film, Radio and Television* 29, no. 2 (2009): 159–80.

Negroponte, Nicholas. *Being Digital.* Vintage, 1996.

Newman, Michael Z. *Video Revolutions: On the History of a Medium.* Columbia University Press, 2014.

Nichols, Bill. "Remaking History: Jay Leyda and the Compilation Film." *Film History* 26, no. 4 (2014): 146–56.

Nora, Pierre. "Monster Events." *Discourse* 5 (1983): 5–20.

Nora, Pierre. "The Return of the Event." In *Histories: French Constructions of the Past*, edited by Jacques Revel and Lynn Avery Hunt. New Press, 1995.

Novet, Jordan. "Google's Plan to Purge Inactive Accounts Isn't Sitting Well with Some Users." *CNBC*, August 19, 2023.

O'Brien, Isabel. "Data Center Emissions Probably 662% Higher than Big Tech Claims. Can It Keep Up the Ruse?" *The Guardian*. September 15, 2024.

Ogden, Jessica. "'Everything on the Internet Can Be Saved': Archive Team, Tumblr and The Cultural Significance of Web Archiving." *Internet Histories* 6, no. 1–2 (2022): 113–32.

Onuoha, Mimi. "What It Takes to Truly Delete Data." *FiveThirtyEight*, January 30, 2017. https://fivethirtyeight.com/features/what-it-takes-to-truly-delete-data/.

O'Reilly, Tim. "What Is Web 2.0: Design Patterns and Business Models for the Next Generation of Software." September 30, 2005. https://papers.ssrn.com/sol3/papers.cfm?abstract_id=1008839.

Osterberg, Gayle. "Update on the Twitter Archive at the Library of Congress." Library of Congress (blog), December 26, 2017. https://blogs.loc.gov/loc/2017/12/update-on-the-twitter-archive-at-the-library-of-congress-2/?loclr=twloc.

Oudart, Jean-Pierre. "Dossier Suture: Cinema and Suture." *Screen* 18, no. 4 (1977): 33–48.

Palmer, Daniel. "The Rhetoric of the JPEG." In *The Photographic Image in Digital Culture*, edited by Martin Lister. Routledge, 2013.

Parikka, Jussi. *A Geology of Media.* University of Minnesota Press, 2015.

Patten, Simon Nelson. *The New Basis of Civilization, Vol. 1.* Harvard University Press, 1968.

Perec, Georges. *Species of Spaces and Other Pieces.* Penguin, 1999.

Perelman, Michael. "Marx and Resource Scarcity." *Capitalism Nature Socialism* 4, no. 2 (1993): 65–84.

Peters, Benjamin. "How Do We Live Now? In the Aftermath of Ourselves." In *Your*

Computer Is on Fire, edited by Thomas S. Mullaney, Benjamin Peters, Mar Hicks, and Kavita Philip. MIT Press, 2021.

Peters, John Durham. *The Marvelous Clouds: Toward a Philosophy of Elemental Media*. University of Chicago Press, 2015.

Peters, John Durham. *Speaking into the Air: A History of the Idea of Communication*. University of Chicago Press, 1999.

Petroski, Henry. *The Pencil: A History of Design and Circumstance*. Random House, 1992.

Phonogram 1 no. 2 (1891): 33.

Pieslak, Raymond F., and Charles M. Jochem. *Magnetic Tape Selectric Typewriter*. Vocational-Technical Curriculum Laboratory, Rutgers University, 1974.

Pinchevski, Amit. *By Way of Interruption: Levinas and the Ethics of Communication*. Duquesne University Press, 2005.

Pink, Sarah, Debora Lanzeni, and Heather Horst. "Data Anxieties: Finding Trust in Everyday Digital Mess." *Big Data & Society* 5, no. 1 (2018): 1–14.

Pitman, Isaac. *A Manual of the Typewriter: A Practical Guide to Commercial, Literary, Legal, Dramatic and All Classes of Typewriting Work*. Isaac Pitman & Sons, 1893.

Plato. *Plato: Collected Dialogues*. Translated by R. Hackforth; edited by Edith Hamilton and Huntington Cairns. Princeton University Press, 1955.

Plotnick, Rachel. "Tethered Women, Mobile Men: Gendered Mobilities of Typewriting." *Mobile Media & Communication* 8, no. 2 (2020): 188–208.

Plotnick, Rachel. "The Unclean Human-machine Interface." In *Computer Architectures: Constructing the Common Ground*, edited by Theodora Vardouli and Olga Touloumi. Routledge, 2019.

Powell, R. J. "Memory of 'White-Out' Shan't Be Erased." *Wall Street Journal*, October 16, 1986.

Preobrazhenskii, N. F. "Vospomenanija o rabote VFKO." In *Iz istorii kino: Materialy i dokumenty*. Akademii nauk USSR, 1953.

Pringle, Heather. "NASA Dives into Its Past to Retrieve Vintage Satellite Data." *Science* 327, no. 5971 (2010): 1322–33.

Pudovkin, Vsevolod. *Film Technique and Film Acting: The Cinema Writings of V. I. Pudovkin*. Translated and edited by Ivor Montagu. Grove Press, 1958.

Pudovkin, Vsevolod, Esfir' Shub, et al. "To All Creative Workers in Soviet Cinema." In *The Film Factory: Russian and Soviet Cinema in Documents 1896–1939*, edited by Ian Christie and Richard Taylor. Routledge, 2012.

Pugh, Emerson W., Lyle R. Johnson, and John H. Palmer. *IBM's 360 and Early 370 Systems*. MIT Press, 1991.

Rajbhandari, Samyam, Jeff Rasley, Olatunji Ruwase, and Yuxiong He. "Zero: Memory Optimizations toward Training Trillion Parameter Models." *SC20: International Conference for High Performance Computing, Networking, Storage and Analysis, IEEE* (2020): 1–16.

Rancière, Jacques. *The Politics of Aesthetics: The Distribution of the Sensible*. Translated by Gabriel Rockhill. Continuum, 2004.

Razinsky, Liran. "The Dream of Absolute Memory: On Digital Self-Representation." *Lit: Literature Interpretation Theory* 31, no. 2 (2020): 182–201.

Renouard, Maël. *Fragments of an Infinite Memory*. New York Review Books, 2021.

Reynolds, C. J., and Blake Hallinan. "The Haunting of GeoCities and the Politics of Access Control on the Early Web." *New Media & Society* 23, no. 11 (2021): 3268–89.

Rheinberger, Hans-Jörg. "Economy of Scribble." In *An Epistemology of the Concrete: Twentieth-century Histories of Life*. Duke University Press, 2010.

Richards, Thomas. *The Imperial Archive: Knowledge and the Fantasy of Empire*. Verso, 1993.

Ricœur, Paul. *Memory, History, Forgetting*. University of Chicago Press, 2004.

Ringel, Sharon. "Studying Absence: The Ephemerality of Digital News Contexts." *Digital Journalism* (2023): 1–15.

Roberts, Sarah T. "Digital Detritus: 'Error' and the Logic of Opacity in Social Media Content Moderation." *First Monday* 23, no. 3–5 (2018).

Roberts, Sarah T. *Behind the Screen: Content Moderation in the Shadows of Social Media*. Yale University Press, 2019.

Robertson, Craig. *The Filing Cabinet: A Vertical History of Information*. University of Minnesota Press, 2021.

Rosen, Philip. *Change Mummified: Cinema, Historicity, Theory*. University of Minnesota Press, 2001.

Rosenberg, Daniel. "Word." In *Uncertain Archives: Critical Keywords for Big Data*, edited by Nanna Bonde Thylstrup, Daniela Agostinho, Annie Ring, Catherine D'Ignazio, and Kristin Veel. MIT Press, 2021.

Sadoul, Georges, and Yvonne Templin. "English Influences on the Work of Edwin S. Porter." *Hollywood Quarterly* 3, no. 1 (1947): 41–50.

Sadowski, Jathan. "When Data Is Capital: Datafication, Accumulation, and Extraction." *Big Data & Society* 6, no. 1 (2019): 1–12.

SalahEldeen, Hany, and Michael Nelson. "Losing My Revolution: How Many Resources Shared on Social Media Have Been Lost?" Presented at "Theory and Practice of Digital Libraries," Second International Conference, Paphos, Cyprus, September 23–27, 2012.

Sargsyan, Sati. "Data Centers and Indigenous Sovereignty." In *Centering the Margins of Digital Culture*, edited by A. Kaun and P. Åker. Södertörn University Press, 2023.

Sarkissian, John. "The Search for Lost Apollo 11 Tapes." *CSIROscope*. March 20, 2013. https://blog.csiro.au/the-search-for-lost-apollo-11-tapes/.

Schawlow, Arthur. Interview with Walter Cronkite. In *The Laser: A Light Fantastic*. Directed by Peter Poor. CBS News, 1967. https://archive.org/details/gov.archives.arc.53891.

Schawlow, Arthur, B. P. Stoicheff, and Suzanne Riess, *Optics and Laser Spectroscopy: Bell Telephone Laboratories, 1951–1961, and Stanford University since 1961: Oral history transcript* (1988). https://archive.org/details/opticslaserspectooscharich.

Schröter, Jens. "Erasure As Planned Obsolescence." In *Obsolescence programmée. Perspectives culturelles*, edited by Ella Mingazova, Bruno Dupont, and Carole Guesse. Presses Universitaires de Liège, 2022.

Schröter, Jens. "The Laser: On the Quantum Materiality of Media in the Twentieth Century." *NECSUS: European Journal of Media Studies* 11, no. 2 (2022): 46–68.

Schüll, Natasha Dow. "Digital Containment and Its Discontents." *History and Anthropology* 29, no. 1 (2018): 42–48.

Schwartz, Stephen A., Ronald W. Beers, Miroslav Dolák, David T. Schwartz, and Darlene D. Rush. "Space Operations: NASA Is Not Properly Safeguarding Valuable Data from Past Missions." Report to the Chairmen, Committee on Science, Space, and Technology, House of Representatives, 1990.

Sconce, Jeffrey. *Haunted Media: Electronic Presence from Telegraphy to Television.* Duke University Press, 2000.

Scott, David Meerman, and Richard Jurek. *Marketing the Moon: The Selling of the Apollo Lunar Program.* MIT Press, 2014.

Sellen, Abigail J., and Richard H. R. Harper. *The Myth of the Paperless Office.* MIT Press, 2003.

"Send Greetings through Record." *Talking Machine World* 7, no. 5 (March 15, 1911): 34.

Serres, Michel. *The Parasite.* University of Minnesota Press, 2013.

Shambarger, Peter. "Cylinder Records: An Overview." *ARSC Journal* 26, no. 2 (1995): 133–61.

Shklovsky, Viktor. "The Work of Re-editing." In *The Film Factory: Russian and Soviet Cinema in Documents 1896–1939*, edited by Ian Christie and Richard Taylor. Routledge, 2005.

Shub, Esfir. "Esfir Shub: Selected Writings." Translated by Anastasia Kostin; edited by Liubov Dyshlyuk. *Feminist Media Histories* 2, no. 1 (2016): 1–28.

Shub, Esfir. "The Manufacture of Facts." In *The Film Factory: Russian and Soviet Cinema in Documents 1896–1939*, edited by Ian Christie and Richard Taylor. Routledge, 2012.

Shub, Esfir. *Zhizn' moia kinematograf.* Iskusstvo, 1972.

Simondon, Gilbert. *On the Mode of Existence of Technical Objects.* University of Minnesota Press, 2017.

Smith, Oberlin. "Some Possible Form of the Phonograph." *The Electric World*, September 8, 1888.

Smyth, Adam. "Errors and Corrections: 'My Galley Charged with Forgetfulness.'" In *Material Texts in Early Modern England.* Cambridge University Press, 2018.

Spigel, Lynn. "From Domestic Space to Outer Space: The 1960s Fantastic Family Sit-Com." In *Close Encounters: Film, Feminism, and Science Fiction*, edited by Constance Penley, Elisabeth Lyon, Lynn Spigel, and Janet Bergstrom. University of Minnesota Press, 1991.

Spigel, Lynn. *Make Room for TV: Television and the Family Ideal in Postwar America.* University of Chicago Press, 1992.

Spigel, Lynn. "Our TV Heritage: Television, the Archive, and the Reasons for Preservation." In *A Companion to Television*, edited by Janet Wasko. Blackwell Publishing, 2005.

Spivak, Gayatri Chakravorty. "Can the Subaltern Speak?" In *Imperialism*, edited by Peter H. Cain and Mark Harrison. Routledge, 2023.

Spivak, Gayatri Chakravorty. "Megacity." *Grey Room* 1 (2000): 9–25.

Srnicek, Nick. *Platform Capitalism*. Polity Press, 2017.

Stallabrass, Julian. *Gargantua: Manufactured Mass Culture*. Verso, 1996.

Stallabrass, Julian. "Trash." In *The Object Reader*, edited by Fiona Candlin and Raiford Guins. Routledge, 2009.

Stallybrass, Peter, Roger Chartier, J. Franklin Mowery, and Heather Wolfe. "Hamlet's Tables and the Technologies of Writing in Renaissance England." *Shakespeare Quarterly* 55, no. 4 (2004): 379–419.

Starosielski, Nicole. *The Undersea Network*. Duke University Press, 2015.

Steinberg, F. J. "IBM Introduces a Typewriter That Erases." *Computers and Automation* (May 1973).

Sterne, Jonathan. *The Audible Past: Cultural Origins of Sound Reproduction*. Duke University Press, 2003.

Sterne, Jonathan. *MP3: The Meaning of a Format*. Duke University Press, 2012.

Sterne, Jonathan. "Television under Construction: American Television and the Problem of Distribution, 1926–62." *Media, Culture & Society* 21, no. 4 (1999): 503–30.

Stevenson, William. "Cutting Remarks." *Film Comment* 26, no. 4 (1990): 70–74.

Steyerl, Hito. "In Defense of the Poor Image." *e-flux* 10, no. 11 (2009).

Stiegler, Bernard. *Technics and Time 1: The Fault of Epimetheus*. Stanford University Press, 1998.

Stiegler, Bernard. *Technics and Time 2: Disorientation*. Stanford University Press, 1998.

Stoichita, Victor I. *A Short History of the Shadow*. Reaktion Books, 1997.

Stoler, Ann Laura. *Along the Archival Grain: Epistemic Anxieties and Colonial Common Sense*. Princeton University Press, 2008.

Stone, Robert, dir. *Chasing the Moon*. PBS, 2019.

Sullivan, Hannah. *The Work of Revision*. Harvard University Press, 2013.

Sutherland, Tonia, and Gailyn Bopp. "The Pacific Futures of Subsea Data Centers." *New Media & Society* 25, no. 2 (2023): 345–60.

Tablang, Kristin. "Thomas Edison, B. C. Forbes, and the Mystery of the Spirit Phone." *Forbes*, October 25, 2019.

"Talking Machines in National Legislature." *Talking Machine World* 4, no. 4 (April 15, 1908): 6.

"The Talking Phonograph." *Scientific American*, December 22, 1877.

Tansey, Eira. "Archives without Archivists." *Reconstruction: Studies in Contemporary Culture* 16, no. 1 (2016).

Taylor, A. R. E. "Future-proof: Bunkered Data Centers and the Selling of Ultra-secure Cloud Storage." *Journal of the Royal Anthropological Institute* 27, no. 1 (2021): 76–94.

Taylor, Richard. "Eisenstein: A Soviet Artist." In *The Eisenstein Reader*, translated by Richard Taylor and William Powell, edited by Richard Taylor. BFI Publishing, 1998.

Taylor, Richard. *The Politics of the Soviet Cinema 1917–1929*. Cambridge University Press, 1979.

Thompson, Emily. "*Machines, Music, and the Quest for Fidelity: Marketing the Edison Phonograph in America, 1877–1925.*" *The Musical Quarterly* 79, no. 1 (1995): 131–71.

Thompson, Kristin. "Government Policies and Practical Necessities in the Soviet Cinema of the 1920s." In *The Red Screen: Politics, Society, Art in Soviet Cinema*, edited by Anna Lawton. Routledge, 1992.

Thorbecke, Catherine. "Why Deleting Something from the Internet Is 'Almost Impossible.'" *CNN*, September 18, 2022.

Thylstrup, Nanna Bonde, Daniela Agostinho, Annie Ring, Catherine D'Ignazio, and Kristin Veel. "Big Data As Uncertain Archives." In *Uncertain Archives: Critical Keywords for Big Data*, edited by Thylstrup et al. MIT Press, 2021.

Thylstrup, Nanna Bonde, Daniela Agostinho, Annie Ring, Catherine D'Ignazio, and Kristin Veel, eds. *Uncertain Archives: Critical Keywords for Big Data.* MIT Press, 2021.

Thylstrup, Nanna Bonde. "The World's Digital Memory Is at Risk." *New York Times*, June 21, 2023.

Tiffany, Kaitlyn. "Flickr Will Soon Start Deleting Photos—and Massive Chunks of Internet History." *Vox*, February 6, 2019. https://www.vox.com/the-goods/2019/2/6/18214046/flickr-free-storage-ends-digital-photo-archive-history.

Trouillot, Michel-Rolph. *Silencing the Past: Power and the Production of History.* Beacon Press, 2015.

Tsivian, Yuri. "The Wise and Wicked Game: Re-editing and Soviet Film Culture of the 1920s." *Film History* 8, no. 3 (1996): 327–43.

Turing, Alan. "Intelligent Machinery" (1948). In *The Essential Turing: Seminal Writings in Computing, Logic, Philosophy, Artificial Intelligence, and Artificial Life: Plus The Secrets of Enigma*, edited by B. Jack Copeland. Oxford University Press, 2004.

Turner, Fred. *From Counterculture to Cyberculture: Stewart Brand, the Whole Earth Network, and the Rise of Digital Utopianism.* University of Chicago Press, 2006.

"Typewriter of the Electronic Era." *New York Times*, November 23, 1984.

Usai, Paolo Cherchi. *The Death of Cinema: History, Cultural Memory and the Digital Dark Age.* Bloomsbury, 2019.

Van Dijck, José. "Datafication, Dataism and Dataveillance: Big Data between Scientific Paradigm and Ideology." *Surveillance & Society* 12, no. 2 (2014): 197–208.

Van Dijck, José. "From Shoebox to Performative Agent: The Computer As Personal Memory Machine." *New Media & Society* 7, no. 3 (2005): 311–32.

Vare, Ethlie Ann, and Greg Ptacek. "Mothers of Invention: For Women, History Is Patently Wrong." Book review. *Chicago Tribune*, January 31, 1988.

Vertov, Dziga. "The Factory of Facts." In *The Film Factory: Russian and Soviet Cinema in Documents 1896–1939*, edited by Ian Christie and Richard Taylor. Routledge, 2012.

Vertov, Dziga. *Kino-Eye: The Writings of Dziga Vertov.* Translated by Kevin O'Brien; edited by Annette Michelson. University of California Press, 1984.

Vertov, Dziga. "We, a Version of a Manifesto." In *The Film Factory: Russian and Soviet Cinema in Documents 1896–1939*, edited by Ian Christie and Richard Taylor. Routledge, 2012.

Vianello, Robert. "The Power Politics of 'Live' Television." *Journal of Film and Video* 37, no. 3 (Summer 1985): 26–40.

Virilio, Paul. *Open Sky*. Translated by Julie Rose. Verso, 2008.

Virilio, Paul. *The Original Accident*. Polity Press, 2007.

Vismann, Cornelia. *Files: Law and Media Technology*. Translated by Geoffrey Winthrop-Young. Stanford University Press, 2008.

Vismann, Cornelia. "Out of File, Out of Mind." In *New Media, Old Media: A History and Theory Reader*, edited by Wendy Hui Kyong Chun, Anna Watkins Fisher, and Thomas Keenan. Routledge, 2005.

Vogl, Joseph. "Becoming-media: Galileo's Telescope." *Grey Room* 29 (2007): 14–25.

"The Volunteer Cutter." *Camera: The Digest of the Media Picture Industry* 11, no. 4 (1919): 4.

Von Neumann, John. "First Draft of a Report on the EDVAC." *IEEE Annals of the History of Computing* 15, no. 4 (1993): 27–75.

Wahl, Robert S. "The History of Punched Cards: Using Paper to Store Information." In *The Routledge Companion to Media Technology and Obsolescence*, edited by Mark J. P. Wolf. Routledge, 2019.

Walker, Shawn, and Sheetal Agarwal. "The Missing Link: A Preliminary Typology for Understanding Link Decay in Social Media." *IConference Proceedings*, 2016. http://hdl.handle.net/2142/89413.

Walworth, Catherine. *Soviet Salvage: Imperial Debris, Revolutionary Reuse, and Russian Constructivism*. Pennsylvania State University Press, 2017.

Wasson, Haidee. *Museum Movies: The Museum of Modern Art and the Birth of Art Cinema*. University of California Press, 2005.

Wayne Jones, "Can Data Really Be Stored Forever?" *ardrive*. https://ardrive.io/can-data-really-be-stored-forever/.

Weber, Max. "Chapter XI Bureaucracy." In *Economy and Society*. University of California Press, 1987.

Weber, Samuel. "Television: Set and Screen." In *Mass Mediauras: Form, Technics, Media*. Stanford University Press, 1996.

Weiss, Allen S. *Breathless: Sound Recording, Disembodiment, and the Transformation of Lyrical Nostalgia*. Wesleyan University Press, 2002.

Wells, Herbert G. "World Brain: The Idea of a Permanent World Encyclopedia." *Encyclopédie française* 18 (1937): 24–11.

Welton, Benjamin. "The Man Arthur Conan Doyle Called 'America's Sherlock Holmes.'" *The Atlantic*, November 20, 2013.

Werrett, Simon. *Thrifty Science: Making the Most of Materials in the History of Experiment*. University of Chicago Press, 2019.

Wershler-Henry, Darren Sean. *The Iron Whim: A Fragmented History of Typewriting*. Cornell University Press, 2007.

Wershler, Darren, Lori Emerson, and Jussi Parikka. *The Lab Book: Situated Practices in Media Studies*. University of Minnesota Press, 2022.

White, Mimi. "The Attractions of Television: Reconsidering Liveness." In *MediaS-*

pace: Place, Scale and Culture in a Media Age, edited by Nick Couldry and Anna McCarthy. Routledge, 2004.

Wiener, Norbert. *Cybernetics: Or Control and Communication in the Animal and the Machine*. MIT Press, 2019.

Wile, Raymond R. "Cylinder Record Materials." *ARSC Journal* 22, no. 2 (1996): 162–77.

Williams, R. John. "Surface Writing." *Representations* 165, no. 1 (2024): 1–36.

Wing, Carlin. "Episodes in the Life of Bounce." *Cabinet* 56 (Winter 2014–15).

Wolf, Mark J. P., ed., *The Routledge Companion to Media Technology and Obsolescence*. Routledge, 2019.

Wood, Bill. "Apollo TV Essay." *Apollo Lunar Surface Journal*. 2005. https://www.hq.nasa.gov/alsj/alsj-TVEssay.html.

Yalkut, Jud. Interview by Sabrina Gschwandtner. *Millennium Film Journal* 42 (2004).

Yampolsky, Mikhail, and Derek Spring, "Reality at Second Hand." *Historical Journal of Film, Radio and Television* 11, no. 2 (1991): 161–71.

Yates, JoAnne. *Control through Communication: The Rise of System in American Management*. Johns Hopkins University Press, 1989.

Zeeberg, Amos. "How Selective Forgetting Can Help AI Learn Better." *Quanta Magazine*, February 28, 2024. https://www.quantamagazine.org/how-selective-forgetting-can-help-ai-learn-better-20240228/.

Zettl, Herbert. "The Rare Case of Television Aesthetics." *Journal of the University Film Association* 30, no. 2 (1978): 3–8.

Zielinski, Siegfried. *Audiovisions: Cinema and Television as Entr'actes in History*. Amsterdam University Press, 1999.

Zittrain, Jonathan, John Bowers, and Clare Stanton. "The Paper of Record Meets an Ephemeral Web: An Examination of Linkrot and Content Drift within *The New York Times*." Presented at Berkman Klein Center for Internet & Society at Harvard University. April 26, 2021. https://ssrn.com/abstract=3833133.

Zuboff, Shoshana. *The Age of Surveillance Capitalism: The Fight for a Human Future at the New Frontier of Power*. Public Affairs, 2019.

ARCHIVAL SOURCES

Ampex Corporation. "V-1000 Videotape Recorder: Industrial Manual." M1230, box 15, p. DRP-1. Ampex Corporation Records, Stanford University.

Brightwater Paper Company. Letter with mailing materials for Cosmic Bond. John G. Callan Collection, Baker Library, Harvard Business School.

Callan, John G. Letter to Henry J. Guild, March 31, 1932. John G. Callan Papers, Baker Library, Harvard Business School.

"Douglas Edwards and the News." Promotional material by Merlin Engineering Works. M1230, box 39. Ampex Corporation Records, Stanford University Library.

Graham, Bette Nesmith. Interview by Ruth Anderson. North Texas State University, Business Oral History Collection, Business Archives Project No. 10, Interview with Bette Graham, August 3, I977.

Graham, Bette Nesmith. Interview by Walt Nielson. Radio Station KXXK, May 10, 1969. North Texas State University, Business Oral History Collection.

Graham, Bette Nesmith. Speech at the New Enterprise Club, Harvard Business School, March 9, 1977. North Texas State University, Business Oral History Collection.

Graham, Bette Nesmith. Speech to Rotary Club, n.d. North Texas State University, Business Oral History Collection.

Guild, Henry J. Letter to John G. Callan, August 9, 1934. John G. Callan Papers, Baker Library, Harvard Business School.

IBM. "Correcting Selectric II." Promotional brochure, n.d. IBM Archives.

Johnson, A. M. Letter to Arthur L. Schawlow, April 7, 1972. Box 81, Arthur Schawlow Papers, Special Collection, Stanford University.

Larsen, Ronald R. Letter with NSF draft to Niels Reimers, January 23, 1973. Box 82, Arthur Schawlow Papers, Special Collection, Stanford University.

Marks, G. Letter to Arthur L. Schawlow, October 25, 1967. Box 82, Arthur Schawlow Papers, Special Collection, Stanford University.

Promotional material for erasable paper. John G. Callan Papers, Baker Library, Harvard Business School.

Reimers, Niels J. Letter to C. Frederick Ekman, August 18, 1971. Box 81, Arthur Schawlow Papers, Special Collection, Stanford University.

Schawlow, Arthur L. Letter to Robert H. Alpen, March 16, 1971. Box 81, Arthur Schawlow Papers, Special Collection, Stanford University.

Schawlow, Arthur L. Letter to Jean-Pierre Dreyfus, December 5, 1975. Box 81, Arthur Schawlow Papers, Special Collection, Stanford University.

Schawlow, Arthur L. Letter to A. M. Johnson, May 22, 1972. Box 81, Arthur Schawlow Papers, Special Collection, Stanford University.

Schawlow, Arthur L. Letter to Eric H. Pinnington, March 28, 1969. Box 82, Arthur Schawlow Papers, Special Collection, Stanford University.

"Statement of Method of Making 'Delible' and Similar Typewriter Bond Paper." Memorandum sent to A. B. Marsh, November 24, 1934. John G. Callan Papers, Baker Library, Harvard Business School.

Wheeler, Katherine D. Letter to Arthur L. Schawlow, February 1, 1965. Box 82, Arthur Schawlow Papers, Special Collection, Stanford University.

LIST OF PATENTS

Amet, E. H. “Erasing Attachment for Phonographs.” US Patent 521,456, issued June 19, 1894.

Austin, Oscar Phelps. “Process of Resurfacing Phonogram-Blanks.” US Patent 429,079, issued May 27, 1890.

Bardsley, E. E. “Attachment for Graphophones.” US Patent 592,758, issued November 2, 1897.

Begun, Semi Joseph. “Apparatus for Demagnetizing a Magnetic Recording-Reproducer Heads.” US Patent 2,538,893A, issued January 23, 1951.

Begun, Semi Joseph. “Automatic Erase for Magnetic Recorders.” US Patent 2,589,035A, issued March 11, 1952.

Begun, Semi Joseph. “Demagnetizing Apparatus for Magnetic Recorders.” US Patent 2,535,481A, issued December 26, 1950.

Begun, Semi Joseph. “Device to Prevent Accidental Erasure of Magnetic Recording.” US Patent 2,508,485, issued May 23, 1950.

Begun, Semi Joseph. “Erase Head for Use with Commercial Alternating Current or Equivalent.” US Patent 2,604,550A, issued January 23, 1952.

Begun, Semi Joseph. “Magnetic Reproducing Device with Means to Prevent Accidental Erasure of Record Medium.” US Patent 2,594,848A, issued April 29, 1952.

Brewington, Grace T., Anthony S. Condello, Daniel M. Bray. “Erase and Writing Continuous for Erasable Media.” Patent US 8,077,191 B2, issued December 12, 2011.

Callan, John G. “Typewriter Paper of Deferred Indelibility and Method of Preparing the Same.” US Patent 1,994,750, issued March 19, 1935.

Dodge, P. T. “Erasing Attachment for Phonographs.” US Patent 449,349, issued March 31, 1891.

Edison, Thomas A. “Burnishing Attachment for Phonographs.” US Patent 382,414, issued May 8, 1888.

Edison, Thomas A. "Device for Turning Off Phonogram Blanks." US Patent 448,780, issued March 24, 1891.

Edison, Thomas A. "Improvement in Phonograph or Speaking Machines." US Patent 200,521, issued February 19, 1878.

Edison, Thomas A. "Method of Preparing Phonograph Recording Surfaces." US Patent 393,465, issued November 27, 1888.

Edison, Thomas A. "Phonograph." US Patent 430,276, issued June 17, 1890.

Edison, Thomas A. "Phonograph." US Patent 430,278, issued June 17, 1890.

Edison, Thomas A. "Phonograph." US Patent 465,972, issued December 29, 1891.

Edison, Thomas A. "Phonograph." US Patent 488,189, issued December 20, 1892.

Edison, Thomas A. "Phonograph." US Patent 609,268, issued August 16, 1898.

Edison, Thomas A. "Phonograph Cutting Tool." US Patent 484,583, issued October 18, 1892.

Edison, Thomas A. "Smoothing Tool for Phonogram Blanks." US Patent 457,344, issued August 11, 1891.

Edison, Thomas A. "Turning-off Device for Phonographs." US Patent 448,781, issued March 24, 1891.

Elbert, D., and G. Waldri. "Adhesively Eradicable Transfer Medium." US Patent 3,825,470, issued July 23, 1974.

Johnson, E. R. "Cutting Tool for Sound-Recording Machines." US Patent 778,975, issued January 3, 1905.

La Mountain, G. C. "Trimmer for Phonograph Records." US Patent 1,032,338, issued July 9, 1912.

Macdonald, Thomas H. "Graphophone." US Patent 654,317, issued July 24, 1900.

Nelles, R. "Phonograph Erasing Device." US Patent 656,366, issued August 21, 1900.

Ott, J. F. "Machine for Shaving Sound Records." US Patent 796,857, issued August 8, 1905.

Pritchard, Charles A. G. "Graphophone-Record Shaver." US Patent 669,207, issued March 5, 1901.

Rockhill, J. D. "Trimmer for Phonograph Records." US Patent 974,435, issued November 1, 1910.

Schawlow, Arthur. "Method of and Apparatus for Erasing." US Patent 3,553,421A, filed November 7, 1968, and issued January 5, 1971.

Steele, John W. "Graphophone Shaving Device." US Patent 668,230, issued February 19, 1901.

INDEX

• • • **Sensing Media**

Aesthetics, Philosophy, and Cultures of Media

EDITED BY WENDY HUI KYONG CHUN AND SHANE DENSON

What does it mean to think, feel, and sense with and through media? In this cross-disciplinary series we present books and authors exploring this and related questions: How do media technologies, broadly defined, transform artistic practices and aesthetic sensibilities? How are practices, encounters, and affects entangled with the deep infrastructures and visible surfaces of the media environment? How do we "make sense"—cognitively, perceptually, and culturally—of media?

We are especially interested in contributions that open our understanding of media aesthetics beyond the narrow confines of Western art and aesthetic values. We seek works that reestablish the environmental connections between art and technology as well as between the aesthetic, the sensible, and the philosophical. We invite alternative epistemologies and phenomenologies of media rooted in the practices and subjectivities of Black, Indigenous, queer, trans, and other communities that have been unjustly marginalized in these discussions. Ultimately, we aim to sense the many possible worlds that media disclose.

—

Steven Henry Madoff, *A Sense of Wholeness: Modernism, Interdisciplinary Art, and Network Aesthetics*

Adrian J. Ivakhiv, *The New Lives of Images: Digital Ecologies and Anthropocene Imaginaries in More-than-Human Worlds*

Maja Bak Herrie, *Thinking Through Data: How Outliers, Aggregates, and Patterns Shape Perception*

The DISCO Network, *Technoskepticism: Between Possibility and Refusal*

Timon Beyes, *Organizing Color: Toward a Chromatics of the Social*

Edmund Mendelssohn, *White Musical Mythologies: Sonic Presence in Modernism*

Ioana B. Jucan, *Malicious Deceivers: Thinking Machines and Performative Objects*

Vilém Flusser, *Communicology: Mutations in Human Relations?*, edited by Rodrigo Maltez Novaes, foreword by N. Katherine Hayles

Mark Amerika, *My Life as an Artificial Creative Intelligence*

The authorized representative in the EU for product safety and compliance is:
Mare Nostrum Group
B.V Doelen 72
4831 GR Breda
The Netherlands

www.ingramcontent.com/pod-product-compliance
Lightning Source LLC
LaVergne TN
LVHW091136080826
845145LV00008B/2173

* 9 7 8 1 5 0 3 6 4 5 2 6 4 *